The Scenography of

Influential contemporary British playwright and director Howard Barker has been engaging with the scenography of the Wrestling School's productions since 1998. Despite this active involvement in the design of set, costume, lighting, and sound, no in-depth published study on this aspect of his work exists to date. This monograph therefore offers the first comprehensive and detailed analysis of Barker's scenographic practice.

Combining aesthetic analysis of play texts and production records with original interview materials, this book presents the first full-length foray into Barker's scenography. It features extracts from conversations with designers working with Barker, and with Barker himself. In addition, it presents the first printed versions of select set and costume designs by Barker.

With the first fully detailed analysis of Barker's scenographic work, this book will be a vital read for scholars and postgraduates of Barker studies, contemporary British and European drama, theatre, and scenography.

Lara Maleen Kipp is an early career researcher, scenographer, and theatre practitioner. Her PhD at Aberystwyth University engaged in an aesthetic analysis of Howard Barker's scenography. Previously, she completed a Master's degree in Practising Theatre & Performance and a joint BA (Hons) in Scenography & Theatre Design and Drama & Theatre Studies. Her work experiences include Vivienne Westwood Studios, the Salzburg Opera Festival, and a lectureship at the University of Derby. She has published with Intellect, De Gruyter, Palgrave Macmillan, Sorbonne University, and Taylor & Francis. Her research interests include scenography, voice and performance, and contemporary European Theatre.

Routledge Advances in Theatre and Performance Studies

For more information about this series, please visit: www.routledge.com/
Routledge-Advances-in-Theatre--Performance-Studies/book-series/RATPS

The Scenography of Howard Barker

The Wrestling School Aesthetic 1998–2011

Lara Maleen Kipp

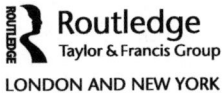
Routledge
Taylor & Francis Group

LONDON AND NEW YORK

First published 2021
by Routledge
2 Park Square, Milton Park, Abingdon, Oxon OX14 4RN

and by Routledge
52 Vanderbilt Avenue, New York, NY 10017

Routledge is an imprint of the Taylor & Francis Group, an informa business

© 2021 Lara Maleen Kipp

British Library Cataloguing-in-Publication Data
A catalogue record for this book is available from the British Library

Library of Congress Cataloging-in-Publication Data
Names: Kipp, Lara Maleen, author.
Title: The scenography of Howard Barker: The Wrestling School aesthetic 1998–2011 / Lara Maleen Kipp.
Description: Abingdon, Oxon; New York, NY : Routledge, 2021. |
Series: Routledge advances in theatre and performance studies |
Includes bibliographical references and index. |
Identifiers: LCCN 2020018870 (print) | LCCN 2020018871 (ebook)
Subjects: LCSH: Barker, Howard, 1946–Criticism and interpretation. |
Barker, Howard, 1946–Aesthetics. | Wrestling School
(Theatre company) | Theaters–Stage-setting and scenery.
Classification: LCC PR6052.A6485 Z79 2021 (print) |
LCC PR6052.A6485 (ebook) | DDC 822/.914–dc23
LC record available at https://lccn.loc.gov/2020018870
LC ebook record available at https://lccn.loc.gov/2020018871

ISBN: 978-0-367-07655-9 (hbk)
ISBN: 978-0-429-02189-3 (ebk)

Typeset in Times New Roman
by Newgen Publishing UK

To Keith LeFever, for laying the foundations that brought me here.

Contents

Acknowledgements

First and foremost, I wish to express my deepest gratitude to Howard Barker, whose generosity with his time and materials has been immense. Without him, this book would not exist.

Further, I thank Prof. David Ian Rabey and Dr. Karoline Gritzner, who guided me through the PhD project that this book is based upon, and continued to inspire me after its conclusion.

Many thanks also to Ace McCarron and Susannah Henry for generously sharing their experiences with me, and allowing me to share them here. Equally, thank you to Rachel Sutton, for kindly and generously agreeing to the posthumous use of Paul Bull's interview materials in this book. Thank you also to Donald Cooper at Photostage UK for his beautiful production photographs, and Jon Primrose at Exeter University for helping me navigate the Howard Barker Digital Archive.

Immense gratitude goes to the Theatre & Performance Research Association, especially the scenography working group, and the Fashion, Costume & Visual Cultures Network, for offering fora in which to air, develop, and refine my thoughts for this book.

Thank you to my editor Laura Hussey at Routledge, and her assistant Swati Hindwan, for guiding me along this process.

Last but most certainly not least, thank you to my partner Samuel, for everything.

Introduction

Two decades of scenographic imagination

The dramatic work of contemporary British playwright Howard Barker has been subject to sustained analysis over many years, but his scenographic involvement with its staging in production has yet to receive the same detailed critical engagement. His playwrighting career spans half a century at the time of writing, and his dramatic work has been subject to keen academic engagement since the mid-1980s at least. The Wrestling School, a company dedicated to staging his work, was formed in 1988, and Barker began directing his own work in 1992 with *Ego in Arcadia*. Others have presented thorough analyses of this directorial work (e.g. Rabey, 2006, 2009, 2012; Reynolds, 2006) and some research has addressed individual aspects of Barker's scenography (e.g. Iball, 2006; Curtin, 2012; Obis, 2013). However, there has yet to be a sustained analysis of the totality of his scenographic work, although this spans two decades and at least 15 productions at the time of writing. This monograph sets out to address this lack.

Critical engagement with, and clear identification of the scenographic working principles that are employed in these influential contemporary theatre pieces will constitute a necessary and overdue extension of the discourse on Howard Barker. This book aims to analyse the scenography of Howard Barker from when he formally began engaging with those aspects of production, namely in 1998 with *Ursula*, to derive a clear sense of Barker's scenographic working principles. I cover productions until 2011 (*Blok/Eko*), as this marks the last time the Wrestling School company performed in full, under Barker's direction. Though there have been a number of productions of Barker's work since,[1] these did not involve Barker in a scenographic capacity, and are therefore outside the remit of my research here. To reduce the material further, full-scale productions by Barker's company the Wrestling School under his direction form the central point of analysis. However, where appropriate and salient as examples, other relevant productions will supplement these core materials. On the one hand, this is to create a manageable amount of material; on the other, it ensures a distinct level of comparability by keeping key variables largely the same, namely direction, production company, scenographic realisation team, timeframe, and available archival materials and their quality.

At the time of writing, many varied resources on the subject of scenography exist and a recent increase in academic publications (e.g. Baugh, 2013; McKinney and Palmer, 2017; Aronson, 2017, 2018; Hann, 2018) attests to the continued and arguably expanding relevance of the field.[2] Similarly, many different definitions for the term also exist. My own definition of scenography is founded not only in the term's historical development and contemporary usage, but also in its etymological origins. Where researchers agree is that scenography 'encompasses a broad and divergent sphere of activity' (Collins and Nisbet, 2010: 1) in contemporary practice and scholarship (cf. Hann, 2018: 3, 5–8). The perception of the term varies in different cultural contexts, and in many Western ones only recently replaced the more common term 'theatre design' (cf. Howard, 2001; McKinney and Butterworth, 2009; Collins and Nisbet, 2010; Hann, 2018) that tended to foreground architectural or painterly processes, but failed to address the active and affective role scenography plays in production (cf. Hann, 2018: 2, 5).

The spatio-temporal, audio-visual nature of scenography demands the development of critical terminology that allows in-depth analysis of individual scenographic proposals within the play texts as well as comparative analysis between textual proposal and realisation in production. While the discourse on discussing the event-stage of scenography is increasingly expanding, analysis rarely includes the implicit stage of scenography as it appears conceptually, as in the case of Barker in the play texts. This book therefore also proposes an approach for developing an appropriate, coherent discourse for the analysis of scenography in both its implicit and explicit manifestations. But first, the multivalent concept at the heart of this research, scenography, requires some context and definition.

The term's linguistic origins are telling: *skēnographia*, as already employed by Aristotle in his *Poetics*, refers, in a literal translation, to writing the scene (cf. Black, 1874: 10–12), though it is often also translated as painting (cf. Butcher, 1902: 19 and Janko, 1987: 78) the scene.[3] The more frequent translation of *graphē* as painting might be a result of the fine art tradition of scenic painting that appeared in Western theatre design from the Shakespearean era onwards, especially with the introduction of perspective painting as a result of the Italian Renaissance. Perspectival scenic painting began in the early 16th century and dominated stages until its gradual decline in the 20th century (cf. Balme, 2008: 55–56). Similarly, the deconstruction of dramatic text in postmodern theatre traditions (cf. Lehmann, 2011) might explain the precedence of painting (visual) over writing (conceptual) in an understanding of the design, organisation, and generation of stage spaces in contemporary theatre practice.

However, approaching the translation of *graphē* as writing allows for a scenographic analysis of materials preceding their realisation in space and time: the dramatic text, too, is writing the scene, implicitly and explicitly. Barker's play texts thus offer a rich scenography that exists alongside the realisation of any given production. Focussing on dramatic text allows me to avoid the process of reification that archival materials might prompt, in which too much importance would be placed on the physical particularities of specific productions. In addition, the existence of said productions as archival materials contains the danger of a false equivalence between the archival artefact and the transient event of the theatrical performance. By returning to the point of origin for both production and archival record, the play text, I can investigate the development of Barker's scenography from its textual iteration, arguably the original scenography as it is written. However, this is not intended to reduce scenography solely to the conceptual. As Hann argues convincingly, although 'scenography is neither exclusively visual nor spatial' (2018: 15), it is fundamentally bound up with theatre-making, that is, staging in space and time (Ibid.: 2, 5, 8). I therefore engage with Barker's scenography in its different iterations, to the extent that is possible, given that the performances lie in the past. I must also note that the subjective interpretation of implicit and poetic scenographic content in the dramatic texts is naturally shaped by my own social and cultural biases. As such, the description and analysis of archival materials allow me to expand my thinking by engaging with specific examples of scenographic realisation. Additionally, the inclusion of original designs by Barker offer the reader an opportunity for more detailed engagement. The inclusion of dramatic text in my definition of scenography enables an analysis of Barker's practice beyond the limited and limiting archival materials that are available; the etymological origins of the term itself set a sound precedent for this approach.

For the purposes of this book, scenography is defined as the deliberate audio-visual, spatio-temporal rendering of space into place. It is both conceptual and affective. Scenography begins in the proposal for an audio-visual rendition of time-space through any medium (sketches, models, text). In this context, on the one hand, space refers to a three-dimensional area that contains material objects and bodies as well as events, both material and immaterial. On the other hand, place is part of space, an area in space with either definite or indefinite boundaries – the latter in particular are crucial in Barker's work, as the reader will discover. Place does require tangible rendering, but might instead arise out of suggestion and association and its boundaries may be conceptual and changeable. In this, I align my thinking with scholars such as Schellow (2013) and Downing (2013). Place therefore shares the temporal three-dimensionality of space. It contains the perpetual oscillation of place, space, and the body as 'a becoming entity' (Anderson, 2013: 114) between the real and the imaginary. Its precarious situation 'between fixity and permanence' (Ibid.: 109) might be at the core of continuing debates concerning a definition that is accepted by scholars and practitioners alike.[4] However, this positioning might simultaneously be considered to contain its solution, not in terms of resolving the tension of this existence 'between', but in an acceptance or even affirmation of scenography's existence in terms of a principle of accumulation and simultaneity (both/and): it is both real and imaginary, fixed and mutable, conceptual and tangible.

This coexistent duality is also the reason for drawing on aesthetic theory, in particular the discourse of the sublime, in my approach to analysing Barker's scenography: it provides a well-established example of critical discourse that is coherent, rigorous, yet non-reductive in its discussion of the subject matter. The wide remit of aesthetic discourse, which includes visual arts, architecture, and installation works, renders it a suitable starting point for the multidimensional practice of scenography. Theories of the sublime, from rhetorical device to descriptor of natural phenomena, and ultimately of human experience beyond reason, offer thorough attempts at critical discursive engagement with an elusive, non-rational, and experientially founded subject matter. This book therefore reassesses the concept of the sublime and its surrounding discourse in the context of Barker's scenography.

Notably, Barker's own theoretical writings and those parts of an academic community focussed on his work share a certain vocabulary that is based in aesthetics, though often without explicit references to this origin. These centre on ideas of the sublime and related terms and include notions of infinity, indeterminacy, ambiguity, possibility, and many concepts prefixed with 'un': the un-speakable, un-representable, un-conscious, un-knowable,[5] and so on (cf. Carney, 2013; Rabey and Goldingay, 2013). Considering the current lack of critical analysis of Barker's scenographic endeavours, one must first forge an appropriate vocabulary with which to ask questions of this aspect of his work. The abundance of terminology that is either directly from, or related to, the discourse of the sublime in existing Barker studies indicates an affinity between those theories and the aesthetics of Barker's work. The particularities of his scenographic approach, which explores the tensions between form and formlessness, light and dark, and soundscapes that blur together the familiar, the uncanny and the abstract, all evidence the significance of the sublime as a guiding concept within his work and therefore warrant analysis in those terms. Before outlining an overview of scenography's development in the 20th century in order to establish Barker as part of a lineage of practitioners, I offer the reader a summary of the key theoretical frameworks.

Approaching scenographic analysis through aesthetics

For the purposes of this book, the sublime is understood as a concept that seeks to address experiences of extreme intensity that result in an ambiguous emotional response, 'an anxiety that unfolds as an inhuman exhilaration' (Lingis, 2000: 161). It exceeds rational thought and instead conjures a sensation of immediacy, resulting in the dissolution of conscious subjectivity in the face of this event. Importantly, the dissolution is not equated with disappearance; instead it affords a 'sublime alienation' (Kristeva, 1982: 9) that challenges the notion of a stable self. The definition I employ in this book has its foundation in a long and diverse history of philosophical engagement with aesthetics, key points of which are delineated below. It should be noted that the definition I propose here is unquestionably postmodern in its foregrounding of the affective and irrational.

The continued presence of the sublime in a wide variety of discourses, even those that oppose its value, is evidence for its continued relevance. Indeed, the criticisms levied by writers such as Elkins (2011) 'can only refer to some inadequacy in the *philosophical concept* of the sublime, rather than signaling the disappearance of the *human experience* to which the concept refers' (Costelloe, 2012: 1; original emphasis). Consequently, these criticisms are in many ways testament to the prevailing and continued influence the sublime possesses. As Timothy Costelloe asserts, 'any farewell to the sublime can be little more than a rhetorical flourish in reference to the purported inadequacy of the philosophical concept' (Ibid.: 7). It is not the aim of this book to engage in detailed analysis of the criticisms put forward against the sublime; instead, it proposes reconsiderations in the context of scenography and perhaps a subsequent reassessment of its value. I therefore position myself in agreement with Costelloe's assertion that the concept and the human experiences it describes cannot disappear, only mutate and be reconceived. The sublime is consequently a crucially and usefully open and difficult concept with which to address the scenographic work of Howard Barker. Thus, I argue for its efficacy in addressing core scenographic principles in Barker's work.

Below the reader finds a brief historical overview of the sublime, centring on those theorists whose ideas form the theoretical backbone of the book. With this contextual knowledge at hand, readers will find themselves well prepared for the subsequent chapters. It should be noted that the scope of this overview is deliberately limited to a trajectory from Immanuel Kant to Jean-François Lyotard and Julia Kristeva. This limitation allows me to establish a through line of ideas (in a Western philosophical tradition) relating to the affective aspects that experiences of the sublime evoke, the development in its relationship to reason and emotion, the notion of subjectivity and its destabilisation in postmodern thought. Further, all three set out ideas on the relationship between the sublime and the beautiful; as the latter concept plays a central role in Barker's playwriting and scenography, this heightens their respective usefulness in this enquiry.

Immanuel Kant's significance in the discourse of the sublime can hardly be overstated (cf. Doran, 2015: 4). Though he diverts the core of the experience away from a physical encounter, spatio-temporality nonetheless plays an important role in his conception of the sublime (Kant, 2007: 76). Kant sees a sublime experience as founded in the superiority of reason, which asserts itself in the face of mortal danger (real or imagined). This runs counter to Barker's emphasis on boundless imagination. Similarly, Kant's attempts to clearly define the sublime and the beautiful as distinct categories (Ibid.: 75 ff.) is in opposition to the crossing over and frequent collapse of these boundaries that takes place in Barker's plays in which beauty can be terrible (cf. Barker, 2014a: 292). Barker conceives of beauty as intricately linked to anxiety, pain, and death (cf. 2005a: 25–26; 2007: 32), presenting a stark contrast to the contained, calm understanding and delight that Kant assigns it (2007: 76). Further, Kant's consignment of women to the realm of the beautiful is in stark contrast to Barker. Additionally, aspects of Kant's ideas on the sublime are deeply problematic from a contemporary perspective, based as they are on patriarchal, Eurocentric ideas of mental capacity and natural superiority (1960: 76–78, 97, 107, 110). The conceptual foundations of these ideas are – plainly put – racist, xenophobic, and misogynistic. This particular heritage of the idea of the sublime must be noted as it shaped subsequent thinking on the subject matter, even when criticised and rejected by later scholars (e.g. Battersby, 2007; Lochhead, 2008; Zuckert, 2012). Nonetheless, Kant's thinking was hugely influential to later scholars, such as Jean-François Lyotard.

Lyotard's ambiguous and densely poetic writings offer a definition of the sublime that is fundamentally embedded in spatio-temporal experience (Lyotard, 1989: 211) and therefore lend themselves to a discussion of scenography. Notably, Lyotard begins to blend Kant's distinct categories together again, proposing an overspill of the sublime into the beautiful and vice versa. To Lyotard, the distinction between beauty and the sublime is a question of intensity (Ibid.: 204–206) whereby it might be more accurate to consider them as gradations on a scale, rather than distinct categories, *pace* Kant. In the case of the sublime, Lyotard foregrounds a negative production of the experience (Ibid.: 198–199, 201, 203–204, 207, 210–211) that arises from incomprehensibility and indeterminacy (cf. Johnson on Lyotard, 2012: 121–123). Rational thought encounters its imaginative limits, precipitating a repeated collapse of the usual sense-making processes. The reader will find that Barker's scenographic strategies deliberately play with such incompletion, as I explore in detail throughout the chapters that follow. This repeated collapse of ordinary meaning-making is also where I see the third philosopher, Julia Kristeva, as essential.

Kristeva offers a full disintegration of the boundary separating the beautiful and the sublime in her articulation of abjection (1982: 210). She also emphasises the crucial importance of language with regard to the sublime (Ibid.: 12), which makes her writing all the more relevant in relation to Barker, to whom elevated language is at the heart of tragedy (cf. Barker, 1997: 29–31). Additionally, she emphasises the role of perception (1982: 12) in the experience of the sublime (and abjection), and discusses at length the origin and nature of subjectivity (cf. Johnson, 2012: 127). The former lends Kristeva a thematic proximity to scenography, the latter to much of Barker's playwriting. To her, language becomes the vehicle by which one may explore the boundaries of imagination beyond conventional linguistic meaning-making strategies (cf. Kristeva, 1982: 14).

Kristeva considers the sublime itself in tension with the abject, as complimentary experiences with a closeness that can render them, if not indistinguishable, as possessing a fluidity that can result in repeated switches between them. Kristeva considers the abject as that which pulls the subject 'toward the place where meaning collapses' (1982: 2), which is instantly relatable to other theories of the sublime, both older and contemporary. The collapse of meaning and the resultant terror which a subject experiences is fundamental to the sublime and the abject alike. Additionally, this rejection of meaning (in a conclusive, rational sense) and its threatened collapse are conceptually reminiscent of Barker's theoretical writings (cf. Barker, 2005a and 2007) and certainly resonate with his scenography that evokes a sense of place, without concretising space. I explore this principle in detail in Chapter 1.

To Kristeva, the sublime is, on the one hand, the (failed) attempt at reasserting boundaries (Kristeva, 1982: 11) after the breakdown in the encounter with the abject:

> The abject is edged with the sublime. [...] For the sublime has no object either. When the starry sky, a vista of open seas or a stained glass window shedding purple beams fascinate me, there is a cluster of meaning, of colors, of words, of caresses, there are light touches, scents, sighs, cadences that arise, shroud me, carry me away, and sweep me beyond the things that I see, hear, or think. The "sublime" object dissolves in the raptures of a bottomless memory.
>
> (Ibid.: 11–12)

Multiple selves appear out of the encounter: "I" does not disappear in it, but finds, in that sublime alienation, a forfeited existence' (Ibid.: 9). On the other hand, she establishes the sublime as a trigger of experience that, in the moment of perception, results in a boundless expansion through perception and words (Ibid.: 12). This endless expansion is crucial to the implicit scenography of Barker's play texts, and their realisation in production. Another resonant aspect of Kristeva's writing in relation to this book is the importance that language, but also crucially sense perception, hold for Kristeva with regard to the sublime:

> Not at all short of but always with and through perception and words, the sublime is a something added that expands us, overstrains us, and causes us to be both here, as dejects, and there, as others and sparkling. A divergence, an impossible bounding. Everything missed, joy – fascination.
>
> (Ibid.: 12)

Although this emphasis on language might initially seem less relevant to the analysis of Barker's scenography, I argue that it is in the indefinite and poetic, yet specific, nature of stage directions that the spectre of a scenographic sublime first surfaces in the plays. Furthermore, Kristeva's insistence on the necessarily sensuous engagement with the sublime not only raises questions about conventional conceptions of subject identity through reason and rational reflection, but also offers connections to scenography which is fundamentally bound up with sense perception and therefore affect. The increasing prevalence of new materialist perspectives in scenographic scholarship (e.g.

McKinney and Palmer, 2017; Hann, 2018) further foreground the relevance of sensuousness as key part of scenography. Despite her particular focus on the abject, Kristeva's writing allows for a critically reflexive engagement with the concept of the sublime in relation to embodied experience and language, both of which are central in the analysis of Barker's scenography as it is proposed in his playwriting and realised in production.

To summarise, the trajectory of this book's theoretical foundation is one that conceives of the sublime as an experience that suspends the capacity for reason (cf. Doran, 2015: 7) through a sensuous and conceptual assault, rather than an experience that reinforces reason's superiority as Kant would argue. The affinity of Barker's theatrical aims with postmodern theories of the sublime such as Lyotard's and Kristeva's becomes apparent in the playwright's own theoretical writings. Before I provide the reader with a short summary of each chapter's contents, I briefly outline a lineage of scenographers alongside whom I situate Barker. This presents a complementary contextual element to the philosophers discussed above.

From Wagner, Appia, and Craig to Wilson, Goebbels, and Barker

My aim here is not to offer a complete overview of the practice of scenography, nor claim to be able to do so, but instead to situate Barker in the context of a still developing discipline, which includes academic scenographic discourse. Here, I begin with the work of Richard Wagner and his notion of the *Gesamtkunstwerk* (total work of art), and more importantly with the principles devised by Adolphe Appia for approaching Wagner's œuvre. I then move from Edward Gordon Craig and Robert Wilson to Heiner Goebbels. I encourage the reader to see Barker's work as an example in a line of practitioners that conceive theatre as a marriage of equals[6] in terms of production elements, thus providing an appropriate historical and thematic context for the book. I therefore examine the scenographers in chronological order, drawing connections to Barker's work in each instance. This provides the reader with a cohesive overview of the field before delving into the analysis of Howard Barker's scenography.

The work of Richard Wagner revolutionised opera and music-drama, and particularly his use of the term *Gesamtkunstwerk* (total work of art) is important to understanding the legacy that informs Barker's approach to theatre making. Further, the historical precedent of Wagner's ideas impacts academic engagement with the field of scenography and Barker's principles of scenography. The book does not investigate Barker's scenography in the specific terms of the concept of the total work of art. Rather, it offers Barker's work as an example of scenography that is situated in a historical context, and that shares points of commonality with other practitioners' works, one of which is the notion of the total work of art and its particular appearance in opera and subsequently theatre. This decision is based on the relatively restrictive effect that the notion of the *Gesamtkunstwerk* could have on the development of the book's argument. In its immediate association with Wagner and the subsequent political implications, a sustained centralisation of the term could potentially inhibit understanding of Barker's works in a contemporary, postmodern context.

Instead, I propose the sublime as a conceptual connection point between contemporary scenography and the *Gesamtkunstwerk*: the overwhelming nature and profound affect (i.e. the emotional and physiological impact as well as the rational confrontation of complex ideas) of a total work of art exceeds the audience's immediate capacity to comprehend fully the entirety of that which they are confronted with. The resulting struggle between rational comprehension, emotional impact, and imagination may very well be considered as sublime. A total work of art may therefore, through an all-encompassing scenography, create a sublime experience that fundamentally destabilises those aspects of subjectivity that are consciously constructed and performed as well as those that are unquestioningly accepted under everyday circumstance.

This does not equate any *Gesamtkunstwerk* with the experience of the sublime, as the former term refers chiefly to a method of production in which all elements serve the expression of a central idea, whereas the latter describes a series of emotional and rational processes that remain crucially unresolved. The main connection between the concept of the *Gesamtkunstwerk* and the sublime consequently lies in the overwhelming nature of both, in which audiences are confronted with an excessive level of sensory stimulation. However, in a total work of art, these all serve to achieve a unified understanding of the core idea. The sublime on the other hand offers an excessive multiplication of possibilities, founded in experience at a level where 'it becomes impossible to articulate [...] unconscious responses to the work' (Oddey and White, 2006: 11). 'Unconscious' is here taken to refer to those reactions that arise from affect,[7] and thus are not rationally accessible in the moment in which they are experienced. However, they may be rationally interrogated and potentially articulated in retrospect. Though the notion of the *Gesamtkunstwerk* unquestionably engages similar ideas, the sublime offers a relatable, yet crucially less constrained, and therefore more suitable concept for the analysis of scenography in the context of this book.

Further, though the term *Gesamtkunstwerk* may initially appear conceptually apt in approaching Barker's work, it is the particular socio-political connotations that Roberts identifies (2011) that make me hesitant in using it in this context: 'The modern idea of the total work of art both intends a critique of existing society and *anticipates a redemptive or utopian alternative*' (Ibid.: 3; my emphasis). While Barker sees theatre as intrinsically political and concedes that this is therefore also the case with his works (in Brown, 2011: 116–117), he repudiates any conscious intent or particular political stance (Ibid.). Consequently, the use of the term *Gesamtkunstwerk* in the context of Barker's work would potentially derail the playwright's conscious disengagement from socio-political intentions.

Barker's working methods are certainly totalising, though notably without a concrete ideological intention: there is no singular message in his plays (cf. Barker, 2014b: 14). The contemplation of possibilities is foregrounded, multiplicities of potential and subjective interpretations are invited. Additionally, Barker's working methods do not have a fully formed, completed, and self-contained goal. The subsequent analyses and overall argument of the book proceed from the very short and selective history of relevant scenographers below, which outlines the heritage of practice which precedes Barker's work and contextualises the principles at play.

The influence of Adolphe Appia's writings on the development of scenography in a Western context, as well as the development of scenographic scholarship, cannot be overstated. One need only look at recent publications such as those by Brandstetter and Wiens (2010), Wiens (2014), Palmer (2015), or Abulafia (2016) to find sustained engagement with the ideas and legacy of Appia. His conception of scenography as a practice that served to realise the 'aesthetic truth of an artistic work' (Beacham, 1994: 16) via a 'mutually subordinated synthesis' (Ibid.: 21) of all production elements remains at the heart of contemporary scenography. The radical shift from an exclusive focus on actors or singers in performance to an image and soundscape in which all elements of production are given overall equal weighting is one of Appia's most important contributions to modern Western scenography (Ibid.: 19). The development of these principles was sparked by Wagner's work, in which Appia saw the 'theatrical form, i.e. its projection in space' (Ibid.: 16) already contained in the manuscript.

To Appia, 'the musical score [was] the sole interpreter' (Beacham, 1994: 16) of an opera's staging through which all actions were determined in their exact timing and rhythm. Following this principle, one might argue that everything that needs to be staged is written in Barker's dramatic texts, including but not necessarily being restricted to specific stage directions. The playwright's style as it appears on the page directly influences its realisation on stage. Indeed, Barker's increasingly poetic presentation of the play text has altered over time, relying less and less on description and more and more on an immediate understanding of fluctuations in emotional states, indicated in verbal formulations to the actor/reader, as well as in evocative stage directions. I discuss this in greater length in Chapter 1. For now, it is sufficient to point out that Barker's scenography is alive with the implied possibilities of how else this space might be, providing set pieces that suggest a locale without specification, such as the recurring park bench in *The Forty* (2014a). He then intensifies this instability of space further by layering different planes of place and time together.

For Appia, such a suggestion of space without concretising place was born from his engagement with Wagner's operas. Appia notably saw this effect achieved through light, which he considered a spatial structuring device. To him, lighting was comprised of two types: 'general illumination and brightness, a *diffused* light, which provided a sort of luminous undercoat

[...] without suggestive nuance [...] but a prerequisite for the second type of *formative* and creative light used in conjunction with it' (Beacham, 1994: 25; original emphases). The latter therefore serves to act as one of the delineating mechanisms by which space is rendered into place (the others being set and properties). This formative light, Appia hoped, would be 'an extraordinarily subtle tool [for] the scenic artist', with which one 'could highlight objects or cause them to disappear; [...] build up or take away; distort, give mass to or dematerialise the physical objects on stage' (Ibid.). The intrinsic connection of space, light, and place, and subsequently space and time is at the heart of theatre-making (cf. Wiles, 2014; Rabey, 2016).

Appia recognised this in his emphasis on rhythm and musicality, which in conjunction with light were to become the core structuring devices of time and space on stage. He furthermore noted the importance of shadows, lamenting that 'an object lit from three or four directions throws no shadow and, from a theatrical viewpoint, does not exist' (in Beacham 1994: 24). In this, Appia's ideas preceded modern lighting technologies and design, the development and implementation of which can be seen in Barker's own approach to lighting, which I discuss in Chapter 2. One might therefore read Barker's plays as a scenographic score, in which 'the performer is given both suggestions for his acting and the precise proportions he has to follow' (Ibid.: 46). The use of light as a spatial and rhythmical structuring device therefore reaches from Appia's writings, particularly those on Wagner, in the late 19th and early 20th century, to Barker's contemporary practice 100 years later.

The contemporary ubiquity of Appia's ideas, in both use of space and lighting, is such that one might easily forget these techniques are not too old in their inception, let alone in their widespread implementation. Other practitioners such as Edward Gordon Craig and Vsevolod Meyerhold similarly expressed discontent with the theatrical *status quo* (cf. Craig, 1956: xx; Braun, 1979: 29) at the time, but it is Appia's eloquence in articulating his criticisms and proposing solutions, his notion of truthful interpretation of the original idea (Beacham, 1994: 16) as well as the decisive emphasis on lighting in his work that make him particularly relevant to the book at hand. Further, Appia's identification of the core role of light in relation to musicality, and its resultant function as spatial structuring device, are principles that one finds echoed in the way in which Barker engages with these elements. I discuss this in detail in Chapter 2.

Appia's emphasis on the artist (dramatist) (Beacham, 1994: 21) and the faithful realisation of their idea through the medium of the actor (cf. Ibid.: 22–23) rings true to Barker's intentions for his own theatre (cf. Barker, 2007: 22–24). In Barker's playwriting this does not result in an elevation of text above all other production elements; instead the text in itself requires its realisation on stage (as speech) in order to become the artwork as intended (cf. Beacham, 1994: 21–22), since ultimately dramatic text is written for performance. Indication and allusion rather than demonstration and representation pervade the scenographic thinking of both Barker and Appia (cf. Ibid.: 23).

Similarly, 'faith in the unconscious' (Ibid.: 42) to work with very few elements presented on stage and complete images through imagination is an apposite formulation of how Barker's sets out to structure the stage space, highlighting the closeness of Appia's and Barker's ideas and practice.

Appia's contemporary, Edward Gordon Craig, shared some similar ideas. Notably, Craig expressed great admiration for the work of Appia, whom he referred to as 'the foremost stage-decorator of Europe' (Craig, 1956: vii) and whose work he considered 'divine' (Ibid.). While the parallels between Appia and Barker can more readily be drawn, the inclusion of Craig serves to acknowledge that the scenographic developments championed by Appia did not exist in isolation. As actor, director, and scenic designer, Craig foreshadowed to some extent Barker's multi-focal approach, utilising the expertise of one role to further another. Craig declared that 'True Art is always discovering marvel in all that does not seem to be marvellous at all, because Art is not imitation, but vision' (Craig, 1956: xviii). In this, an immediate parallel to Barker's aim of continuous invention can be drawn (see Appendix 1: 191). In the same vein, Craig exalted 'imagination, that only power which achieves true Freedom' (Ibid.: xxiii). This echoes Barker's convictions against naturalism (e.g. 1997, 2005). The concurrent development of related ideas (suggestion of locale rather than illustration, work with levels, space structured by abstract shapes, musicality in lighting, etc.) by Appia and Craig at the turn of the 20th century indicate extreme changes in the conceptualisation of theatre, its aims, and its potential functions. An awareness of this evolution is crucial to any appropriately contextualised and detailed study of Barker's work as scenographer.

Like Appia, Craig saw inspiration in 'music and architecture' (Craig, 1956: 5), yet accorded primacy to nature (Ibid.). His understanding of the scene as 'a place which harmonizes with the thoughts of the poet' (Ibid.: 22), primarily constituted through 'lines and their direction' (Ibid.) suggests an approach similar to Appia's, which has become so commonplace in contemporary theatre: a simplification that works by suggestion, not by naturalistic implementation of detail. Craig's conviction was that '[a]ctuality, accuracy of detail, is useless upon the stage' (Ibid.: 27). Barker champions this principle, too, claiming that '[t]here is no problem that is not resolvable in terms of design' (Appendix 1: 180) as long as metaphor and poetry, not literal-mindedness, are engaged (Ibid.).

Like Barker, Appia appreciated the suggestive power of incompleteness, and favoured it over literal representations on stage. Craig on the other hand considered the incomplete outside the vast remit of beauty (Ibid.: 37). Incompleteness however is a crucial theatrical device in Barker, whether it is in the setting of the scene, in language, or in traditional character and plot. Even if one reconsiders Craig's rejection of the incomplete to refer to incoherence, it still remains apart from Barker's aim to 'be only ever proximate' (2005: 5), to repudiate meaning and instead embrace the ecstasy of its vanishing point (Ibid.: 14). However, incoherence – the impossibility of rational and complete understanding – does not equate to inconsistency. The scenographic and directorial decisions in Barker's production work are entirely deliberate, and come together in an internal logic of their own, even if that logic does not reveal itself explicitly, immediately, or readily to the audience.

Further, Craig's dismissal of the human voice (1956: 49) expressing 'greater admiration' (Ibid.) for instruments 'outside [the] person' (Ibid.) clashes with Barker's deliberate and sustained elevation of language and orchestration of actors' (vocal) skills as instruments in their own right (cf. Barker, 2007: 15). Additionally, Craig's emphasis on the visual aspects of theatre making (1956: 141) is at odds with Barker's increasingly totalising approach, in which sound, especially performed language,[8] is crucial to the overall result. The connection of Barker and Craig is therefore more focused on their shared conceptual ideals of what theatre might be and do, than on stylistic preferences and the specific realisations of their scenographic endeavours.

It becomes clear then that Barker's engagement with scenography and its realisation in production draw on a heritage of theoretical and practical developments beginning in the late 19th century. The above examples demonstrate how Barker's work finds clear predecessors in some of Craig's writings, but even more clearly in Appia's proposals for Wagner's operas. Similarly, the signature works of Robert Wilson in the late 1960s and early to mid-1970s illustrate wider developments in the theatre that were contemporary at the time – famously identified by Lehmann as 'postdramatic' (1999 first German ed., 2006 first English ed.) – which engaged with principles that had been outlined by Appia and Craig.

I take a moment here to briefly recapitulate the characteristics that Lehmann ascribed to the 'postdramatic': fragmentation of narrative, stylistic heterogeneity, hyper-naturalistic, grotesque, and neoexpressionist elements are among those aspects that he perceives as part of the postdramatic trend (cf. Lehmann, 2011: 26), though he emphasises that it is the constellation of such elements that ultimately decides whether a piece is postdramatic (Ibid.). The close relationship between the postmodern and the postdramatic that Lehmann identifies (cf. Ibid.: 29 ff.) stands in some contrast to Barker's theatre, which may be perceived as anachronistic in its elevation of the dramatic text, and its most frequent presentation of materials in a traditional proscenium arch arrangement. However, Lehmann's further identification of principles of layering, multiplications of meaning, 'opening up' (cf. Ibid.: 32), and so forth resonate very strongly with Barker's theatre, despite the latter's more traditional conception through singly authored play texts.

The influence of Lehmann's publication on academic discourse can hardly be overstated, as it continues to offer a comprehensive and provocative vocabulary for describing a diverse range of production modes in contemporary theatre and performance practice. However, in terms of Barker's theatre, its usefulness is significantly limited: after all, Barker continues to work with classically conceived dramatic texts, singly authored, finished before production begins, and with lines usually assigned to specific figures. Barker's modes of production are therefore the reverse of much that Lehmann analyses and categorises as postdramatic; it is in content and presentation that affinities can be identified. Since Lehmann uses the work of Robert Wilson as an example in his analysis, and I propose to place Barker into a scenographic lineage with Wilson, the influence of *Postdramatic Theatre* remains notable, if not immediately relevant to this book.

Wilson's training in fine arts and architecture, detailed on his website, has thoroughly shaped his approach to theatre making. Consequently, his theatre emphasises visual aspects over textual approaches insofar as 'written text is only a small part of this larger text [of performance]' (Holmberg, 1996: 39) in which Wilson connects the words 'not on a surface, but on a deep level' (Ibid.) as he considers any imposition of interpretation 'aesthetic fascism' (Ibid.: 62). This way of working, with its emphasis on individual meaning-making, continues until the present day. Visual layering in Wilson's work is more immediately obvious than in Barker's. Nonetheless, the inconclusiveness and abstraction that Barker's pieces present visually, in combination with their soundscapes and overwhelming spoken texts, result in a layering that is similarly resistant to conventional narrative meaning-making. In both Barker and Wilson's works, the multiplication of meanings obliges the audience to choose where to focus their attention. German scenographer Goebbels, who I discuss in more detail below, describes Wilson's work as achieving 'unity by radical independence of the theatrical means' (2015: 62). Such collage is perhaps less foregrounded in Barker's work than in Wilson's, yet the depth of Barker's scenography similarly refuses reduction to immediately understandable situations in terms of traditional plot. Rather, Barker's scenography offers multiple focal counterpoints to the plays' figures, their speeches, and their actions. Both the creation of striking and emotive visual imagery and an emphasis on the musicality of language are principles shared by Barker and Wilson.

Further, language was a constitutive part of the overall soundscapes in Wilson's earlier works, rather than playing a traditionally communicative role. This approach remains predominant in his work (cf. Goebbels, 2015: 63). The primacy of language as a tool for sense-making and the advancement of narrative is suspended in Wilson, as it is in Barker. In the work of the latter, though language is expressive, it acts more on an experiential and sensually expressive level than by fulfilling a direct, communicative function (e.g. the overlapping speeches of Pindar and Tot in *Blok/Eko,* Barker, 2011: 60). Where a communicative function is employed in Barker's writing it tends to be ambiguous, filled with associative and emotive content (e.g. Isonzo's war memories; Barker, 2012a: 67–68). In particular, Barker's non-textual exordia, which he began implementing from the 1990s onwards and which are often developed late in the rehearsal process, display a notable resonance with the haunting living tableaux of Wilson's works such as *Deafman Glance* (1971).

Another shared feature of Wilson's and Barker's work is the distension of time that both practitioners employ; this is intricately bound up with the indeterminacy of space that pervades their work. In these aspects, Wilson and Barker both present conceptual challenges to the audience and require that spectators submit themselves to an ordeal of intensity and of duration (cf. Barker, 2005a: 25). Barker privileges anxiety and 'unknowing' (Ibid.: 11), for his characters as much as for his audiences: there is a sense of on-going discovery within the world of the plays. Barker invites a continued struggle for meaning, even or especially, if it remains fruitless. Equally, Wilson's work may be described as dreamscapes, emphasising visual storytelling through 'architecture [...] in time and space' (Wilson in Shevtsova, 2007: 42), in which the internal logic of the piece is apparent to those that present it, yet 'requires the spectator to suspend the search for meaning' (Holmberg, 1996: 60). The requirement that audiences submit themselves to the logic of each piece, and suspend their everyday understanding of space and time, is apparent in both practitioners' works.

Additionally, the importance of expressive gesture arises in both. In Wilson, the choreographic nature of actors' bodies, set pieces and properties on stage, and their interactions in time and space come together as scenographic compositions that exist and function outside of, as well as alongside, textual components (e.g. *Einstein on the Beach*, 1976, and *Hamletmachine*, 1986). In Barker, gestures are both physical and verbal: each utterance is a manipulation, an attempt to elicit responses from other figures on stage or to explore possibilities of self (cf. McArthur in Rabey, 2013). They 'try on' and 'try out' subjectivity through speech, or as Freeland phrases it, '[s]peech is first of all a mode of bodily presence in Barker's theatre' (2011: 78). This use of language in Barker is complemented and contrasted through movements that become 'what perhaps cannot be said [...,] a gesture toward the unseen depths of thought' (Ibid.: 91). Notably, Wilson's working method is much more prescriptive to the actors (cf. Otto-Bernstein, 2007), whereas Barker trusts the ensemble of the Wrestling School to find resonant and often archetypical gestures in response to, and through, the text they are performing (cf. Appendix 1: 191–192). However, the precise lighting that both practitioners employ places restrictions on the actors' freedom of movement and requires exact, repeatable physical choreography. Wilson often begins with a structure based on geometrical shapes (Holmberg, 1996: 82), pre-imposing certain spatial arrangements on the actors; this is not the case with Barker, though he specifies that 'the rhythm of the writing oblige[s] the placing. The one follows the other. It is spiritual. If you can't do that, you can't direct my work. It is a spiritual thing. That line means he is there, she is there' (see Appendix 1: 187).

In addition, both Wilson and Barker explore sound as a multidimensional element that affects time and thereby space; it is 'privileged for its referential ambiguity and polyvalence' (Curtin, 2012: 269). The complexity of Wilson's soundscapes is comparable to those of Barker, though the latter emphasises heightened performed language and 'the ecstasy of vanishing meaning' (Barker, 2005a: 14) over explicit linguistic deconstruction.[9] Both (largely) suspend the exchange function of dialogue on stage. Nonetheless, language may occur as a negotiation, manipulation, and seduction in Barker (cf. Lamb, 2005: 69 ff.), utilising the particular surrounding soundscape's 'potential strangeness as a signifying agent' (Curtin, 2012: 269) to multiply associative possibilities for the audience. The pieces of Wilson and Barker admit their artifice, and demand to be encountered on their own terms. Similarly, the work of German scenographer and theatre maker, Heiner Goebbels, foregrounds an experiential encounter with his works.

Goebbels deliberately seeks to work with incongruity and distance (2015: ix) and to engage with the 'value and integrity of all media' (Ibid.: xv) involved in the production; his work aims to foreground materiality (Ibid.), and 'trust in the intelligence of the audience' (Ibid.: xvi). He does this by presenting works that possess openness, 'non-representational, non-referential theatricality' (Ibid.), and invite individual interpretation and imaginative engagement. The parallel timeline of Goebbels' and Barker's scenographic practice[10] and the distinctly European character of both point towards the continuation of a scenographic tradition that is inextricably linked to Appia and Craig (cf. Ibid.: xvi). The crucial difference from Barker is that Goebbels does not necessarily work with (play) text, nor does he use actors as primary expressive media (cf. Ibid.: xv). However, *Aesthetics of Absence: Texts on Theatre* (2015) offers reflexive writings by Goebbels that are akin to Barker's theorisations on theatre in their poetic presentation (cf. Barker, 2005a, 2014b, 2016). Since Goebbels' works present an influential example of contemporary scenographic practice, and the texts presented in *Aesthetics of Absence* offer a rare insight into a scenographer's theorisation around their own work, the monograph constitutes an outstanding contemporary example of discourse in the field. It indicates the significant developments in scenography in terms of its increasing recognition as a worthy field of research, and the ways in which theatre itself is conceived, among other things. Goebbels' scenographic works, but more importantly in the context of this book, *Aesthetics of Absence*, offers a relevant contemporary example of the developments in scenographic discourse that further situates Barker within a European lineage of scenography, as well as in contemporary scenographic practice.

In summary, it is clear that developments in theatre and performance in the mid to late 20th century Western world took on many iterations in which scenography's development from design for performance to design as inextricable and constitutive part of performance became increasingly distinct. Howard Barker's work as discussed within this book therefore exists in a lineage of scenographers that have thought out, delineated, and experimented with similar principles in their practice. It is thus possible to use these in order to appropriately contextualise Barker's work and support analysis by drawing on historical materials in addition to the selected plays. As the reader is now contextually briefed, both in terms of the philosophical grounding of this book, and its existence in the developing discourse of scenography, I conclude this introduction with an overview of the subsequent chapters' content.

Chapter 1 reiterates and expands on the intersecting definitions of space, place, and set, and outlines the ways in which Barker's scenographic use of space results in a deliberate conceptual and visual destabilisation of place. It draws on key examples throughout the time period specified, offering insights into the developments of Barker's spatial scenography both conceptually in the text and as realised in production. The chapter identifies core working principles of Barker's spatial scenography, drawing on play texts as well as archival materials of relevant productions. In particular, the tension between physical space and imaginary place is analysed in detail, considering the relationship between the conceptual and actual, as well as onstage and offstage. The analysis is complemented by interview materials from a conversation held with Howard Barker for the purposes of this research.

Chapter 2 engages in a detailed analysis of light and darkness in Barker's scenography. It considers Barker's lighting in conjunction with its effects on space. The chapter engages with principles of light and darkness in a Western art historical and philosophical context, and contrasts these to Barker's personal philosophy. The notion of the *Ganzfeld* effect (cf. Abulafia, 2016; Karasek, 2010) appears as a useful descriptor of some of the effects generated through lighting in Barker's scenography. It is connected to the previously outlined framework of aesthetics, in particular the sublime. The chapter therefore also explores the connections between lighting and darkness in relation to their significance in terms of the conception of subjectivity and the limits of perception, which offers strong links to postmodern theories of the sublime. The tension between the visible and invisible is similarly analysed in relation to the preceding chapter (what is on stage, what is not) and in terms of the theoretical framework. Where possible and relevant, the chapter draws on available archival materials to expand the analysis of key play texts. It furthermore offers observations by long-standing Wrestling School associates Ace McCarron and Helen Morley, whose lighting work with Barker covers most of the chosen examples.

Chapter 3 expands the visual aspect of Barker's scenography as analysed in the preceding two chapters to engage in detail with costume, styling, and the processes of (un)dressing. It draws connections between stage space, place, and the costumed performing body. It considers the construction of character and subject identity through processes of dressing and undressing and makes connections to the theoretical framework with a particular emphasis on boundaries, their transgression, and the generation of selfhood (cf. Monks, 2010). The chapter engages in detailed analysis of the reciprocal influences of stage space, lighting, and costume regarding time period, geographical location, and cultural markers of gender and status. This analysis is used to derive core working principles of Barker's costumes as part of the visual scenography. Like the preceding chapters, Chapter 3 draws on salient examples from a selection of play texts, supplemented by analysis of available archival materials where possible. Furthermore, the analysis is expanded by materials from the interview with Howard Barker, which was conducted as part of this research, and presents an exclusive look at Barker's design sketches.

Chapter 4 considers sound as part of Barker's scenography. It establishes the term aurality (cf. Kendrick and Roesner, 2011b) and offers definitions for the discussion of different categories of sound that arise in Barker's sonic scenography. The chapter analyses the rhythmical and choreographic qualities of both sound and silence in Barker's work in relation to the visual aspects of scenography. It considers the ways in which sound contributes to structuring time and space on and off stage. Sound and silence are also analysed in terms of the generation of tension regarding the limits of perception on the part of the audience. Furthermore, the chapter analyses the sonic function of performed text in Barker in conjunction with other sounds. The notion of the ubiquity effect (cf. Augoyard and Torgue, 2005; Home-Cook, 2015) appears in this chapter as a sonic complement to the *Ganzfeld* effect discussed in Chapter 2 to enable a more detailed comparative discussion of the respective scenographic elements in Barker's work. In establishing non-visual scenographic working principles, this chapter rounds off the individual analyses of different aspects of scenography. As in previous chapters, archival materials are used to supplement the textual analysis. In addition, Chapter 4 includes materials from an interview with the late Paul Bull, a long-standing Wrestling School associate and award-winning sound designer.

The conclusion offers a recapitulation of the aims of the book before synthesising the findings of the research, drawing connections between Chapters 1 to 4 in order to articulate the general working principles of Barker's scenography.

Notes

1 Examples include the National Theatre's 2012 production of *Scenes from an Execution* and *Lot and His God* at the Print Room, both in London and the world premiere staging of *The Forty (Few Words)* at Theatr Y Castell, Aberystwyth, in the same year. *Victory* and *The Possibilities* in a double bill at Glasgow's Tron Theatre in 2013. *Innocence* at Théâtre des Célestins in Lyon, *Ursula: Fear of the Estuary* at the Riverfront Theatre in Newport, *Seven Lears* at Warwick Arts Centre and the revival of *The Forty (Few Words)* at Emily Davies Studio, Aberystwyth University, all took place in 2014. 2015 saw a double bill of *The Twelfth Battle of Isonzo* and *Judith: A Parting from the Body* at the Arcola Theatre in London, and *Und* at Théâtre Olympia, Tours, touring through Paris in 2015 and 2016. 2016 also saw Theatre N16's London production of *Gertrude – The Cry*, and Théâtre des Célestins presented *Scenes from an Execution* in Lyon. The Print Room, London, staged *In the Depths of Dead Love* in 2017. In the same year, Randolph College students performed *Wounds to the Face* at Toronto's Annex Theatre in 2017, while in New York Potomac Theatre Project staged *Pity in History*. PTP then staged *The Possibilities* in 2018, while Red Tape Theatre presented *I Saw Myself*. Despite the Wrestling School's hiatus, Barker's work continues to be performed internationally.
2 These are all examples that actually contain the term 'scenography' in their title; there are many more that engage related terminology, e.g. Malloy, 2014 and Klingelhoefer, 2017, and resources outside the English language context.
3 Rachel Hann notes that variations of the term skēnē translate as 'stage' in various continental European languages (2018: 3). Here, I set this etymological complication aside for clarity's sake.

4 This is not to suggest that the two are mutually exclusive ways of working with scenography, quite the contrary.

5 Compare also Rabey's discussion of this regarding Rudkin's work (1997).

6 It should be noted here that Barker conceives text and language as the heart of his work (Barker and Houth, 2007: 15); however, he acknowledges the necessity of all other elements of production in order to achieve the expressiveness he seeks (Barker in Brown, 2011: 81).

7 'Affect' here refers to prerational responses – physical and emotional – that impact on bodyminds (cf. Schalk, 2018) as a result of various stimuli (cf. Clough and Halley, eds., 2007).

8 Performed language in this context extends beyond speech to include song and utterance, among other forms of verbalisation that may use words, but do not necessarily fulfil a communicative function.

9 Deconstruction here refers to ways of employing language in a fragmented, often repetitive form that privileges rhythm and sound over rational meaning, often obscuring recognisable words by the way in which they are spoken. The intensity and density of Barker's poetic play text may very well be perceived as deconstructive in terms of meaning, whilst generally refraining from formal deconstruction (*Charles V* presents a notable exception; Barker, 2012b).

10 Goebbels' first music-theatre piece, *Schwarz auf Weiß*, premiered in 1996; Barker's scenographic engagement with his own playwriting began in 1998.

1 Space and place

Howard Barker's scenographic work is a contemporary example of the practice of scenography as a fundamentally constitutive part of performance in theatre making. Though the different underlying principles of his scenography manifest across all aspects of it, discussing them in separate chapters enables a closer look at the particularities of their practical manifestations. I begin with space as defined in the introduction, since theatre is 'a space of spaces'[1] (Waldenfels, 2014: 24; my translation) that possesses the potential to be anywhere, although the physical dimensions of any stage naturally impose some constrictions. However, stage space holds the possibility of creating infinite imaginative places. These exist by their very nature alongside and within the physical space in which they arise. Tatari's describes the emergence of such places on stage as 'an opening-up of places that are not given places nor can they become given, absolute, which also means inequivalent places as pulsing openings of space-times' (2014: 95; my translation).[2] She highlights this irresolvable, inconclusive nature as a fundamental and productive aspect of stage space. Over the course of this chapter, the reader will find immediate meeting points with Barker's spatial scenography in this idea. Arguably, all scenographic elements are spatial to a degree, as audio-visual perception requires 'somewhere' in order to happen (cf. Eke, 2014: 31), even if said space is virtual or imaginary. It is therefore prudent to begin analysis of Barker's scenography with a focus on stage space, place, and set.

One of the express aims of this book is to identify some core working principles of Barker's scenography in relation to the concept of the sublime. Thus, we may consider the possibility of a scenographic sublime that enables suitable description and analysis of Barker's scenographic work. The unquestionable spatiality of the theatre, and consequently Barker's dramatic scenography, necessitates an analysis of the ways in which the limitlessness and conceptual upheaval of boundaries at the heart of postmodern conceptions of the sublime (cf. Johnson, 2012: 122) offer salient meeting points with the necessarily limited, and physically defined stage space, and theatrical places that arise through use of set in said space. In this chapter, I draw on examples across roughly 20 years, from when Barker first engaged as a scenographer (*Ursula*, 1998[3]).

The first section focuses on what I have termed landscape plays, loosely following Gertrude Stein's notion of a landscape theatre of ongoing beginnings (1926: 2). This offers the reader an understanding of Barker's scenography for plays on an epic scale. I then discuss what I call Barker's chamber plays, beginning with the solo piece *Und* (1999). The chamber plays explore the particularities of scenographic space on a seemingly domestic scale, which is fundamentally complicated by the specific ways in which Barker utilises spatial scenography to destabilise these apparently familiar and familial scenes. The conclusion draws together the different types of plays, identifying the underlying spatial principles. The notion of atmosphere arises as a concept related to both landscape and the postmodern sublime, tying together contemporary developments in scenography and aesthetics. The scenographic principles of Barker's work are complex; therefore, this chapter focuses on spatial instability as a core performative feature, the deliberate oscillation of place through indeterminate space, the seemingly opposing principles of emptiness and excess, and placelessness.

Landscape plays

In 1998, the Wrestling School staged *Ursula* under Barker's direction at Birmingham Repertory. This marked the first time that he also took on scenographic responsibilities, designing the set under the pseudonym Tomas Leipzig. In a 2016 interview, he explained his move into design as follows:

> ...with that first *(Uncle) Vanya* show, 1996 I think that was, I told the designer what I wanted. [...] I told him 'do you mind if I show you? It can't be a Chekhovian set, because it is an anti-Chekhovian play. Can we set it in an old, sunken freighter, a rusty freighter, with decks and iron staircases?' [...] he was very cooperative. [...] Having done that, I then thought, [...] I might as well do it, and work with someone as an assistant who knows the technical stuff, and can go to the workshops and can do what I can't do: make the stage models, do the arithmetic. [...] So, I did half the designer's job, I did the design and handed the practical stuff to somebody else. That's how that happened; I just kept doing it. Because I am a painter, I have got a visual sense, of course. I wouldn't let anyone else design now.
>
> (Appendix 1: 174)

While *Ursula* perhaps lends itself more readily to analysis in terms of sound, the fact that its 1998 Wrestling School production marked the beginning of Barker's scenographic stage work, necessitates some consideration of its spatial premises, and their realisation in production.

The staging at Birmingham Repertory utilised a traditional proscenium arch arrangement, with a black, polished stage floor cut across by thin lines. On record, these appear to be either thin strips of metal set into the floor or bright white paint. As the surviving visual materials are of limited quality, a more exact description is unfortunately not possible. However, I do again recommend the reader seek out the Wrestling School's YouTube channel, as it hosts extracts of *Ursula,* among other examples discussed in this book.

The back of the stage disappeared into darkness, evoking the *chiaroscuro* effects of Renaissance paintings, a recurring lighting technique I discuss in more detail in Chapter 2. This empty stage space was at times augmented by wheeled set pieces reminiscent of portable hospital screens. Otherwise, locations throughout the play were brought to live through verbal description, such as when Placida imagines the estuary, 'lapping water and one solitary curlew crying' (Barker, 2008a: 87). Notably, this description, as many others throughout the play, foregrounds sound. More on this in Chapter 4.

The entrance of 'a nun' (Ibid.) by which the play opens, suggests the setting of a convent in all probability through costume, even if place is not concretised through spatial markers. In many ways, Placida's line 'Don't look I'll look for you' (Ibid.: 88) is an invitation to the audience as much as an instruction to the novices: it is through the rich descriptions that places come into being on stage.

The lack of concrete signifiers not only allows for easier transitions between spaces and places, for example from inside the convent to outside on the riverbank, but also individuates the scenes through each spectator's imagination. In *Ursula*, place is important chiefly in terms of its evocative power. Though frequent descriptions of landscape appear throughout the play text, their physical appearance on stage is not important. The titular estuary, like the river the nuns travel on, is important mainly for its liminal quality. Similarly, the suggestions of wildness and unpredictability associated with these landscapes are in deliberate contrast with the ordered and tightly structured nature of convent life. As such, the convent, the river, the estuary, and the castle become merely textual descriptors of atmospheres, which in production are evoked not by set, but by other scenographic means.

The notion of atmosphere has gained significant traction in theatre and performance studies in recent years, due to the rising prominence of affect theory (cf. Gregg and Seigworth, 2010) and new materialist thinking, especially in the field of scenography (cf. McKinney and Palmer, 2017; Hann, 2018). I propose that the notion of atmosphere, due to its undeniable presence, but indefiniteness, can be employed productively in the analysis of Barker's spatial scenography. Further, I propose that atmosphere is conceptually linked with Lyotard's notion of landscape, which is in turn tied to postmodern conceptions of the sublime. All three engage the non-rational, experiential encounter of subjects who are literally ecstatic, in the original sense of the word as being outside oneself. The atmospheric landscapes of Barker's scenography refuse being fixed places, yet they do not become wholly unrecognisable either. Where *Ursula* uses several liminal locations to generate spatial instability, my next example engages this principle somewhat differently.

While limited to one location, *A House of Correction* similarly depends on spatial liminality. The play proposes certain spatial premises, which are dismantled over time. In the play, the courier Godansk puzzles 'What is this place ...?' (Barker, 2010b: 113), a question that remains without definite answer. From the start, the play establishes a vertical expansion of the stage space beyond the visible to a possibly infinite, open sky through a 'storm of leaflets' (Ibid.: 89) cascading into 'a damaged room' (Ibid.). This immediately establishes an instability of traditional boundaries separating inside and outside, which renders the visible space vulnerable. The physical and conceptual boundaries by which such differences are commonly defined are literally broken, but do not vanish completely, resulting in an unsettling overlap. This is particularly apparent in the juxtaposition of the 'snowfall of leaflets' (Ibid.: 92) with the 'haggard, pale' (Ibid.: 90) figure of Hebbel in his bed (Figure 1.1). The presence of a character who is visually coded as physically fragile in a potentially hostile environment heightens the sense of wrongness: logic dictates that they belong to separate spaces and yet they are presented as elements in a single, coherent, but certainly unsettling environment. This compounds a sense of peril that has no concrete object to fix upon as its source.

In *A House of Correction*, the attempted withdrawal from outside influences is subverted and continually disturbed by the leaflet raids and repeated appearances of the courier Godansk. This physical dismantling of

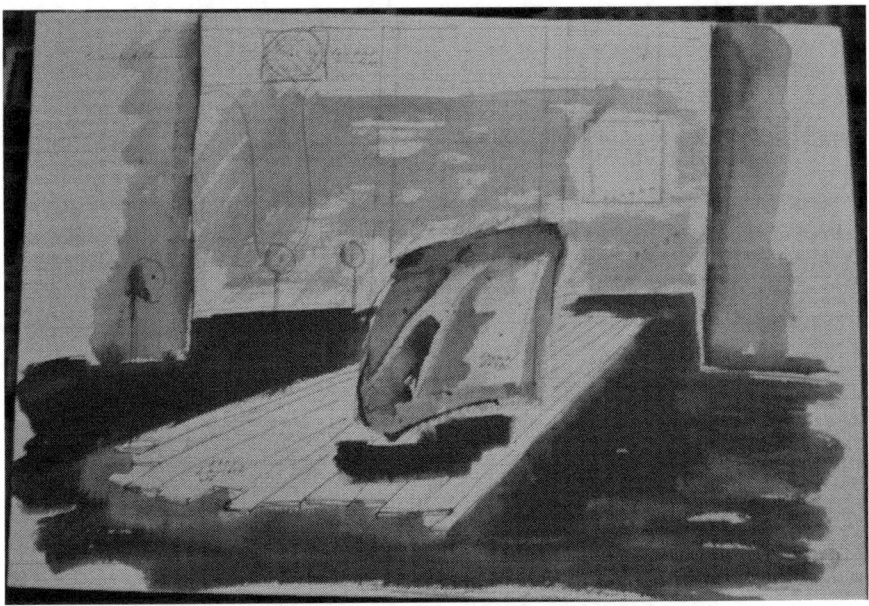

Figure 1.1 Set Design for *A House of Correction*. © Howard Barker

borders echoes the 'dissolution of all distinctions' (2012: 116) that Guyer discusses in relation to Nietzsche. Nietzsche considered it conditional to the sublime as 'experience of the dissolution of rationality' (Ibid.), which follows the breakdown of concepts that usually exist by virtue of definition against one another: inside is 'not outside', and vice versa. The spatial scenography therefore becomes a question of 'both/and' rather than 'either/or', resulting in an uneasy coexistence of potentially contradictory concepts.

The imaginary infinite extension upwards is matched by an equivalent expansion downwards through the offstage well that Hebbel is thrown into later in the play. This imagined extension of space downwards brings to mind Aronson's assessment of the stage as an abyss, and one that 'returns the gaze' (2005: 1). Though located offstage, the well intrudes onto the stage through characters that report back their interactions with it. The premise of a (in some Barker plays explicitly named) bottomless well challenges the limits of imagination. In the words of Kristeva, it pulls the subject 'toward the place where meaning collapses' (1982: 2). This is aggravated by confronting audiences with a situation that is defined by its 'lack of referentiality' (Lyotard, 1989: 188) to concrete experiences and the laws of physics.

Particularly by being offstage, and thus intangible in every way, these interruptions of the imaginary landscape draw attention to the active engagement of an individual's imaginative facilities, and their limitations. Spectators' imaginations run up against the idea of limitlessness, which necessarily cannot be contemplated in its entirety, even as it can be conceptually understood. The deliberate removal of these unthinkable spatial occurrences, such as a truly bottomless well, from the visible, and audible, grasp of the audience forces a displacement of the encounter with the thing from the stage world into an individual's imagination. There, the impossibility of its existence in the physical world and the simultaneous possibility of its existence in imagination expose a fault line in the constitution of subjectivity. Namely, that it is predicated on being able to set out clear rules by which its boundaries, and thus its being, are established. This, as Kristeva phrases it, results in these imagined spaces and places to be 'situated outside the domain of meaning', turning them into 'an external essence...a sublime object' (Kristeva, 1996: 203). In refusing conclusive meaning, and instead forcing audiences to repeatedly attempt to make sense of the overwhelming strangeness of the stage space, in particular its invisible and imaginary aspects (whether it is the depth of the well, the expanse of sinister yet seductive buildings, or invading hordes offstage), Barker offers a sequence of potentially sublime objects for the individual spectator to contend with.

The onstage space in *A House of Correction* is further complicated by frequent references to the 'puzzling nature of the courtyards, none of which are connected to another except in a wholly arbitrary way' (Barker, 2010b: 114). This suggested labyrinthine nature of the play's setting expands the imagined place far beyond the confines of the visible playing area. The vague but supposedly vast place of the play's action offers the audience spatial uncertainty for contemplation: while the place of the play is constant (the entire action takes place in the same room), its boundaries are perpetually shifting as the offstage world is expanded not only beyond the spatial boundaries of the acting area, but also supposedly beyond the realm of physics (e.g. through the bottomless well). This unstable stage space thus imaginatively overwhelms the audience by scenographic means that are suggested verbally. This principle already emerged, if more subtly, in *Ursula*. Confronted by an ever-expanding, yet resolutely elusive setting, an individual may draw close to the 'abyss of the mind' (2007: 33) that Gritzner sees at the core of tragedy.

This destabilisation of the limited and limiting frame of the visible perform-ance area is a driving force in the increasing uncertainty that the characters face. The continuous and progressive upheaval of conceptual space on stage becomes the impending crisis that the characters expect to happen at any point. The effects of this crisis not happening (until the very end at least, des-pite Shardlo's assertion that Godansk is the crisis, Barker, 2010b: 146), but its sustained threat, render the instability of the stage a source of perpetual terror that brings Lyotard's conception of the sublime acutely to mind: the 'possibility of nothing happening' (Lyotard, 1989: 198) opens an immense void that imagination desperately attempts to fill, yet never succeeds in doing so completely (cf. Ibid.: 147).

Though *A House of Correction* does not offer an audience the same false comfort of apparent stability that other plays like *Und* initially do, its characters accept the leaflet bombings as normal, framing them as regular parts of the onstage world. However, as the play progresses and people get lost in a maze of courtyards (supposedly like the one that is visible before the audience) there is an increasing sense that this acceptance is a desperate attempt at making sense of something that is beyond understanding.[4] This culminates in the discovery of the well, the attempted murder of Hebbel in it, and the subsequent failed attempt to fill it up with rubble. The strange but benign fall of poetry is shortly thereafter replaced by gunfire (2010b: 183), a further threat of and to the space, this time deadly. The strange and frail logic that the place of the play initially appears to follow is destroyed: whatever that place is, it operates not just outside of conventional logic and predict-ability but also outside any logic its characters may have attempted to impose upon it.

The 2005 play *The Fence in Its Thousandth Year* (hereafter *The Fence*) con-tinues Barker's principle of suggesting certain spatial premises and parameters, only to devolve or undermine them throughout the play. Kristeva's notion of leaking bodies (1982: 102) might be usefully adapted to consider the effects of Barker's spatial scenography as 'leaky spaces'. It is not only a notion of fluidity that affects visual and conceptual boundaries in Barker's spatial scen-ography, but the concept of leaking implies an uncontrolled, unintended, and potentially infectious quality. This suitably links to Barker's notion of the theatre as 'house of infection […] in the age of social hygiene' (1997: 182) that might allow for ways of creating productive anxiety (cf. Ibid.: 188–189).

At the heart *of The Fence* is the premise of a structured, civilised duchy enclosed by a 'frontier fence' (Barker, 2005b: 7) that keeps out the 'thieves' (Ibid.) of the surrounding area. However, as Mangan notes: '[the play] weaves together an extraordinary variety of themes: the personal and the private; intimacy and power; limits and taboos; [...] freedom and constraint' (2013: 90). Many of these themes centre on the image of the fence, which is 'an intrinsic part of the set design' (Ibid.) that remains visible throughout the play. It also sets out the complexity of conceptual and narrative threads through its striking opening image in which an elegant woman submits to copulation with several desperate figures through a wire fence (cf. Barker, 2005b: 7). As transpires in the next scene, the woman is in fact the duchess Algeria, whose realm is protected by the fence.

The play hinges on the notion of boundaries, physical and social, and the ways in which they invite their own violation (cf. Ibid.: 17) by virtue of their existence. Further, the play explores the parallels between physical and mental boundaries, such as when Photo observes that 'it is the idea of the frontier that you judge offensive' (Ibid.: 19). The notion of social and mental barriers is crucial to the relationship of Photo and Algeria: though he is – he thinks – her nephew, they have an intense incestuous relationship: 'I kiss my aunt I strip my aunt I put my lips between her legs' (Ibid.: 12). This serves as the manifestation of their privilege: where others are bound by social rules, 'in this as in so many things' (Ibid.) those in power may redefine the boundaries at will, or simply exceed them. It later comes to light that Photo is in fact Algeria's son, not her nephew (Ibid.: 14), begotten by a blind thief in one of her night-time encounters at the fence. These therefore become parallel violations of the body politic of the duchy and of Algeria as representative thereof. As Mangan phrases it: 'the site of resistance to authoritarian structures [...] is the body and the mode of resistance is desire' (2013: 91). This also resonates with Kristeva's observation on the 'prohibition placed on the maternal body (as a defence against autoeroticism and incest taboo)' (1982: 14), which Algeria repeatedly and continuously defies through her actions. The result is a 'non-distinctiveness of inside and outside [...], a border passable in both directions by pleasure and pain' (Ibid.: 61). The concurrent presence of pleasure and pain that arise in an unnameable transgression recalls Lyotard's writing on the sublime as that which 'consciousness cannot formulate' (1989: 197).

In *The Fence*, the anxiety caused by this 'impossible bounding' (Kristeva, 1982: 12) is expressed in the cyclical appearance, maintenance, decay, and reinstatement of the physical, visible boundary of the wire fence. The omnipresent set piece both attests to an outside and a beyond which supposedly expands past the visible stage space and simultaneously attests to the invariable, though perhaps not immediately apparent limitations of boundaries, be they socially or physically constructed: 'High is the fence [...]/Long is the fence [...]/HOW DEEP IS IT THOUGH' (Barker, 2005b: 29) muses Kidney after observing the duchess with the thieves. The question of depth is a recurring one in Barker, as discussed earlier with reference to the repeated image of the (bottomless) well he employs. The impermeable nature of the boundary therefore becomes a matter of perspective.

The 2005 Wrestling School production's spatial organisation was fundamentally confrontational: the fence cut nearly straight across the stage space, suggesting on the one hand a substantial expansion of it,[5] and on the other hand providing a greater sense of depth. This was amplified by cross-lighting that enabled an emergence of figures from the darkness beyond. Consequently, the central notion of a boundary of questionable stability is conceptually explored as well as spatially presented and interrogated through the characters' interactions with the fence.

Lyotard's conception of the landscape as an interruption to narrative (1991: 187) becomes, in the context of *The Fence*, an interruption of the dominant narratives of stability that are predicated on a clear distinction between two opposing poles of a dichotomy. The fence (as an object) becomes the manifestation of its own idea: the possibility that boundaries can not only be clearly identified, but also maintained. However, the deliberate transgression of this boundary by those who supposedly ordered its construction undermines this certainty. This is where Kidney's questioning of the fence's depth comes to bear: the visible may attest to a clear and well-maintained distinction, but it is in those aspects which lie beyond the immediately apparent that the precariousness and fluidity of its existence are most strongly implied. Notably, the proliferation of blind characters in the play supports the fallible logic of those that assert the stability of visible boundaries (cf. Barker in Gritzner and Rabey, 2006: 32). The thieves' realm therefore becomes a landscape in the Lyotardian sense, as that which exists '[b]eyond the pale, beyond the cultivated land, beyond the realm of form' (Lyotard, 1991: 186) and threatens the cognizable, domesticated in its indeterminate, infinite character (cf. Ibid.: 184–185).

Where the spatial stability of *A House of Correction* is conjured by the way in which the play sets up specific expectations regarding its location (which are subsequently infringed upon tangibly and conceptually), *The Fence* is more abstract in its approach to renditions of place within a single stage space. On the one hand, the play presents changing locales, such as a cemetery (Barker, 2005b: 7), 'a bedroom in the ducal palace' (Ibid.: 21), a 'park of babies and sunshine' (Ibid.: 30), and a zoo (Ibid.: 39), returning to the frontier again and again in changing seasons (cf. Ibid.: 26–30) and times of day. The wire fence therefore becomes a constant theme, which in production served as the backdrop to various locations, such as the cemetery, zoo, and the mental institution – crucially, all fenced, and the latter two dependent on a fence in their functions – that Algeria is later imprisoned in.

As such, the themes of inside/outside, us/them, self/other visibly manifested alongside the character's explorations of the concepts in a broader context such as the identification of sterility (Ibid.: 53) and madness (Ibid.: 59) as metaphorical fences that separate the normal population from those who suffer these circumstances. Notably, it is Algeria as a (initially) powerful woman who in her sterility rejects continuing prevalent notions of the worth of women predicated on their fecundity. Similarly, the institutionalisation of women transgressing the established social order has long-standing historical precedents that demonise female sexuality and self-determination. Photo identifies the cost of social stability that offers 'freedom *from* therefore not freedom *to*' (Ibid.: 70; original emphasis), and crucially the manifestation of desire as freedom (Ibid.) which degenerates under the restrictions of social order and the resulting sense of responsibility (Ibid.).

Another way in which Barker explores the themes of the play lies in the mutual transgression of the boundary: not only is it violated by Algeria's behaviour, but also through the strange ritual of throwing watering cans across (Ibid.: 15) in a futile attempt to entice the thieves to 'CO-PY' (Ibid.) honest agricultural behaviour. From the other side, the border is transgressed through the throwing of infants inside (cf. Ibid.: 27). This practice seems to have been going on for a substantial amount of time, since the duchy now contains '[t]hree fields of baby thieves and it started in a garden' (Ibid.: 34). The substantial presence of the infants from the outside taking up, and perhaps taking over the inside of the duchy (spatially as well as perhaps genetically), invalidates the very purpose of the fence, since 'a holed fence [...] [is] the very definition of impotence/futility frustration and redundancy' (Ibid.: 24).

As in other Barker plays, *The Fence* sets out spatial parameters that are subverted over the course of the action. However, unlike in *A House of Correction*, the undoing of the premise is begun explicitly in the opening image of *The Fence*, though in the former, the 'damaged room' (Barker, 2010: 89) already evokes a sense of instability and precariousness. In the latter, the circularity of the 'frontier fence' (Barker, 2005b: 7) that becomes 'rotted and thick with clinging litter' (Ibid.: 45) until the mental asylum's fence 'falls, pristine' (Ibid.: 56) implies a continuation of this pattern of perpetually reasserting imperfect boundaries. Though the fence disappears gradually, the play concludes with the promise of a new frontier as a surveyor and his assistant (Ibid.: 71) measure out the new boundary and 'the sound of tapping travels over the landscape' (Ibid.) as guiding pegs are set into the ground. As in other Barker plays, this non-resolution of conflicts results in a conceptual lacuna, which the audience must contend with. Similarly, the suggestive and incompletely prescribed places, which Barker's spatial scenography conjures, remain to haunt the imagination long after the lights have faded.

The next play I discuss, *Found in the Ground*, draws on imaginative hauntings of a slightly different kind. Roughly following the burning of a former Nuremberg judge's library at his behest, the play draws on a distinctly European memory by evoking imagery of the spaces and places of the Second World War: concentration camps, bombed out cities, and seemingly tranquil landscapes marred by memories of death and violence.

This is established from the offset, as the exordium of *Found in the Ground* presents an immediate excess of sound and imagery that is subsequently multiplied throughout the play. To the soundtrack of an unceasing yet unspecified industrial process, a naked, headless woman perambulates through an unidentifiable landscape (Barker, 2008b: 123). In production, images of bombed out cities were projected onto hanging screens behind her. This woman, listed in the credits as Macedonia, is merely one example of Barker's combination of the alluring and the repulsive in ways which recall Kristeva's proposition that 'the abject is edged with the sublime' (Kristeva, 1982: 11). The oscillation between attraction and repulsion lies at the heart of the sublime experience in which fear and pleasure are simultaneously encountered by a subject that is overwhelmed by encountering that which inspires these emotions. We are riven with potentially contradictory and violent emotions in response to clusters of meaning that overwhelm, strain, and distort our self-perception. Macedonia's erotic, yet disturbing appearance as part of the play's opening landscape consequently becomes a miasmatic black hole 'bearing [...] expressive witness to the inexpressible' (Lyotard, 1989: 199), to use the words of Lyotard.

The play's complex subject matter, ambiguously presented and amplified by the equally complex scenography, confronts and overwhelms its audiences by the simultaneous existence of different planes of reality and timelines. This is aggravated by the juxtaposition of figures that are recognisably from different times, such as the octogenarian former Nuremberg judge Toonelhuis and Adolf Hitler (Barker, 2008b: 196). The place of this play is, as in the plays discussed previously, evocatively 'like' other places, but it is also always not like them. By textually referring and visually alluding to recognisable places, the stage space of *Found in the Ground* is thoroughly evocative yet decisively indefinite, refusing an easy conceptual completion by audience members. This repeated layering of associative content in imagery contributes to the overall excess in Barker's spatial scenography. This is further exacerbated by the soundscape (see Chapter 4), but also by the projections that bring the desolate landscapes they depict onto the stage. It remains uncertain whether they form part of the play's action – which never moves from the strangely multidimensional estate of Toonelhuis – in the sense that they appear to surround onstage events, present historical context, or whether they are an evocative visual component of the stage images.

The excess of conceptual content and actual imagery on stage is exacerbated by the deliberate absence of concrete spatial boundaries. The 2009 Wrestling School production at the London Riverside Studios followed Barker's design very closely (Figure 1.2). The stage was stripped back to the bare wall of the theatre, necessitating a long approach for the actors, visible to the audience. In this, Barker once more engaged with the image of 'the longest possible entrances' (Barker, 2007: 73), illustrating a keen awareness of perspective and duration. Space, as indicated in the play text, lacks definite boundaries and clear identifiers, creating a sense of limbo, an uncertainty of location, without sacrificing a sense of *somewhere*. In the words of Lyotard, it engenders 'a lack of referentiality for the whole set of experiences, an impossibility of making them topographically contingent' (1989: 188).

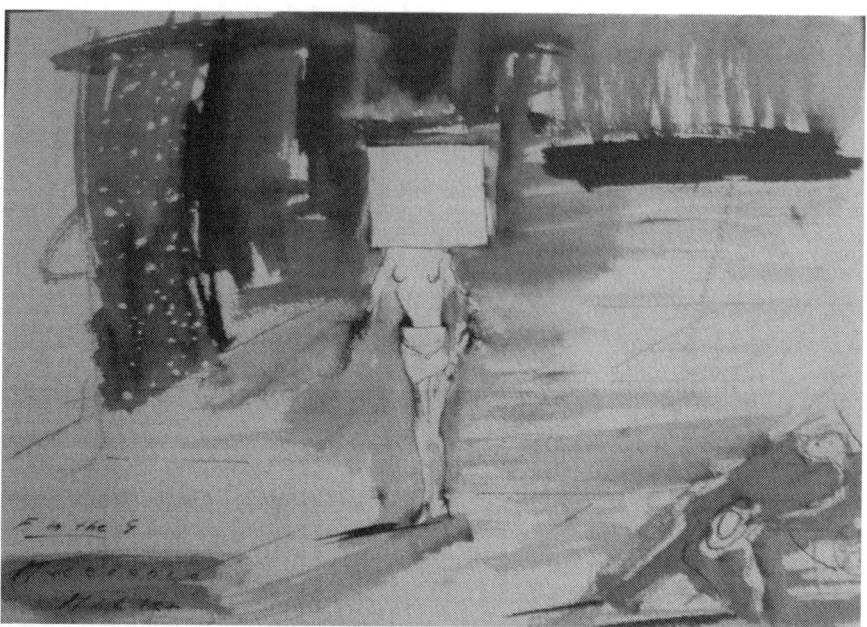

Figure 1.2 Set design for *Found in the Ground*. © Howard Barker

In production, the stage space was nearly empty, broken up only by the diagonal tracks of the mechanical dogs from upstage right to downstage centre, and the open trapdoor with the smouldering fire downstage right. The workman's line of approach was through an upstage trench, gently sloping upwards to stage level on the right. High vertical metal bars on both sides and one crudely draped swathe of fabric, like a broken curtain, at the centre back served to generate an unsettling environment by virtue of their materiality and textures: the metal gleamed cold and dull, uninviting and reminiscent of prison and military or mental institutions. The fabric appeared patch-worked and of a dull, nonspecific colour, indicating ageing and neglect. The screens descended on wires when needed, to disappear again thereafter, their existence precarious and transitory.[6] Another crucial aspect of the spatial arrangement and the visual impact of the staging was the contrast of the materiality of the actors' bodies, with the brutality of the set's materials, for example, the jagged metal of the mechanical dogs and the gaping maw of the fire pit (replacing the original stage of a pyramid of smouldering books; Barker, 2008b: 123). The spatial indeterminacy of the near-empty stage was intensified through the few select objects and set pieces that served mainly atmospheric rather than loca-tional functions on a physical as well as a conceptual level. The gap between the tangible realisation of the stage space and the imaginary space created by the audience's engagement with the fully realised piece is a productive one;

the oscillation between what is actually on stage and what is present through suggestion only engages the imagination actively, yet without resolution.

The repeated return to key scenes, such as Toonelhuis' attempt at eating the earthly remains of Nazis he sentenced to hanging, do not become any clearer over time, despite or perhaps even because of the slow introduction of further details. Furthermore, these all take place in the same space, which suggests ostensibly the same place to the audience, too. Consequently, it is likely that the recognition of preceding materials, visual and aural, seduces the audience into repeated attempts at meaning-making, even though they will be frustrated. In their incompleteness, and in the case of *Found in the Ground* also their inconclusiveness in terms of rational thought and conventional narrative, the spatial scenography draws on 'untameable states of matter' (Lyotard, 1991: 186) to engage the spectator with 'an excess of presence' (Ibid.: 187), which Lyotard considers a condition of landscape. This, in combination with Stein's idea of perpetual beginnings, leads me to term plays such as these as landscape plays.

The circularity of events in each case and the instability of their stage spaces – both physically and conceptually – may serve to seduce the audience into a drifting state in which the previously mentioned 'dissolution of all distinctions' (here/there, now/then, offstage/onstage, inside/outside, etc.) serves as a trigger for the 'dissolution of ordinary reason itself' (Guyer, 2012: 116). The juxtaposition of evocative and strangely familiar imagery (that nonetheless refuses complete recognition) with fragmented action and figures that defy traditional characterisation confront us with an 'erasure of support' (Lyotard, 1991: 189). This support would serve traditional modes of meaning-making, but severance from it leaves us stranded in contemplation of the catastrophic landscape of the play instead. While the final landscape play that I discuss here does not engage the same multidimensional layering as *Found in the Ground*, its epic scale spanning multiple years, and – for Barker unusual – presentation on a thrust-stage warrant some attention.

I will discuss *Blok/Eko* (2011) at greater length in Chapter 4, as sound is a key scenographic aspect of the play. However, since it presents the final full staging of a Wrestling School production under Barker's direction and scenographic imagination, it would be remiss not to touch upon it. The play's setting is an unspecified kingdom, whose ageing despot queen has banned medicine and instigated the mass murder of all doctors, nurses, and other medical practitioners in her domain. By this, she hopes to reintroduce pain into life and, with that, poetry. The play spans roughly a decade, from the murder of the last surgeon to the reintroduction of medicine after Eko's death.

The play opens on 'a vast floor, empty' (Barker, 2011: 7). The Wrestling School production, co-produced by Exeter Northcott and the University of Exeter's drama department in 2011, was staged at the Northcott theatre. Its curved, raked auditorium seats 460 (Exeter Northcott website, 2019) and features a semicircular thrust stage that extends just over 3 m (meters) in front of the proscenium arch, covering an orchestra pit (Ibid. Stage Dimensions

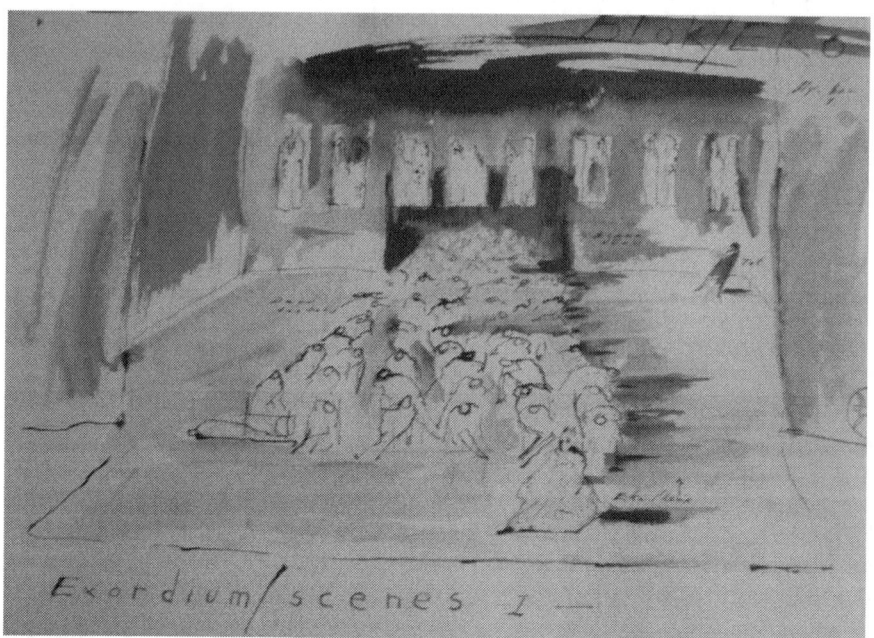

Figure 1.3 Set design for *Blok/Eko*. © Howard Barker

Diagram). The production of *Blok/Eko* appears to have used this forward extension of the stage space to the full, as can be gleaned from the play extracts presented on the Wrestling School's YouTube channel, and Barker's designs (Figure 1.3). This forward extension of the space was matched by a backwards extension through a corridor at the centre upstage. The physical extent of this passage was obscured by shadow, allowing for an imagined continuation way beyond the physical confines of the theatre.

Similarly, the play text immediately expands upwards and downwards, as Eko 'rises through the floor' (Barker, 2011: 7) while a 'slatted grate containing the bodies of two surgeons descends' (Ibid.) from above. Later, a 'tree descends, roots first' (Ibid.: 87). The conscious theatricality of these movements opens up the spatial dimensions of the action. It is not necessary to attempt to impose the structures and physical laws of everyday life upon the action on stage – they are simply not relevant. The intensity of the experience and the beauty of language are at the heart of *Blok/Eko*. The absence of any permanent set pieces quite literally makes space for the audience to absorb this. In this, *Blok/Eko* engages the same principles as Barker's design for *Ursula*, in a return to a primary emphasis on atmosphere over locale.

Just as there are no distinct temporal markers that suggest a particular era, there are no concrete geographical markers to the place of the play. However, references to Odysseus and the character Nausicaa create a tenuous link to Western Europe. Similarly, the descriptions of weather phenomena like 'squalls and showers' (Ibid.: 52) or Blok's appearance 'clad for winter' (Ibid.: 53) suggest a place with distinct seasons. References such as '[r]ooks complain' (Ibid.: 57) are more likely to evidence engagement with evocative sounds, than fix the action in Eurasia. In this, the spatial scenography of the play provides just enough recognisable elements to sustain audience engagement. As will become clear to the reader by this point, such flickers of familiarity are recurring throughout Barker's work. They deliberately tap into a sense of pan-European aesthetics that are fundamentally shaped by the Renaissance, Industrial Revolution, and two World Wars (cf. Barker in Brown, 2011: 129–130).

The sweeping placelessness of the play's setting is complemented by the sheer extent of time passing over the course of the play. Not only are there several suggestions that the extermination of medical professionals, instruments, and literature took substantial time (cf. Ibid.: 88), but Tot reappears after his seven-year jail sentence. He references events from the beginning of the play as 'going back eight years' (Ibid.: 67). Breaking the Aristotelian unit of time is not unusual for Barker. However, it is through the combination with the bleak, unfixed landscape of the action that *Blok/Eko* becomes particularly elusive. Barker seduces the audience into repeated attempts at meaning-making by virtue of just enough familiar material, be it in a character name, or a sound cue with subconscious geographical associations. The audience's struggles for meaning are continually frustrated by virtue of the deliberate failure to present conventionally conclusive materials. The particularity of the theatrical form enables Barker to 'inundate an audience with experiences which attack all the senses' (Ibid.). In the words of Karoline Gritzner, this results in an encounter with the sublime as 'an intensified experience of presence that produces cracks in the flow of time and distortions in space; [...] which causes a dissolution of subjectivity' (2012: 342). It is in the simultaneous presentation of too little (empty space, somewhere that is nowhere in particular) and too much (years and years of time, cacophonies of hyperarticulate characters in situations of extreme emotion) that Barker's scenographic principles thus find meeting points with the postmodern sublime. Considering that *Blok/Eko* arose out of research into the twin principles of plethora and bare sufficiency (cf. Mangan, 2012), the radical emptiness of the physical space presents the ideal contrast to the sonic intensity and overabundance of evocative imagery in the play.

While the plays in the next section seemingly possess greater spatial stability on a tractable scale, I will show how Barker subverts their apparent domesticity. By making the homely and familiar strange and unsettling, he once again employs principles of spatial scenography related to the idea of the sublime as a rupture of self and space-time.

Chamber plays

The first of the chamber plays I discuss is a piece for a solo female performer, *Und.* In it, the titular character supposedly awaits a gentleman caller. In time, the audience discovers that he 'gathers Jews' (Barker, 2012a: 11) and that our protagonist is 'not an aristocrat' (Ibid.: 21), but Jewish. The pretence of a romantic teatime encounter crumbles alongside the spatial stability of Und's parlour, as she, and the audience along with her, hurtle towards catastrophe. The seemingly familiar setting and the focus on a single female performer evoke intimacy and domesticity, luring spectators into a false sense of familiarity and comprehensibility.

We meet Und in 'an interior' (Ibid.: 9), a sparse description at best, barely alleviated by the presence of a laden 'tea tray' (Ibid.). These objects, evoking genteel propriety and everyday structure, in conjunction with the protagonist's attitude of waiting, seemingly locate the action in an aristocratic woman's parlour. Consequently, the audience expects the spatial conventions of such a place. However, this seemingly domestic and realistic space is disturbed within the first 18 lines of the play by the 'swift descent of a mirror' (Ibid.) that intrudes upon the stability of the parlour by its sudden and unexplained appearance. As the protagonist does not register its arrival as strange, it becomes an accepted part of the onstage world, though the mirror remains somewhat uncanny by its inexplicable and intrusive appearance. Similarly, it upsets the notion of a fourth wall as it reflects 'her face to the audience' (Ibid.), deepening, expanding, and extending the stage image beyond the confines of the onstage space. The visual depth and reflected image of Und's face in the mirror therefore confronts us with the fallacious stability accorded to visible spatial boundaries.

In the 1999 Wrestling School production, this was exacerbated by *chiaroscuro* effects created through light that rendered even the visible spatial boundaries onstage somewhat fluid.[7] This is a recurring technique: by emphasising darkness and employing a graduation from shadow to light in the style of Renaissance paintings, Barker creates a skewed perception of depth. A thorough discussion of Barker's lighting techniques in text and production follows in Chapter 2. Still confronted with the troubling presence of the mirror, our understanding of space is further troubled by the invisible servants that Und bids 'Go away/I did not ring' (Ibid.: 10). These unseen addressees of – as the play progresses – increasingly contradictory commands evoke an imaginary offstage space. This offstage space forms part of the interior where the play takes place: a logical extension of the spatial expectations raised at the very beginning.

The mirror also serves to distance Und from the audience; it offers only an indirect glimpse of her face, framed in darkness. As she gradually revokes and recharacterises her identity before the audience, her surroundings simultaneously distort. As her unseen personnel desert her, we remain confronted, as Battersby phrases it in her discussion on the sublime and its 'others', not with 'the constancy of the self, but its disappearance' (2007: 17). In this disappearance we might then find those worlds beside and apart that Lyotard identifies in Paul Klee's work in which monstrosity and formlessness are conditional to the sublime (cf. 1989: 202). The dark expanse of the auditorium, reflected in the mirror, might attest to such a world. Similarly, the gradual disintegration of Und's surroundings from something recognisably familiar echoes the dissolution of stable subject identity that she performs over the course of the play.

The doubled binary of inside/outside space which initially appears to correspond to onstage/offstage space is upset by increasingly frequent intrusions by set pieces.[8] This simple dichotomy is quickly expanded from the extended interior of Und's supposedly grand house to include the outdoors of the 'rural districts' (Barker, 2012a: 17) of her descriptions. The relative stability of this conceptual spatial understanding that conflates onstage with 'inside' this particular room and offstage with 'outside' is infringed upon by the non-naturalistic appearances of set pieces and objects such as the mirror, and subsequently the appearances of flying trays. These bear more and more absurd and disturbing contents, ranging from a letter to yellow flowers covered with stained cloth, and a heap of fresh earth. The dissolution of seemingly stable spatial boundaries on stage is further undermined at one point by a 'deluge of sordid fluid' (Ibid.: 42) that pours down from above, drenching Und. Her initial interaction with the space as 'an interior' (Ibid.: 9), despite the intrusion of the flying trays – which could conceivably be considered as a non-naturalistic image for a dumb waiter – and the mirror, misleads the audience's perception into a false sense of spatial stability, which is increasingly troubled as the play progresses until it is questioned in its entirety. The play concludes with rain falling 'steadily, heavily' (Ibid.: 48), which ultimately unravels the spectators' initial and intuitive reading of the stage space according to theatrical conventions: onstage is *inside*, but also not; offstage is *inside as well as outside*, whatever that may be in the world of the play. The isolation of Und as the only human audiences actually see in the play intensifies a sense of disorientation: once Und loses control of the space, with increasingly strange and violent events disrupting her make-believe, we are lost, too. The next play I discuss disorientates by different means, namely untrustworthy narration and a dangerous game of one-upmanship.

The Twelfth Battle of Isonzo, performed by a duo of one man and one woman, also operates from a domestic spatial limbo. However, it lacks the physical intrusions by set pieces that characterise *Und*. It is perhaps more helpful to consider *The Twelfth Battle of Isonzo* as situated between placeless limbo and evasive domesticity. Howard Barker's scenography in this play again evokes a sense of place, without concretising space, resulting in unsettling affects. I use the word affect here to emphasise the joint emotional, physical, and rational impacts of the works to avoid falling into a perpetuation of the still pervasive Cartesian mind-body schism.

Following the first encounter of an old man, Isonzo, and his young bride-to-be, Tenna, *The Twelfth Battle of Isonzo* charts the expectations, fears, hopes, and manipulations of the two figures in their fateful encounter. The notable absence of a concrete location and the sense of a claustrophobic emptiness that pervades the action allow for an analysis of Barker's spatial scenography as evocative environment in which these events take place.

The play begins with a decidedly non-prescriptive and indeterminate setting: 'A blind bride seated' (Barker, 2012a: 55). Barker provides no indication where or on what Tenna sits, let alone if inside or outside, nor geographical and historical location. The latter two may be alluded to in costuming, but the implicit staging as identifiable in the text makes no concrete prescriptions. The 2001 Lurking Truth English-language premiere production (directed by Barker and designed by his alter ego Tomas Leipzig) in Dublin maintained this spatial ambiguity by choosing a chair that might equally be found in an interior or exterior context: lacquered wood, appearing black in the stage lights, without a cushion. By lack of any further stipulation of locale, the play effectively allows for any rendition but invites a scenic realisation that maintains the resonant emptiness of the stage directions. Denying an audience easily identifiable reference points regarding time (of day and historical period) and place (geographical as well as regarding locale) focuses them instead on the encounter of the two figures and its development over time.

The Barker/Leipzig productions furthermore engaged contrasting signifiers of the domestic and the industrial: whilst the chair suggested a homely atmosphere, a raised metal grille centre stage and jagged metal poles towards the back conjured a rather more hostile environment. The setting in which these figures encounter one another is not recognisably the expected one of a church or secular equivalent. The absence of any witnesses to the impending marriage further makes the situation strange. The soundscape extended this ambiguity. For example, 'the sound of shuffling feet' (Ibid.: 56) precedes Isonzo's onstage appearance by a good page, sonically expanding the expanse of the stage space beyond the visible, thereby unsettling its overall stability. The lack of a concretely defined back wall on stage (other than the back wall of the venue itself) resulted in a porous spatial border. This became a suitably ambiguous realisation of the temporal and geographical indeterminacy suggested by the simplicity of the opening stage direction.

In the stillness and emptiness of the play, the stage space is expanded verbally by conjuring the depth of the figures' bodies, especially Tenna's. Isonzo makes repeated and frequent references to 'the streams and cataracts of [her] landscape' (Ibid.: 58). He notes that by 'virtue of [their] sightlessness' (Ibid.: 58) they 'make no distinction anymore between the surface and the depth' (Ibid.). The emptiness of the stage is therefore imaginatively filled, not only with the faraway places Isonzo references throughout, but also with the evocative imagery he applies to his bride's body which emphasises depth, darkness, and mystery. Useful comparisons can be made to the recurring image of the abyss that abounds in Barker's plays[9] and literature on the sublime (cf. Lyotard: 1989; Battersby: 2007). Rabey quotes Greenblatt in this context, referring to a 'play on the brink of the abyss' (2006: 22) that denies audiences and characters certainty: neither quite know 'where to place [their] feet' (Barker in Gritzner and Rabey, 2006: 34). The resultant exhilarating anxiety (cf. Ibid.) approaches a state of sublime experience in which the subject is riven with contradictory and overwhelming emotions that suspend rational thought and instead foreground emotional expressiveness in a changing, unstable environment.

The concentrated spatiality of the action – we never move from the place of Isonzo's and Tenna's meeting – in conjunction with the increasing intensity of their encounter serves to engender a mounting pressure on the audience. Combined with the lack of reassuring and recognisable spatial structures indicative of a particular place, Barker's play conjures up a claustrophobic emptiness: overwhelmed by the plethoric language of the figures and the ambiguity of their actions (seduction and threat lie very closely together) the audience's imagination has no concrete tools at their disposal for making sense. Nor can they rein in the verbal, conceptual, and imaginative onslaught that the play presents. As Booth asserts for audiences of *King Lear*: 'we leave one logic and slip into another' (2001: 46). Such slippage serves to reset the stage throughout *The Twelfth Battle of Isonzo* and 'demonstrates that all categorization [...] is an arbitrary and unreliable mental convenience' (Ibid.: 44). In that respect, the space of *The Twelfth Battle of Isonzo* becomes fundamentally destabilised.

The play provides some of this destabilisation through set pieces, such as the gaps of the back wall formed by metal rods intensifying a sense of depth. Additionally, in the 2002 production Isonzo moved through the narrow corridor formed behind them during the exordium, escalating a sense of permeability first evoked by the irregular arrangement of the set's materials. Furthermore, this spatial presentation of set called into question the distinction of onstage and offstage, as it visibly made use of the back wall of the performance venue. This technique also featured in the 2009 production of *Found in the Ground*, as discussed earlier.

In *The Twelfth Battle of Isonzo*, multiple possible places exist simultaneously in the figures' speeches and the audience's imagination. If indeed 'forms domesticate [space into place]' (Lyotard, 1991: 185) and 'make it consumable' (Ibid.) and therefore comprehensible in its entirety, the absence of clearly identifiable forms in the play's staging precisely refuses this domestication. Instead, it draws near to the 'nothingness of being-there' (Ibid.: 188) in the sense of a perpetual, repeated throw-back to the moment in which narrative is interrupted (Ibid.: 187). This state might be characterised as a productive *not-knowing*, triggered by the 'excess of presence' (Ibid.: 187) of multiple possible places contained in the play, which is conjured by verbal overabundance and subtraction of fixed spatial content. This is furthered as the figures' blindness is conceptually imposed upon spectators through the emptiness of the space.

Images of places real ('Naples/Nice/Cadiz'; Barker, 2012a: 59) and imaginary, such as the 'dense weed in railway yards' (Ibid.: 80) that Tenna envisages for her wedding night, abound throughout the play. The audience is therefore transported verbally from place to place in the empty and mostly static space of the stage. Movements, where they do occur, are simple and often repetitive, such as Tenna's crossing and uncrossing of her legs (Ibid.: 61, 64, 69). Isonzo's movements are slow and 'laborious' (Ibid.: 64) and repeatedly he claims to have moved when he has not (Ibid.: 59, 63). Excessive descriptions of movement in the spoken text, particularly those referring to unseen processes such as 'the traffic of [Tenna's] bowel' (Ibid.: 58) or '[t]he music of the veins' (Ibid.: 87), highlight the contrasting stillness of the figures on stage. The contrast of verbally conjured overabundance (of images and sounds) and the reality of a near-empty stage on the one hand highlights the distance between the two figures, charging the bare space with their emotions, intentions, and openly admitted attempts at manipulation. On the other hand, it enables a constant and fluid imaginative reconfiguration of the space into multiple places with changing connotations.

The continued upheaval of imaginary place in the realised space on stage results in a doubled sense of violent dissolution of tangible boundaries and simultaneous claustrophobia as the desolate stage space becomes more and more suffocating: the absence of set and concrete place markers comes to life as the 'possibility of nothing happening' (Lyotard, 1989: 198), a threatening lack demanding to be filled by something. This results in repeated and sustained displacement through the imaginary places conjured in the figures' speech. These treat historical occurrence (Barker, 2012a: 68) and fictional musing (Ibid.: 80) equally, highlighting the constructed nature of the former and fundamentally unsettling the perceived stability of space and places. For example, 'the war' (Ibid.: 66) that Isonzo refers to is likely the First World War, since he references '[p]oetry and poison gas' (Ibid.: 68). However, we know him to be an unreliable narrator by this point (Ibid.: 70). The geographical and historical location is further undermined by the sparse reference points given through speech: the historical battle of Thermopylae (Ibid.: 70) is equally present as the real-world locations Isonzo recounts, and the future places Tenna imagines. The play oscillates between placeless limbo (some time, somewhere) and an evasive domesticity (the only concrete thing is the exchange between bride and groom), both of which resolutely deny audiences fixed meanings. The next play I discuss, *Dead Hands*, expands from duo to trio and features another essential rite of passage: mourning. It similarly taps into emptiness as a spatial strategy, yet also utilises the unstable claustrophobia encountered previously in *Und*.

The opening stage directions of *Dead Hands* specify '[a]n open coffin on a table' (Barker, 2004: 7), nothing more. In the 2004 Wrestling School production designed by Barker, this was realised by suspending a large mirror slightly left of centre stage, upon which lay an immaculately suited corpse. The play follows the deceased's two sons, Eff and Istvan, and their father's former mistress, Sopron. Right from the start, Eff develops an obsessive sexual attraction to Sopron, which intensifies over time. When he discovers that his brother Istvan has had and continues to have an affair with her, both brothers first attempt to leave the situation behind. This fails, as Eff considers his obsession an inheritance of his father's situation: 'Inheriting the property of one's father one inherits both the pride and agony of it' (Ibid.: 70).[10] Sopron also attempts to leave, only to be informed that the train station no longer exists (Ibid.: 51–52). The action consists of an ongoing rotation of the three individuals, though Eff begins and ends the play alone on stage, addressing the corpse. Further, he spends significantly more time alone on stage than his brother; Sopron on the other hand is present on stage the least, and never alone. The play's location is limited to a singular room, though references to upstairs, downstairs, and to places outside feature. Further, the three characters all leave the stage at various points throughout the play but fail to leave for good. This claustrophobic set up is intensified by the continuous, unaltered presence of the corpse.

In many ways, this play is reminiscent of Sartre's *No Exit*, insofar as the focus is on the relationships between three characters in a singular, unspectacular room. The only stage objects are the corpse and a chair, which is only present by inference as Eff enters and after his first line sits (Ibid.: 7). Barker's characters leave the room at various points, either to other locations within the house (e.g. Ibid.: 69) or in the case of Sopron, to attend to banal tasks of her everyday routine, such as a dentist's appointment (Ibid.: 32) or a charitable community visit to a sick former colleague (Ibid.: 42). This contrast of the continuing ordinariness of everyday life outside, and the extraordinary events of grief and desire playing out inside, render the play's location curiously out of joint with normal spacetime (cf. Lingis, 2000: 117 ff). There is no sense of a specific time of day, though we learn that 'it's Thursday' (Ibid.: 42). We have no idea of geographical location, but reference to a barbershop's 'red and white pole' (Ibid.: 58) offers a familiar image. It is by the juxtaposition of quotidian details, such as this, with the unprecedented actions of the characters, such as Sopron's repeated performances of grieving 'naked beneath a coat' (Ibid.: 11, 26, 49), that space and place are repeatedly unsettled. As Lingis argues, a 'catatrophic event destroys the time of work and reason, and opens up the empty endurance of void' (2000: 121). It is this monumental event, grief in all its complexity, to which audiences can relate. However, though this recognition might hook spectators, the action that unfolds is probably unlike any wake they have ever attended. The death of the looming patriarch does not suspend his power in *Dead Hands*, rather we witness echoes of fraught familial relationships as they entangle the characters on stage to a point of no return. Or rather, a point of no escape.

In the 2004 Wrestling School production at the Riverside Studios in London, Barker's set design under the name of Tomas Leipzig rendered the simple interior uncanny through suspending multiple tarnished mirrors of varying sizes along the edges of the playing area, back and sides (Figure 1.4). These doubled, deepened, and distorted the stage space beyond its physical dimensions. This design choice echoed the suspended mirror that disturbs the domesticity of Und's parlour early on in the play of the same name. The bizarre abundance of mirrors further increases the strangeness of the space, as widely diverse conventions – from the Victorian age to contemporary Judaism – would dictate they be covered for the period of mourning. Consequently, the immediate impression of the stage space is deliberately distanced from recognisable conventions of mourning, and interior design. Each mirror also

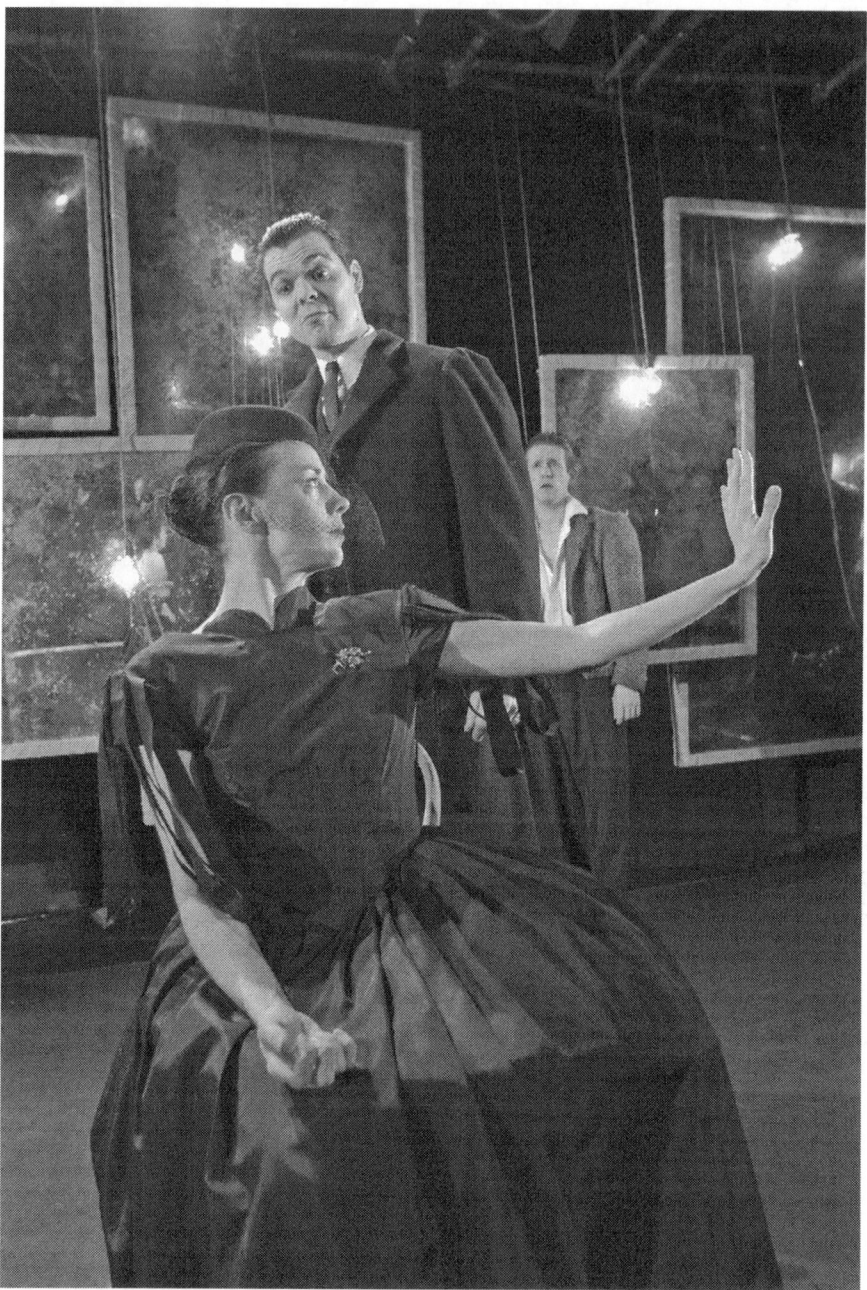

Figure 1.4 Dead Hands; l-r Biddy Wells (Sopron), Justin Avoth (Eff), Chris Moran (Istvan). © Donald Cooper, Photostage UK

featured a naked lightbulb suspended in front of it, which lighting designer Helen Morley used as 'points of interest in the staging', instead making 'the dead body the source of light in the room' (in Kipp, 2016: 264).

Dead Hands provides just enough localising pointers to avoid complete alienation for the audience. From the three characters' interactions and references, the place is identifiably a domestic one. However, the pervasive emptiness of the space, rendered especially unstable in production, renders this everyday location uncanny. Like *The Twelfth Battle of Isonzo*, this play is focussed tightly on interpersonal relationships; the environmental factors one might expect in a naturalistic play are stripped away, leaving only the barest, most banal, and therefore ultimately intangible references to where and when these events are happening. The figure's eloquence speaks to a deliberate theatricality, in which they perform their mourning and their desires as much for each other as for the audience. The conscious absence of spatial and locational particularities pulls our attention to the here and now. The when and where do not matter, only that 'it happens' (Lyotard, 1989: 197). Lyotard sees this happening configured through privation: in order to experience the 'temporal ecstas[y]' (Ibid.) of *now*, conscious thought 'must be disarmed' (Ibid.). This focus on immediate, individualised experience is deliberately encouraged by Barker through his spatial scenography, which resolutely refuses to be pinned down into spatio-temporal, historical, or geographical specifics. Nonetheless, his stage spaces provide just enough concretising spatial markers that draw the spectators' eye, and spark fragmented, nagging impressions of recognition. This is a particularly strong feature in the next play I discuss, *I Saw Myself* (2008).

As in *Und*, the opening image of *I Saw Myself* indicates a domestic setting as '[f]our women weave a tapestry' (Barker, 2008b: 11). Unusually, the play text offers seemingly more concrete information in addition to this stage direction as it specifies '[t]he setting of the play is Europe in the thirteenth century' (Ibid.: 9). However, more relatable to reality this descriptor may seem, it is still decidedly indefinite. Considering the multitude of conflicts of the 13th century, ranging from the Mongol invasion of Europe, numerous crusades and various succession and secession wars, Barker's directions once more conjure up a spectre of likeness. This sense of relatability is ultimately unstable, as the historical context serves to free both action and characters from a perceived obligation to be recognisable to the audience and fixed to a concrete place. Set in a single room over a period of 'eight years' (Ibid.: 64) during which the women gradually age and lose their sight and Sleev's granddaughter grows from 'infant' (Ibid.: 13) to ten years old (Ibid.: 78), the play appears to present a stable dichotomy of inside/outside, comparable to other plays discussed here. However, as with these other plays, there are ways in which Barker destabilises the visible onstage setting, conceptually and physically.

The domesticity of the opening scene is quickly expanded: on the one hand, the estate of Sleev appears to expand beyond the confines of the visible stage space, as Guardaloop makes reference to the 'orchard' (Ibid.: 13), and Sleev herself mentions an 'upstairs' (Ibid.: 18) as well as 'gardens' (Ibid.: 26) among other places. As with the blind characters in *The Twelfth Battle of Isonzo* and *The Fence*, Sleev's deteriorating eyesight contrasts with the complexity of the stage images, both as they are visually presented and conceptually expanded over time. One such extension takes place through the repeated mentions of 'the war' that 'is nearer' (Ibid.: 25). Offstage threats of violence are a frequent stage mechanism in Barker's playwriting, for example, in *A House of Correction*, *Und*, *Slowly*, *The Dying of Today*, and *The Brilliance of the Servant*, among others. On the other hand, and crucially in the case of *I Saw Myself*, the space is also expanded inwards through the continuous presence of the wardrobe (Ibid.: 11), in which a 'naked man' (Ibid.) appears to reside.

Once its contents are revealed at the beginning of the play, the wardrobe becomes a truly enclosed space within the supposedly enclosed space on stage; it attains an aura of intrusiveness, as the suspected continuous presence of Sleev's lover hovers in the background of the women's private conversations. In production, this was furthered by the physical elevation of the wardrobe on a raised podium with three steps leading up to it. The light wood of the wardrobe, steps and tapestry frames presented a stark contrast to Sleev's and Sheeth's black costumes and stood out against the stage space's dark background of indeterminate depth. For a visual reference of this, I point the reader to the extract presented on the Wrestling School's YouTube channel, as the resolution of the recording is too low for inclusion in print. The repeated uncanny opening of the wardrobe (Ibid.: 26, 29, 38), without any visible manipulation by its (then still mute) inhabitant echoes the flying trays of *Und*, in which the space becomes an active co-player to the actors. Sleev confirms this in the ways in which she addresses the wardrobe and its silent inhabitant, considering the opening of the door an invitation at one point, an unwanted interruption out of concern at another (Ibid.).

The seemingly domestic setting of *I Saw Myself* is further destabilised by the mirror on the wardrobe's door (Ibid.: 11), which – as in *Und*, and the Wrestling School's 2004 production of *Dead Hands* – serves to double the stage image and undermine the stability of the supposedly contained onstage space through visual extension. Additionally, the depth of the mirror's surface – all the more tangible if it shows only the auditorium's darkness behind Sleev's face – becomes a black hole, 'a brutal nothing' (Ibid.: 34) in the onstage space that perpetually attests to the fragility of visible spatial boundaries.

The offstage threat of the war gradually draws closer, first only conceptually by way of the repeated statement that 'the war is nearer' (Ibid.: 25, 36, 37, 40, 49, 51, 53), until it 'is here' (Ibid.: 66) at the final stitch of the tapestry[11] and 'THE ENEMY IS IN THE GARDEN' (Ibid.: 67). Ultimately, the conceptual approach of this offstage threat is expanded to the sonic dimension as 'the sounds of wanton damage come from the outside' (Ibid.: 70), in which outside is equal to offstage. The war furthermore becomes an actuality of the onstage space through the reappearance of Modicum, who in the Wrestling School's 2008 production was not, as in the stage directions, naked (Ibid.: 69), but instead wore black combat boots and black riding trousers. The startling contrast of these garments to the light wood of the wardrobe and the actor's fair skin emphasised the intrusiveness of his reappearance. He was no longer a harmonious part of the onstage environment, but a disturbance, visually as much as conceptually. As Modicum 'discovered speech' (Ibid.: 70), he also left the confines of the wardrobe, the only time this movement from inside to out was visible. Though Modicum appears once before outside the wardrobe (Ibid.: 22), this earlier instance is upon his return to it (Ibid.) and thus does not contain this movement from inside to outside the wardrobe. Importantly, we do not see him enter the wardrobe, instead he 'loosens the belt of his gown and goes behind the wardrobe' (Ibid.). It is therefore only towards the end of the play that he takes the step that violates the boundary between inside and outside the wardrobe, and simultaneously this marks the arrival of the amorphous and uncertain offstage threat of the war. In this, the domesticity of the play's action, precarious throughout by virtue of the impending violence, is finally imploded.

From the beginning, Sleev's actions indicate that *I Saw Myself*, as so many of Barker's plays, ultimately presents an exploration of subjectivity and a radical questioning of existing moral and social structures, for example, when she couples with her daughter's husband (Ibid.: 13). The transgression of boundaries at the heart of *I Saw Myself* is echoed in the spatial set up of the piece that balances uneasily between concrete, tangible objects (the empty frames, the wardrobe) and abstract, conceptual infringements (the perhaps-present hidden lover, the offstage war) that nonetheless have real impact on the way in which the characters engage with the space and each other.

The excessiveness of Sleev's life cannot be contained by the social and moral order that Ladder attempts to maintain, even to the very end (Barker, 2008b: 63). Sleev's actions therefore have 'the power to disrupt our models of rationality and selfhood' (Battersby, 2007: 99) and become an example of a female sublime experience that is not predicated on male experience as norm, in which catastrophe serves to reaffirm the subject's identity in the face of a fear of death (cf. Gritzner, 2007). Instead, the creation of 'a consciousness of the abyss of the self' (Ibid.: 48) through deliberate engagement with the rifts between social expectation, subjectively experienced reality, and constructed historical narrative allows Sleev to open up 'opportunities for ecstatic self-[exploration]' (Gritzner, 2012: 339). The ambiguity of physical and conceptual space serves to focus in on the protagonist's 'excessive, intense and extreme inwardness' which 'leads to a subversion of the boundaries between subject and object, the self and the world' (Ibid.: 341). At the same time, the physical boundaries of the stage space are destabilised; however, without being abolished. This imperfect process recalls Kristeva's abject as 'something rejected from which one does not part' and which 'disturbs identity, system, order' (1982: 4).

Though spatial rendering is simple in *I Saw Myself*, and central parts of set and place presented only conceptually (e.g. the visually absent but elaborately described tapestry, the protagonist's expansive estate, and the marauding enemies present onstage only through 'sounds of pain and ruin' (Barker, 2008b: 71), it is in the contrast of sparse tangible presentation and verbally evoked, sonically supported overabundance that the play draws, as so many of Barker's, on opposing principles of emptiness and excess in its staging. The simplicity of the set demands an actively engaged imagination of its audience by drawing on the rich imagery of Barker's complex language.

The doubled dichotomy of inside and outside as presented through the relationships of the wardrobe to onstage, and onstage to offstage space, once more engages a fundamentally unstable conception of space that throws into question the physical and conceptual markers by which we determine not only where we are, but also more importantly who we are. *I Saw Myself* therefore engages modes of spatial structuring that provide just enough locational information for the audience to consider it as somewhere not entirely unknown, without offering them the comfort of any more concrete information. The deliberate denial of a definite place through an indefinite and – in other plays more physically obvious – unstable space offers up a liminal experience (cf. Gritzner, 2015 and Suthor, 2014) that is not reducible in terms of its potential meanings. In *I Saw Myself* specifically, as in Barker's theatre at large, 'thought's wrestling with the boundless is translated into the actuality of dramatic stage action' (Gritzner, 2015: 128). However, the rendering of the stage foregrounds the immanence of this translation and points towards the 'threatening void' (Lyotard, 1991: 84) of the sublime. The excess of potential meanings, proliferated by the lack of a domesticating framework (cf. Ibid.: 185–187), positions the subject (protagonist and spectator) at the 'edge of non-existence and hallucination' (Kristeva, 1982: 2). The excess of language and the imaginative excess triggered by the deliberate '*incompleteness of its prescriptions*' (Rabey, 2004: 4; original emphasis) may then be described in terms of the sublime, and be claimed to constitute a scenographic sublime that exists in the aporia of consciously indeterminate physical renditions of the stage and the incommensurability of the ideas they hint at.

Conclusion: not nowhere, but …

As shown in this chapter, the landscape plays and chamber plays share certain underlying spatial principles, though they also diverge in the ways in which these principles manifest. A chamber play here refers to an ostensibly stable, and potentially somewhat claustrophobic, domestic setting in which the stability of the plot unravels sequentially alongside the seemingly fixed identity of the play's characters. Further, it also concerns itself with apparently domestic concerns of familial relations and duties. Landscape plays on the other hand figure on a more epic scale, both in terms of the evocative spatiality of their settings and in terms of temporal expansiveness. In that regard, *I Saw Myself* might be considered a hybrid of the two categories; however, its domestic location and theme triggered my decision to include it among the chamber plays here. Where the landscape plays frequently appear to operate on multiple temporal loops, the chamber plays generally focus on one situation that intensifies and becomes less and less connected to the everyday as time passes. However, much of the scenography of Barker's chamber plays and landscape plays functions on the same principle of spatial instability.

Many plays of both categories are essentially entropic in the sense that they begin in a seemingly stable state, though at different points of decline into disorder. Barker's spatial instability reverberates into the temporal dimension: the usual rules are not to be trusted, space and time are *other*, yet recognisably close to the real world that audiences inhabit. These plays exist in the oh-so-close yet intangible 'world apart' (Ibid.: 202) that Lyotard outlines in relation to Paul Klee. Such destabilisation of conventionally linear time is another scenographic device Barker frequently employs.

Placelessness is a further recurring strategy in Barker's work, where his stage directions and their realisation in production provide just enough to draw the audience in with something recognisable (it is 'like' a strange vestry in *The Twelfth Battle of Isonzo*, it is 'like' a manor house in *Und*, the clifftop is 'like' Beachy Head in *The Forty (Few Words)*, etc.), without ever giving them concrete or finished signifiers. Even when reasonably explicit stage directions appear (e.g. the recurring park bench in *The Forty (Few Words)*, Barker, 2014a), the circumstance of the characters' situations and their actions serve to make something familiar strange again, cutting loose meanings so that they float and multiply in each new iteration. Additionally, even such seemingly precise directions contain an implicit placelessness by virtue of their banality. The multiplication of possible meanings is instigated through the figures on stage, in the ways in which they refer to and interact with the space, but also through the layered scenography, in which lighting and sound function primarily evocatively, not descriptively. It is in this suggestive, deliberately elusive quality that the notion of atmosphere as discussed by Böhme (2017) gains resonance. Notably, he specifically links the atmospheres created through scenography to ecstasy in its original meaning (Ibid.: 108) in terms of stepping outside oneself. This in turn finds immediate meeting points with the postmodern sublime that throws the subject outside themselves, overwhelming reason by an excess of immediate experience (cf. Lyotard, 1989, 1991; Johnson, 2012).

In layering multiple meanings atop one another, Barker's spaces continually shift and refocus into multiple possible places (cf. Reynolds, 2015: 153). This perpetual oscillation between what is initially presented as a recognisable space and the 'formal estrangement' (Rabey, 2006: 16) that follows forms another central spatial working principle. This is achieved through 'denaturalizing imagery' (Barker in Gritzner and Rabey, 2011: 124). The fragmented and cyclical nature of a play's exordium will already have undermined conventional understanding of stage space to some extent and instead foregrounded an experiential and – to a large extent – image-based mode of theatre spectatorship (cf. Barker in Gritzner and Rabey, 2011: 124).

Similarly, Barker uses indicators of domesticity (like the tea tray in *Und*, or a bed in *A House of Correction*, to name but two) and isolates them in an ambiguous environment, highlighting the constructed nature of meaning that depends on socially agreed cross-referencing of signifiers: for example, a park bench is associated with outside; chairs and a table, depending on their materials and shape, indicate inside; a bed is commonly understood as something encountered inside; and so on. By stripping away other reference points, Barker forces the audience's imagination into a state of free play, with meanings emerging and morphing as the events of the plays unfold.

Though overall one might consider Barker's works in those two categories, chamber plays and landscape plays, they share similar underlying principles: firstly, the deliberate absence of concrete spatio-temporal markers. This refuses a recognisable identification with a particular time and place; there is no 'immediately, readily or completely recognisable world' (Rabey, 2006: 13). Further, Barker always seeks a deliberate historicisation in his work, to increase his imaginative freedom, though the plays are 'clinical in their absence of direct historical context' (McCarron, 2015: 69). Instead they seduce the audience into a moment-by-moment engagement with the pieces on their own, theatrically specific terms (cf. Dyble-Kitchin in Rabey, 2015: 239–240). Indications of (fictional, ambiguous, and non-naturalistic) time periods are more prominent in costuming (cf. Barker in Gritzner and Rabey, 2011: 124). The stage space is kept as empty as possible, with few structural elements that usually lie at the core of each piece, such as the fence in the play of the same name, or the tapestry in *I Saw Myself*.

Scenographically then, Barker's stage spaces operate on a few distinct foundational principles: spatial instability, indeterminate spatial rendering, and the utilisation of the seemingly opposing principles of emptiness and excess in achieving the first two, resulting in a multiplication and destabilisation of place on stage. The indeterminacy of Barker's 'essentially divisible, foldable, and catastrophic' (Kristeva, 1982: 8; cf. Rabey, 2006: 20) onstage spaces is achieved by employing a few, select set pieces, which refuse clear identification in terms of historical and geographical location as well as conceptual and physical intrusions from offstage. By refuting spatial identifiers that audiences might use to construct a concrete sense of recognisable location, Barker's stage spaces become 'contaminated, condemned, at the boundary of what is assimilable, thinkable' (Kristeva, 1982: 18).

The distinction between Kristeva's abject (and thus by extension Lacan's *jouissance*) and Lyotard's postmodern sublime becomes ever more blurred, after all the 'abject is edged with the sublime' (Ibid.: 11). If indeed the 'postmodern resurrection of the aesthetics of the sublime is ultimately an attempt to represent [...] the properly unimaginable complexity' (Johnson, 2012: 130) of contemporary human existence, then Barker's scenographic engagement with stage space – consciously incomplete, indeterminate, and in its imaginative overabundance beyond rational comprehension – is an artistic manifestation of this development. Barker, too, establishes the relationship of pain and pleasure, suffering and joy (cf. Barker, 2005a: 33), the simultaneous experience of which might be a desirable loss (cf. Ibid.: 41) of rational self-control: 'The gesture of tragedy is so sublime as to make the prospect of judgement unthinkable' (Ibid.: 89). His aims for an art of theatre that is 'Infinite/Functionless/ Intractable/Nowhere/Incalculable/Illogical/Arbitrary' (Ibid.: 93) echo the vocabulary applied to the sublime; his scenographic methods are designed in a manner as to evoke these associations and thereby may be said to trigger a sublime experience. In refusing illustrative spaces on stage, Barker's plays 'conjur[e] spectres of known times and places' (Kipp in Rabey, 2015: 236) in which the 'layering of a social, collective memory as construed by dominant historical discourses with individual memory gives a sense of incomplete recognition, inviting the spectator to identify the known, yet thwarting the process of that recognition' (Ibid.), instead standing 'emancipated from any settled placement' (Dyble-Kitchin in Rabey, 2015: 237).

The guiding principles and physical manifestation of Barker's spatial scenography – indeterminate place through conceptually and physically unstable space, juxtaposition of contrasting textures, particularly with regard to the performers' bodies, and estrangement through use of unusual or ambiguous stage objects – aim towards a dissolution of concrete spatio-temporal markers and engage a 'total aesthetic' (Barker, 2007: 41) that springs from a single, unified, and as far as possible uncompromising imagination (cf. Barker, 2011: 101–102). What is on stage and shown is equally responsible as that which is not (cf. Reynolds on Barker's 'imagined space', 2015: 168). Barker's scenography decidedly lies between the visible, tangible and the invisible, intangible. The seemingly opposing principles of emptiness (in spatial rendering) and excess (in unfixed and changing audio-visual and conceptual content), amplified by spatial instability (physical and conceptual), result in theatrical stage spaces that contain a 'multiplicity of current times' (Lyotard, 1989: 186). These are, in Lingis' sense, catastrophic and destroy 'the time of work and reason, and [opening] up the empty endurance of the void' (2000: 121–121). Faced with this abyss which attests to the 'incommensurability between thought and the real world' (Lyotard, 1989: 201), the visible stage space and its imaginative extension beyond (aided by sound) becomes a site of infinite possibility in which rational thought is disarmed (cf. Ibid.: 197) and subjective experience elevated to the point of sublime rapture.

Notes

1 'einen Raum der Räume'.
2 'Eröffnung von Orten, die keine gegebenen Orte sind oder werden können, absolute, d.h. auch inäquivalente Orte als pulsierende Eröffnung von Raumzeiten'.
3 Performance dates given, unless quoting from the play texts.
4 This acceptance of incomprehensible circumstance reappears in other plays such as *Und*, *The Fence in its Thousandth Year*, and *Found in the Ground*, too, to name but a few.

5 At one point, Kidney refers to 'all three hundred miles' of the fence (Barker, 2005b: 24).

6 I recommend readers seek out the Wrestling School's YouTube channel, thewrestlingschool, for short samples of production recordings. Only very limited production photographs exist.

7 Unfortunately, archival materials for this production are exceedingly limited; the statements here are based on production photographs Howard Barker generously shared with me when I interviewed him (see Appendix 1: 191).

8 Sound cues also intrude, see Chapter 4 for detailed discussion.

9 Conceptually (cf. Barker, 1997: 116, 172; 2005a: 16, 26) as well as a recurring stage device, for example the bottomless wells of *A House of Correction* and *In the Depths of Dead Love*.

10 I cannot discuss the inherent misogyny of this casual objectification here but must note the problematic identification of Sopron as property.

11 Importantly, the tapestry is never shown; in production, empty frames served to conjure it without concretising it as an object. The imagery it supposedly depicts is exclusively evoked verbally by the characters.

2   Light and darkness

This chapter explores the particular scenographic contribution that lighting makes to a production, by drawing on relevant play texts and on archival production materials. It considers light's role in the creation of an evocative scenography, and engages with the underlying scenographic principles at play in Barker's use of light and darkness. The chapter draws on Abulafia's proposal for detailed academic analysis of lighting design as well as on Palmer's and Crisafulli's publications (2013 and 2013 respectively) on light.

It must be noted that the existent (academic) discourse on the matter of light in scenography is still significantly limited in terms of reflexive theorisation (cf. Moran, 2016: 1). Abulafia's monograph marks a crucial departure from practically focussed guides. Those identify the generating components of performance lighting, yet tend to pay little attention to the analysis thereof, let alone generate methods for doing so. This is not to detract from the unquestionable usefulness of primarily instructive materials regarding colour theory, technological developments, and the practical effects of different lenses, or the processes of pitching a design and subsequently plotting it, for example. However, in the context of this book, it is less the specific realisations that I am interested in, and more the underlying scenographic principles that each of the production elements attests to in order to engage in an aesthetic analysis of Barker's scenography.

It is through light that a performance becomes visible as such in the first place, be it through daylight or carefully controlled and plotted stage lighting; light is a 'fundamental element and cogent force in the creative process' (Abulafia, 2016: 10). Whether it is used architecturally, by structuring space (cf. Appia's proposals for Wagner's operas), or poetically, through expressive uses that foreground experiential engagement for spectators (cf. Olafur Eliasson's *Your Black Horizon* at the 2005 Venice Biennale), light acts as a fundamental element of scenography, with physiological and psychological effects on the spectator. Its fluid qualities and potential for subtlety allow it to impact deeply on both space and time in performance, since light is inextricably bound up with both: it requires the limitations of space in order to become visible (cf. Moran, 2016: 26), even if this entails encountering an object along the way, rather than stopping at a surface. It is only through light's interaction with physical objects that spectators are able to identify its direction, intensity, and colour (cf. Zyman in Abulafia, 2016: 55). Its progression – whether in movement across space or developments in intensity – subsequently links light with the perception of time (cf. Abulafia, 2016: 9; Palmer, 2013: 66). The surrounding darkness of Barker's stages, which so often spills onto the stage, too, is of course fundamentally bound up with the lighting design, as neither exists in isolation from the other. Notably, discussion focussed on darkness on its own, rather than merely as a side-effect of light, is a recent development in scenographic discourse (cf. Alston and Welton, 2017; Welton, 2017; Graham, 2016 and 2018; Palmer, 2017). I therefore want to emphasise that any discussion of the scenographic working principles of Barker's lighting comments on his engagement with darkness, too.

The difficulty of discussing light is a central concern of scenographic scholarship, recently addressed admirably by Yaron Abulafia (2016). His conceptual framework for the analysis of light, which addresses the phenomenological-cognitive and semiotic aspects of light from a spectator's perspective (cf. Ibid.: 100), is central to this chapter. I draw on technical descriptions of production footage regarding direction, intensity, colour tonality, and cueing progression over time, before engaging with the semiotic implications of these elements in a broader context. Then follows a phenomenological analysis of the lighting states. It should be noted that these processes are deeply entwined and therefore not literally sequentially discussed. Nonetheless, I start with a technical description of notable lighting states throughout a piece before moving to an aesthetic analysis, without guessing at authorial intention or being prescriptive with regards to meaning or affect.

My aim here is to consider the textual implications of Barker's playwriting for the development of lighting design in the creation of an evocative scenography in conjunction with their realisation in production. As before, I have to stress the limitations of archival materials, particularly in the discussion of lighting, as the quality of recordings severely impacts the possibility to accurately describe colour and intensity. The human eye is much more sensitive than digital video equipment, so certainly some subtleties of the lighting are lost in the archival record. Nonetheless, the Wrestling School's (and Lurking Truth's) video recordings are useful complementary sources to the play texts, particularly as much of Barker's lighting is implicit (cf. Moran on the difficulty of writing about light, 2016: 22 ff.). Once again, I point the reader in the direction of the Wrestling School's YouTube channel, and videoed production materials on Vimeo. In addition, the Howard Barker Digital Archive at the University of Exeter offers access to a number of production records discussed here.

In order to appropriately consider the realisation of light in the Wrestling School's productions in conjunction with the scenographic proposals contained in Barker's play texts, I expand the framework outlined by Abulafia into the realm of aesthetics. This move to philosophy has historical precedents in the analysis of visual arts, installation art, and also theatre pieces (cf.

Abulafia, 2016: 43). In terms of the analysis of lighting, its contribution to the overall scenography, the evidencing of underlying scenographic principles implicit in Barker's play texts, and their realisation in production, aesthetic discourse offers a well-established vocabulary that lends itself to description and analysis of visual artistic expression. The lack of a similarly coherent language for lighting (cf. Moran, 2016: 25) can thus be alleviated. Theories of the sublime, with their particular links to notions of imagination, and historically to reason, are also fundamentally bound up with Western philosophical traditions that are founded on visual metaphors (cf. Sloterdijk in Keller, 2010: 287–288). The notion of the sublime is thus implicated in any analysis of meaning-making processes in terms of stage lighting.

Chiaroscuro and side-lighting

Considering the development of contemporary lighting techniques from the industrial revolution onwards in conjunction with philosophical shifts to postmodernity in the wake of two World Wars, it comes as no surprise that 'theatre-makers sought alternative forms of expression that would be closer to the "sublime", to the essence of ideas beyond their materialized forms' (Abulafia, 2016: 24). The newly developed creative potential of lighting, which increasingly prevailed over its illustrative function, led to 'metamorphoses of the stage space through a poetic use of light' (on Svoboda, Ibid.: 34) in the mid-20th century. This development can also be seen in the ways in which Barker's play texts invite ambiguous staging, complete with lighting that creates the 'impression that space [is] monumental and [has] no boundaries of height and depth' (Ibid.: 25). Though not schooled in the plotting and implementation of stage lighting, Barker's painterly approach (cf. Morley's anecdote about beginning the working process of *Found in the Ground*, see Kipp, 2016: 257) brings a visual imagination to the working process that engages very consciously with lighting and its effects in dramatic productions. Barker subsequently relies on trained lighting designers and technicians to develop an appropriate visual vocabulary in response to the play texts and – where they precede the lighting process – set as well as costume designs.

It should be noted that Barker implements a deliberately limited colour palette in his designs and prefers to '[use] materials, as far as possible, in their raw state, rather than as a result of scenic effect' (Henry, 2019: n.p.). These same restrictions also apply to lighting (in design, and in instructions to the lighting designers he works with, cf. Appendix 1: 181). Scenographer Susannah Henry, who worked with Barker between 2004 and 2009, notes that working with Barker enabled her to see 'the power of a limited palette (i.e. colour or material)' (2019: n.p.). There are consequently some fundamental principles regarding the structuring of space through light. The goal is to 'lose the horizons' (Appendix 1: 182), creating *chiaroscuro* effects from which figures emerge, obscuring the spatial dimensions of the stage through darkness (Ibid.). Additionally, he seeks to isolate the performing bodies of the actors on stage (Ibid.) by minimising the stage floor's visibility. This principle of *chiaroscuro*, 'the technique of defining areas of light and shade as a way of revealing three-dimensional form' (Palmer, 2013: 59), which in visual arts manifests as lighter tones emerging from a dark base, plays tricks on the spectators' visual perception, harnessing the natural attraction to areas of light that appear to offer concretising points for orientation. This principle of visual emergence in an uncertain space derives from Renaissance painting conventions. On stage, it is often achieved by side-lighting, which enables selective illumination, minimising light on the stage floor and walls of a performance space. This creates a suggestive, deliberate, undefined expanse. Zyman discusses similar principles in her analysis of Eliasson's light art, and notes that such spaces suggest a 'loss of physical presence and corporeity. Distance and the configuration of space become illegible, and the space can only be measured by the movement of one's body' (2006: 478). Since her analysis at that point engages with an installation piece, the notion of measuring space through the movement of one's body cannot be directly extrapolated to Barker's scenography (with its usually clear distinction between performance and audience space). However, the movement of actors through sparsely lit space presents spectators with an approximation of spatial dimensions, which are deliberately thrown into question in Barker's work, both visually and conceptually (cf. Chapter 1). The body of the actor, in passing through light, and becoming sculpted by it, becomes a visual anchor for the spectator, albeit one that remains decidedly strange in its supposed recognisability. All of the techniques I outline above are at work in the different plays analysed in this chapter. Their particular appearance and affective impact in specific productions are discussed individually, though a general statement on the intended effects of these techniques can be summed up as heightening the consciously theatricalised appearance of the stage image (cf. Barker's comments on denaturalisation in Gritzner and Rabey, 2011: 124; and Appendix 1: 179).

The plays discussed below are, as is the case throughout this book, merely some of the most salient examples, expanded upon by references to other works, and should be considered neither exhaustive nor exclusive. Below follows a chronological analysis of the plays *The Twelfth Battle of Isonzo, The Fence in its Thousandth Year, I Saw Myself, Found in the Ground*, and *The Forty (Few Words)*. These come together in an attempt to establish fundamental and recurring principles of lighting in Barker's scenographic work, whilst simultaneously charting their development over time.

The Twelfth Battle of Isonzo (2001) offers a fruitful example of the ways in which lighting plays a central role in Barker's scenography, even where the textual references to it are sparse. The 2001 Dublin production's lighting design is credited to Nick McCall and Jerome Devitt in the production's programme (kindly provided by Professor Rabey). Charting the tense meeting of a teenage bride and her much older groom, the play explores the desires and manipulations of these two blind characters. Their blindness (frankly stated in the play text, Barker, 2012a: 55, 57) creates a much more pronounced sense of voyeurism for the spectators, as Isonzo and Tenna are presumably invisible to one another. Though one might subsequently assume a pronounced emphasis on text alone, all productions of *The Twelfth Battle of Isonzo* (2001 in Dublin, and the 2002 tour through Cork, Cardiff, Newtown, and Aberystwyth, which adapted the original design to the various venues) utilised light in a musical manner, to support but also to counterpoint the character's actions and words.

The opening state of the piece out of the exordium into the play proper appeared cold and blue: more interrogation room than wedding venue. The artificiality of the lighting induced a sense of being underground, or at the very least away from direct daylight. This state then shifted to a cold white, top down spot on Tenna's chair, with slightly warmer low-level side-lighting as filler. This served to draw particular focus to the by-then still figure of Tenna during her opening monologue. Shifting into a medium-level side-lighting from the opposite direction, positioned high enough to catch the actress' face and torso just prior to Isonzo's entrance complemented the sonic precedent of his appearance. His deliberate steps onto the metal platform upon which Tenna was seated was accompanied by another drastic shift in lighting, back to colder bluish-white lighting from the back and side.

These quick and very noticeable changes in lighting achieved several things: the tonality of the lighting set up an uneasy and potentially even antagonistic atmosphere, if not between the characters themselves, then between them and their environment. Additionally, the drastic successive shifts undermined habitual ways of perceiving space and time on stage, as expected correlations between the passage of time as experienced through daylight and the stage environment are clearly not applicable: time and place are suspended in this strange duet/duel. Furthermore, the surreal qualities achieved by obviously directional lighting of differing intensities resulted in a denaturalisation of the stage space, but also the actors' bodies on stage as they were abstracted and fragmented through extreme and distorted shadows. The deliberate use of extremes of light and darkness[1] offered spectators a much more painterly stage image, in which conventional understanding of time and space was suspended in favour of affective visual content that was presented alongside the dense, poetic spoken text.

After Isonzo's entrance, the lights quickly shifted again to the other side, with more yellow and straw tones in the stage area most often occupied by the youthful bride, with the ancient groom occupying the colder, bluer fringes that lent his skin tone a pale, cold, grey pallor and deepened lines (accentuated by simple stage make up): a haunting of the lively by the almost-dead, circling restlessly. Light in this instance yet again served several purposes and certainly more than merely making visible. It set up a complimentary, but possible slightly antagonistic relationship between the two performers in a more subtle way than their contrasting (though by no means unexpected or inappropriate) attire (see Chapter 3 on costume for more details). In addition, rather than merely considering the individual lighting states throughout, one has to consider the effects of transitions: the lighting in production had a pronounced change whenever Tenna achieved a sense of her own performativity (cf. Barker, 2012a: 63, e.g. her acceptance and embrace of lying), usually to colder tones, and back into warmth when she faltered in her own convictions (cf. Ibid.: 64; the shift in production occurred when she was 'suddenly afraid' [Ibid.] and later again as she questioned Isonzo's wartime memory; Ibid.: 68). Yet another shift accompanied Isonzo's sudden and uncanny 'terrible cries' (Ibid.: 66). As such, lighting in this production served as a kind of rhythmical punctuation that ran parallel to the emotional developments of the characters, as the decidedly non-natural lighting states avoided bathetic lapses of the ongoing tension between Tenna and Isonzo. At the same time, the lighting did not manipulate the spectators' emotions in terms of sympathising with the characters: their visual fragmentation by side-lighting and resulting harsh shadows (intensified by stage make up) resulted in an uncomfortable, yet mesmerising, abstraction. Tenna and Isonzo are not like the audience, and their theatricalisation by means of lighting heightened this perception as much as their elevated language and careful gestures did.

Beckett's *Play* springs to mind, in which the interrogating light triggers the heads in the urns to speak; in *The Twelfth Battle of Isonzo*, light shifted attention between Tenna and Isonzo, such as the single, cold, top-down spot illuminating Isonzo's face resting in Tenna's hand whilst he pondered the after-effects of a long-gone war (Ibid.: 66–67). In this particular instance, the visual separation of the characters in two separate pools of light after Tenna withdrew her hand (Ibid.: 67) accompanied their contrasting story-telling: Isonzo's gruesome war memories, dubiously detailed, gory and dramatic (Ibid.: 67–68), strikingly different from the romanticised, simple, and nostalgic images Tenna describes of her grandmother's youth (Ibid.). In the recurring instances of storytelling, whether it be Isonzo's descriptions of the war and various travels or Tenna's journey to the department store to pick out underwear for her wedding (Ibid.: 72), the lighting zoned in on the speaker, demanding full attention to the details they were offering to the other person on stage, and – by extension – the audience. In this instance, the stage direction 'they dream' (Ibid.: 73) was not only accompanied by a sound cue, but also by low lighting, tinted with straw, and what appears on the video recording as tints of red or purple. Mixed with the white spotlight, this spilled onto Tenna's wedding gown in the very 'SHELL PINK' (Ibid.: 73) the characters are dreaming about at that particular point. As soon as the sequence was interrupted by Tenna's laughter (Ibid.), the scene returned to the clinical lighting state first encountered at Isonzo's opening lines: cold, white, with a general wash from above and the front, eradicating the subtle shadows the top- and side-lighting of the dream sequence held just moments before. This state of lighting, sustained until Tenna's removal of her underwear (accompanied by a variation of the eerie sound cue from the dream sequence just previously), was interrupted by the loss of her shoe (Ibid.: 77), fading to a white spot on Tenna, with some harsh but low-level whitish-blue side-lights hitting the shoe and her bare foot, spilling stark long shadows across the stage, and deepening the shadows of the gaps in the grid upon which Tenna sat on her chair. Once more, the tonal shift was accompanied by a shift in lighting state: the perfect performance of undressing that Isonzo demands is abruptly destroyed by his bride's clumsiness.

The lighting in the play's production served as a visual score accompanying the intense and often musical verbal exchange between the two blind characters, supporting but also counterpointing their words. This offered audiences a further layer of potential associative meanings through repeated and recurring shifts of obviously non-naturalistic, highly theatrical lighting states. These are not generally specified in the play text itself, with one notable, and crucial, exception: at the actual disrobing of Tenna (whose nakedness is discussed in detail by Isonzo prior to the actual occurrence of undressing) 'the room is plunged in darkness' (Ibid.: 89), finally putting audience and performers on par. The voyeuristic gaze of spectators is frustrated in the very moment that could have been its climax. Notably, in production this 'darkness' consisted of a low-level blue wash from the top on the metal grille. In combination with low-level side-lighting grazing the actress' shoulder and hip, the reflection of the light on the metal actually resulted in sound visibility, though the naked body, steeped in deep shadows and only hints of light became 'highly theatrical' (Obis, 2013: 73): more abstracted shape than unclothed subject. This was immediately followed by bright backlighting at Isonzo's 'terrible wail' (Barker, 2012a: 89), before the blackout specified in the text. This sudden switch and the deliberate blinding of the audience would certainly result in an even more acute sense of darkness in the moments that followed. Considering Health & Safety Regulations requiring the perpetual visibility of emergency exits, the flash of backlighting could serve as visual overstimulation in order to achieve the desired effect of making the naked Tenna invisible.

However, the production returned to very low-level white side-lighting and a low-level top wash at Isonzo's repetition of 'CAN'T SEE' (Ibid.: 90), much earlier than the 'slow dim light' (Ibid.) the text calls for some 21 lines later. Though this might jar with or lessen Isonzo's lamentations of blindness (no longer shared by the audience) and lessen the severity of his (seeming) revelation 'I am not blind' (Ibid.), the fact that the production offered a spatial arrangement that saw Isonzo facing away from Tenna and threw his revelation into question, since he had not actually looked at Tenna's naked form.

Particular importance is attached to light in this play, since the two characters are (ostensibly) blind; the verbal preference for auditory aspects, particularly regarding the invisible, the underneath, and the inside (of Tenna, and her clothes, cf. Ibid.: 58), invites lighting solutions that support and/or contrast the vivid storytelling that Isonzo engages in (Ibid.: 58–59; 70), later matched by Tenna's imagination (Ibid.: 80). Lighting sets the mood of the characters' relationship visually for the audience, yet also acts to exclude spectators from the strange erotic intimacy that the two characters appear to share by virtue of their blindness, and their consequently heightened sense of hearing and smell. Similarly, the visual contrast of stark side-lighting (a frequent technique in Barker; see Appendix 1: 182) and the characters' austere attire with the vivid and sensually affective descriptions of colour (Ibid.: 73–77) requires active imaginative engagement from the audience: their visual sense has to incorporate both the stage as is visible, and the multiple and diverse scenes the characters set for each other and the audience over the course of the play. Additionally, lighting serves to carve out in more detail the contrasting materialities of the stage set, the costumes, and later the naked body of the performer portraying Tenna. It contributes both to the abstraction of the actors' bodies through harsh shadows and to the resulting fragmentation of the human form and perhaps more importantly also face. Simultaneously, it highlights their vulnerabilities as they prey, play, and construct their separate subject identities in repeated attempts to assert power over one another. Ultimately, it is Tenna who emerges from the encounter victoriously, though not unscathed: 'Nose bleeding' (Ibid.: 109) she attempts to flee the room (successfully in production), leaving behind the strangely undead form of Isonzo, 'kick[ing] his legs like a doll' (Ibid.), as the scene of their encounter fades to invisibility. In a setting that could potentially be constructed as a realistic chamber play, the heightened performances of self by the characters were accompanied in production by a lighting design that refuted any such association, instead offering bodies and space as surreal and abstracted shapes in which the imaginations of the spectators were set to roam free. The next play I discuss here, *The Fence in its Thousandth Year* (hereafter *The Fence*), utilised the destabilisation of spatial borders through selective lighting to a similar effect.

The Fence offers – conceptually and visually – a much larger scale than the play discussed earlier. Its opening sequence already demands lighting solutions as the duchess Algeria visits the 'frontier fence at night' (Barker, 2005b: 7), offering herself to 'a dim rush of figures' (Ibid.) from beyond the barrier; after the act, a 'light traverses' (Ibid.). The particular setting of the scene requires lighting that offers the information to the audience without attempting an accurate or realistic representation of a night time frontier fence. It is light's task 'to make the action visible, and make visible in an interesting way' (Morley in Kipp, 2016: 260) without 'trying to create an environment that is real' or 'show[ing] anything outside of what is in the words and what is put on the stage' (Ibid.). Helen Morley utilised the depth of the stage in order to allow figures to emerge from the shadows beyond the titular fence,[2] though their approach was caught occasionally by side-lights used to highlight the wires and (apparently) concrete posts of the fence.

This technique offered several visual cues to the spectators: on the one hand, it brought the central stage piece to life by highlighting its materiality; on the other hand, the fragmentary illumination of the figures beyond othered them in comparison to characters on the nearer side by reducing them to mere shapes without faces. Though dressed in what appears on video as muted colours, the 'thieves' were nonetheless costumed in shades that allowed their bodies to appear in graduations of grey and dirty browns through the side-light, avoiding a separation of their heads and faces from the rest of their bodies as darker clothing would have caused. In this instance, the stripes of medium- to low-level side-lighting came together with the costume designs to enable a *chiaroscuro* emergence of shapes from the dark background, the depth of which was unknowable both visibly (by being steeped in darkness) and sonically (through a disorientating and surrealistic layering of live sounds and pre-recorded aspects of the soundscape; see Chapter 4 for detailed discussion).

The night time scenes at the fence were dominated by side-lighting from the wings that rarely exceeded the actor's body height, giving sharp cuts of illumination across the body. It appears on video that colder tones dominated, with true white and hints of blue. The daytime pastoral scenes inside the duchy offered a much warmer, softer palette of straw tones. In addition to lower strength side-lighting, these also utilised a top wash from the front and side, softening and splitting shadows on the floor, whilst offering clear illumination of actors' faces. The production's lighting designer very consciously utilised the scene changings and flying set pieces in order to play with the objects' shadows 'in such a way that [they] became part of the set pieces' (see Morley in Kipp, 2016: 261). For example, for the watering can ritual (Barker, 2005b: 15), the 'frontier by day' (Ibid.) was initially established by a medium level and backlighting of warm colour tonality from a medium-height angle, hitting the flying fence at touch-down, spreading its ominous shadow across the downstage area, populated moments later by women in light coloured dresses and headpieces, crossing through the dark lines thrown by the set piece. At the same time, the angle of lighting picked up the fence's wires quite strongly, once more emphasising its materiality visually and thereby generating a plethora of potential associations for the spectator: whether the fence is perceived as martial, threatening, or reassuring, there is no question that the deliberate expansion of its presence through its shadow and the attention-drawing accentuation of its constituent parts through highlighting made it a central visual and thematic force through lighting techniques.

Similarly, the 'park of babies and sunshine' (Barker, 2005b: 30) connected the flying set pieces (suspended wicker Moses baskets) to the overall stage space through lighting: by adding warm top-lighting to the overall more yellow-orange wash from both sides of the stage at the front, the cribs' shadows dotted across the softly lit floor,[3] offering a cohesive stage picture through colour similarity (of the baskets' material, the light and Photo's coat as well as Lou's dress) as well as visual composition. Additionally, Morley recalls a colour distinction in lighting employed to distinguish inside and outside settings (in Kipp, 2016: 261–262), subtly shaping the spectators' understanding of the stage space through lighting in the absence of concrete or naturalistically illustrative spatial markers. The deliberate creation of shadows through directional lighting also tied together the sparse set, the stage space, and the costumed bodies of the actors. The transitions between different lighting states varied, from subtle to more sudden changes; the latter usually denoted the end of one scene and beginning of another, which in *The Fence* frequently also coincides with a change of locale. Since the basic spatial arrangements remained mostly stable (with the fence running across the stage into the darkness of the wings), the altered lighting became a fundamentally spatial clue that attested to changed location, time of day, and season.

Where lighting changes were subtle and more continuous, they reflected dramatic shifts in the action of the play, rather than become indicative of the passing of time. This is not to suggest that the lighting became a narrative device that provided spectators with prescriptive emotive content. Instead, selective highlighting through narrow, focussed beams served to focus attention on the expressive (speaking) body, concrete yet elusive in the unfixedness of the shadows that surrounded it. Like *The Twelfth Battle of Isonzo*, the lighting in *The Fence* once more engaged an explicit theatricality in the visual presentation of materials on stage. The predominance of shadows in contrast to deliberately limited, yet starkly illuminated areas and the conscious creation of *chiaroscuro* effects, particularly through the interplay between light and costuming, are at the heart of the next play discussed here, *I Saw Myself*.

Following the quiet revolution of the wealthy widow Sleev, who weaves her life's transgressions in a pursuit of ecstatic self-discovery, the overall aesthetic of *I Saw Myself* in the 2008 Wrestling School production was clearly reminiscent of Renaissance paintings. It opened on a low corridor of light on the floor upstage right at the back, however without exposing the full dimensions of the stage: the back wall remained unlit, and the corridor of light disappeared behind the podium mid-way downstage, stage left, on which the wardrobe was dimly visible. Cold lights caught suspended balls of yarn at the very front from downstage left and right; the yarns appeared white, pale green, or straw coloured and blue-tinged, no noticeably bright colours, with the exception of Ladder's yarn: a deep red. The unlit mirror on the lightly coloured wooden wardrobe appeared as a black hole. At Sleev's entry, a cold top-down frontal wash from downstage left and right brightened the stage, catching the descending frames (matching the wood of the wardrobe and the steps leading up to it) and splitting the actresses' faces into half dark, half light. Though the steps were then also illuminated, the top half and mirror on the front of the wardrobe remained relatively dark, as did the back of the stage space, giving no clear indication as to its depth or height. This was furthered by a slight echo that pervaded the space, possibly induced by hidden microphones that suggested a space of enormous proportions, the edge of which was invisible.

Sleev's mourning garb effectively offered her form as a dark hole amidst the bright shapes of her maids (for a detailed discussion of costume see Chapter 3). Over the next minute or so followed a slow fade up on the wardrobe from angled lights positioned downstage left and right, top down, and middle height (the right one slightly stronger) catching the wardrobe eaves' contours without illuminating the mirror, thereby avoiding accidentally blinding the audience, or creating glimpses of their reflections and deepening the darkness of the mirror in contrast to its surroundings. The inside of the wardrobe was lit warmly from the top down, casting deep shadows along Modicum's face and body below the shoulders. The movement of the mirrored door caught the frontal lighting, resulting in a brief glare towards the auditorium. A corridor of light existed at the back of the stage falling across the space from stage left; invisible without anything to intercept it (cf. Barker's desire to avoid lighting the floor, Morley in Kipp, 2016: 258), it offered illumination to the many entrances from stage right, such as when it partially lit Sheeth's face and upper torso behind one of the suspended frames, strongly and anachronistically evocative of Dutch Renaissance painting, thereby alluding visually to the setting outlined in the text, namely 'Europe in the thirteenth century' (Barker, 2008b: 9).

The deep, dark backgrounds of the stage and subsequent extreme contrasts of costume to dark space, and also of (dark) costumes to skin (especially in the case of Sleev and Sheeth's attire) drew the spectators' eye in, offering them a succession of paintings that attest to a rich history and even richer stories the full extent of which cannot be accessed, merely glimpsed. The mirror offered a similar framing, the light wood offering a bright frame to the dark pool of the glass in which pale faces are reflected, most often that of Sleev, who returned to the mirror again and again in search of insight into herself, a 'self-consciousness that [can] be relieved by scrutiny' (Ibid.: 13). The lighting states of the Wrestling School production were fairly stable, offering the characters thin strips of light here and there to seek out. These were tightly bound up with the blocking that most frequently aligned performers along a diagonal across the space, maximising distance between bodies. Whilst the frames and yarns downstage dipped into darkness, the suspended frames (doubled in number for Act 2) upstage were always dimly lit. Similarly, the wardrobe remained lit throughout the piece, with more or less emphasis on the door and the darkened mirror at its centre.

The notable exception was a fade to low lights plunging most of the rooms in dim twilight, with only a small white spill across the downstage corner of the steps upon which the wardrobe was placed, giving an eerie impression of emptiness, and perhaps night time before Ladder berates Modicum at the end of Act 1, and when Hawelka and Ladder discuss the encroaching war in Act 2. The lights faded back up as Ladder muses on the necessity of personal sacrifice in art: 'when women are no longer blinded something will go from weaving' (Ibid.: 60). Though the lights came up, they did not illuminate the downstage frames, but rather pooled top-down around the wardrobe, the dark centres of the suspended frames visually echoing the dark mirror. More importantly perhaps was the slow concentration of lights on the isolated figure of Sleev in the final moments of the play, gradually closing in on her as the other women take down the tapestry (cf. Ibid.: 80). Her dark clothing contrasted with the bright wood of the stairs and wardrobe, as well as actress Geraldine Alexander's pale face and blonde hair: a shadow, isolated in an increasingly dark space without visible boundaries. The dark interior of the wardrobe (on previous occasions warmly illuminated) contrasted the bright line of reflected light that the mirror traced across the space at the last opening of the door (Ibid.: 81) before the 'light [died] in the room' (Ibid.).

In *I Saw Myself*, the proportionally larger abundance of darkness illustrated Italian lighting designer Crisafulli's assertion that 'shadows are the substance of vision' (2013: 11): in the negative spaces they create, the audience's imagination is invited to roam. In *I Saw Myself*, the textual references to lighting within the play itself are exceedingly sparse. Nonetheless, the play evokes a sense of spatio-temporal limbo in which the women weave, with the catastrophe drawing nearer until finally it is just offstage. The deliberate blurring of scale (with regard to visible space, the dimensions of the tapestry, and the timespan in which it is woven) and the lurking horror of the invisible war might usefully be considered in terms of Lyotard's notion of the sublime: 'optical pleasure when reduced to near nothingness promotes an infinite contemplation of infinity' (Lyotard, 1989: 204). This formulation brings to mind the *Ganzfeld* effect, in which the shocking absence of discernible patterns may result in an 'intensification of [the spectator's] conceptual and emotional capacity, an ambivalent enjoyment' (Ibid.: 206). The nebulous, intangible, and borderless world of *I Saw Myself* offers a 'world apart' (Ibid.: 202) to the everyday reality of spectators' lives, which is in no small part created through the actual and metaphorical shadows at the edges of the stage (cf. Morley in Kipp, 2016: 262).

These principles of absence and borderlessness are also at the core of the next play discussed here, *Found in the Ground*, which structurally is possibly Barker's most challenging piece. Its fragmented formal bricolage offers not only different timelines and places in disorienting succession, but occasionally even presents them simultaneously. The play's particular placelessness contrasts those scenographic aspects that, though specified in the stage directions, were rendered in production through light in view of budget, feasibility, and health and safety regulations, such as the smouldering 'pyramid of books' (Barker, 2008b: 123) that dominates the conceptual stage space, and is a core element of the action. The Wrestling School production realised this scenographic proposal through a trap door downstage right, lit from below in flickering warm yellow, red and orange tones. By evoking the fire through lighting (with additional help through smoke effects), the production maintained this crucial feature in a manner that stayed in accordance with safety regulations as well as offering a reasonably economic, yet elegant solution to the problem posed by the stage directions. The fire's colours contrasted with the eerie blue that heralded the haunting presence of the undead war criminal Knox. The production's lighting designer Helen Morley described her choices thus: 'Knox was lit with an intense blue, because he occupied a different world, or possibly timeline. There had to be a separateness [sic] to the character's appearance' (in Kipp, 2016: 261).

Similarly, the lighting of Macedonia's recitations (e.g. Barker, 2008b: 149; 153) focussed tightly on her naked form, especially her torso, sharply and coldly side-lit from stage left. The figures on stage in *Found in the Ground* were visually as fragmented as the layered timelines and places they inhabit. Coherence was deliberately and noticeably disrupted on all scenographic levels. Though light tied the different locales (the site of burning books, the dogs' kennels, Toonelhuis' haunt, and the locations of Denmark and Burgteata's encounters) together to a minor extent – simply by virtue of occasionally making them visible at the same time, especially when parallel scenes coexisted on stage (e.g. Knox's promise to 'get [Tonnelhuis] Hitler' [Ibid.: 181] and the sunbathing nurses) – the selective illumination of smaller parts of the stage (such as the nurses lit in warm colours, contrasting with Burgteata's ghostly appearance as bride), and the narrow beams of side-lighting actually reinforced the sense of spatio-temporal disjuncture that centrally pervades the text. This is furthered by the deliberate difference in colour choices for lighting different characters (most notably Knox, Macedonia, and the nurses in the bikini scene; Ibid.: 173), which heighten the audience's sense of visual disparity.

This was immediately apparent in the production's exordium in which Macedonia was grazed by very low-level side-lighting in what appears on record as a reasonably warm straw colour (though one should cautiously note that low-level lighting frequencies always warm up colours); this was complemented by the low glow reflected on the propped-up trapdoor downstage right and contrasting the cold black-and-white, bluish tinged projections of war time photographs projected onto a screen suspended at standing height stage left. As the projections and low-level side-lighting faded, the audience was momentarily left with only the suggestive glow illuminating the trapdoor. The subsequent entrance by the nurses was backlit with cold side-light along the entry passage upstage left (appearing white on record), brightly reflecting off their white dresses. This corridor of light for their entrance offered a subtle colour contrast to the small, warm top- and front-lit pool that Toonelhuis wheeled into. Already the principle of a general visual isolation and fragmentation of the different figures' bodies on stage was established: the lighting afforded partial glances, no more. Even when an actor's body was lit, the sharp angles of lighting and resulting shadows rarely afforded, more than barely, adequate visibility of the body's entirety. Where bodies were brightly lit, they appeared abstracted not only through fragmentation, but also through the luminescent quality the directional lighting imbued the actors' skin with. The precise carving out of smaller, separate spaces within the overall stage space was especially apparent in the very bright top and front lighting on Toonelhuis' eating ritual.

Lighting in *Found in the Ground* was instrumental in generating unsettling atmosphere and directing the audience's attention without ever providing clear indication of time of day or year, or locational clues (inside/outside; geographical position), despite Toonelhuis' references to these things (e.g. 'It's noon/It's autumn'; Ibid.: 178), whenever he demands to be fed. There existed a notable contrast between the (barely) living Toonelhuis, lit by straw-coloured tones, warm but not welcoming, and the undead Knox, in colder blue tones. The other haunting occupant of the stage, Macedonia, appeared similarly colour-coded in contrast to the living members of the cast. Additionally, the nurses frequently appeared to occupy not only their own stream of narration (unrelated to the obfuscated strand of action that charts the progress in burning the library), but were repeatedly cordoned off by lighting from other figures. The stage space was therefore carved up into several interrelated, and interacting, spaces, the precise nature of which was never fully identifiable.

The Wrestling School production of *Found in the Ground* offered crucial interplay of costume, set, and light throughout: the nurses' dresses, Burgteata's dressing gown (mustard yellow), and Lobe's valet jacket all picked up the dim beams crossing the stage by virtue of their light colouring, whereas Toonelhuis' attire (in particular, the loose reddish-purple dressing gown) offset his pale skin and white hair, offering a much more subdued and tightly focussed point of attention. The blue lighting accompanying Knox's repeated appearances also caught on the vertical metal grille running along the left-hand side of the stage, highlighting the set piece's cold, hard materiality, and evoking imprisonment and a state of insecurity, or perhaps hostility within the stage environment. This cold, looming presence stood in direct contrast to the warm, unsettling glow of the trapdoor swallowing wheelbarrows full of books across the diagonal of the stage, offering an oppositional colour scheme as well as inverse vertical extensions of the stage (the grille upwards into the shadow, the trapdoor downwards into invisibility).

In this, the lighting and set of *Found in the Ground* together achieved a conceptual extension of the stage space beyond the (deliberately obscured) visible boundaries of the onstage area. The directional implications of the set pieces were supported by the suggestive lighting solutions that offered inconclusive visual information regarding the exact dimensions of the set and therefore the stage. Working once more with *chiaroscuro* effects, this production – though offering the audience the bare back wall of the theatre, and long, visible entrances by various characters – nonetheless also engaged in a repeated sense of emergence (of figures from the shadows or background, and also of new information regarding cyclical scenes scattered throughout the piece) that was never brought to a full conclusion. Instead, one moment of emergence (conceptual or visual) was overlaid with the next, as images and words piled up in a complex sensory assault.

In the production, overall strong side-lights, other directional lighting, and low levels of illumination were employed to achieve the *chiaroscuro* effect of singled out, emphasised visual content, acting as a theatrical equivalent to filmic zoom: the human eye is attracted to differences in stimuli, so that in contrasting areas of light and dark it will privilege what is lit over what is not (cf. Moore and Zirnsak, 2017), and draw the audience's attention consciously and unconsciously to what has been chosen to be visible. These strong visual highlights were in use even when a more traditional general frontal top-down wash was employed (e.g. in Act 1, Scene 18), offering select points of emphasis.

Secondly, setting up the stage in a manner that offered performers bands of light and dark enabled them to emerge (and disappear) from positions across the space. In a piece as complex and conceptually overwhelming as *Found in the Ground*, the directional guidance of spectators' attention through lighting simultaneously enables performers to take up positions technically already on stage, though hidden in shadows. Usually drawing on a limited colour palette (echoing the mostly monochromatic costume designs and equally restrained sets), Morley recalls that *Found in the Ground* demanded a slightly different approach: the existence of Knox and the necessity to mark his otherness in a non-reductive, non-explanatory manner was solved through colour tonality. Similarly, the stand-alone scenes of the nurses – setting counterpoints to the cyclical actions of Toonelhuis and the Workman – required on the one hand responsiveness to stage directions (e.g. 'Wind. Rain.'; Ibid.: 160), on the other a sensibility of distinguishing these figures from those that might conceivably be identified as the protagonists of the play.

Morley recalls she 'used bright orange sunlight on the nurses in the bikinis, but [...] would not have done that had they not been in those. It was something about their nature that demanded this colour' (in Kipp, 2016: 261). There are very few explicit lighting cues within the play text (e.g. Barker, 2008b: 183), and only some implicit (such as the time of day or season), leaving extensive interpretive freedom to the lighting designer. Barker's scenography therefore requires responsive engagement with the play text that does not impose limitations upon the play that foreclose the audience's imaginative engagement with multifaceted content on stage. Though Barker's work in general refuses a clear identification of geographical location and time period, *Found in the Ground* in particular requires a realisation on stage that demonstrates sensitivity towards the fundamental ambiguity of his writing and offers staging solutions in practice that engage with this, foregrounding the experiential and affective qualities of theatre, without resorting to reductive, easily recognisable imagery. This principle is pervasive in Barker's works even where some more concrete locational information is required by the play text, such as in *The Fence in its Thousandth Year*. The poetic capacity of lighting to hint at changing locales, to suggest ambiguity of mood, to sculpt set and performers in a painterly manner are all crucial elements to the realisation of the next texts considered here: the collection of plays titled *The Forty (Few Words)*.

This particular set of very short, poetic, and intense playlets requires immense scenographic flexibility when staged in one space in quick succession (cf. Kipp in Rabey, 2015: 236). The changing locales are as much conjured by costuming and sound as they are by light. This particular collection of plays offers some of the most ambiguous stage directions in Barker's writing. Their poetic appearance also extends to the explicit and implicit lighting cues contained within the play text. *The Forty* has been staged twice, once in 2011 under the direction of David Ian Rabey with third year students of the Theatre, Film and Television Department at Aberystwyth University, and again under his direction in co-production with that same department and

Lurking Truth Theatre Company in 2014. Despite the absence of a Barker-directed Wrestling School production of this text, the particularity of its scenographic proposals nevertheless renders it a salient example for analysis in the context of this research. This is compounded by my involvement in both productions (taking on the roles of costume designer, assistant director, actress, and set adaptation in the latter). This provides me with insights that can be extrapolated and related to various Wrestling School productions.

Gareth Weaver, the lighting designer for both productions of *The Forty*, offered the following contemplation in 2011: 'The lighting [...] was particularly inspired by the natural phenomena of sunset and sunrise, which in their climatic moments create such dramatic shadows, inextricably linked to change, endings and new beginnings' (Rabey, 2012: 294). He furthermore identified the principle of 'a definite, but undefined space: a playing space with a particular mood, without being literal: with a more specific casting of shadows. By using haze and light in counterpoint, the bodies were heavily outlined, making them appear hyper-real' (Ibid.). The crucial significance of shadows is as pervasive in Weaver's thinking as it is in Morley's: both use them to shape the stage space and create visual points of interest, creating lines through the interplay of light, the performing body it encounters in space, and the shadows this generates both in the space and on the body.

The textual ambiguity of Barker's œuvre requires precisely that flexibility to play and explore. The lighting utilises the deliberate un-fixedness (of visual and conceptual boundaries) to open up the stage space, even in instances where it may be segmented (cf. *Found in the Ground*). Nonetheless, each of these locales retains a fundamental ambiguity in terms of time period, geographical location, season, and often even time of day. For example, playlet 11 of *The Forty* merely specifies 'bad light' (Barker, 2014a: 297) – a challenging proposal for any lighting designer. In this instance, it adds to the central theme of secrecy (it arises in the course of the play that the audience are witnessing the discovery of an extramarital affair), which the text offers without resolution, and more importantly without moral opinion. It falls therefore to the lighting design to create a space for these extremes of emotion to play out, without prescribing a precise, recognisably quotidian situation that would invariably shape the audience's expectations (e.g. the cuckolded husband takes revenge) and emotionally manipulate their reading of the situation (the woman is reprehensible; the husband pitiful, etc.).

In other instances, stage directions are more precise, and yet deny the audience's narrative conclusion. One pointed example of this is playlet 24, which opens with '[m]oonlight and its shadows' (Ibid.: 318) and closes with '[t]he moon moves on, the shadows alter. Dawn arrives in the form of the chorus' (Ibid: 319). Whilst at a glance this may appear to require a more realistic setting than the previous example, the strangeness of the action (an old man attempts suicide by exposing himself to the cold at night) and the distinct lack of a locational description once more engage the degrees of likeness that are at the heart of this collection of plays. In addition, *The Forty* consists in large parts of stereotypical snippets of parlance (e.g. 'So sorry' constitutes the entirety of spoken text in playlet 3; Ibid.: 285) that come forth in moments of extreme emotions; their utter inadequacy regarding truthful, meaningful expression for the characters becomes apparent in each iteration. The extraordinary nature of all these pivotal moments that the collection presents was crucially expressed in both productions through non-naturalistic lighting states that engaged the possibilities of dream-like states, of deliberate displacement (the audience does not know where a scene takes place; it is likely the characters do not either). By offering evocative visual content, rich in contrast and filled with dramatic shadows that illustrate the tense distances between performers (cf. Weaver in Rabey, 2012: 295), *The Forty* was always 'like' somewhere, but never concrete in its precise location: 'this time is somewhat like the 1930s or 1940s, this place is perhaps like Beachy Head' (Kipp in Rabey, 2015: 236), always somewhat, never quite.

The collection deals in degrees of approximation in order to afford the audience a maximum of associative possibilities. The ambiguity of lighting is particularly well-suited to engage these imaginative capabilities, since the physical reality of our eyes' attraction to light may result in a confrontation with disturbing images that we are nonetheless seduced to look at, simply by virtue of the way they are lit (cf. Johnson, 2012a: 50). In low visibility our minds may very well be seduced to attempt completion of a partially glimpsed image. This '[m]ulti-channeling of information sets the relationships between the media in a constant, unstable movement and uncertainty with regard to possible meanings' (Abulafia, 2016: 2), which in Barker's scenography is intentional and lends validity to the individual spectator's response to the material. In this, Lyotard's notion of a presentation of the unpresentable (1989) through approximation via affective suggestion resurfaces, as it does with regard to Barker's sets: *The Forty* presents a parade of fragmented worlds *between* (cf. Lyotard, 1989: 202) that are neither realistic nor entirely removed from the lives of spectators. It is both familiar and strange, offering a multiplication of possible individualised meanings through indeterminacy. Though 'patterns, colours and structures of light may provide a dynamic articulation of space', in the expressive scenography that Barker's texts invite 'they rarely bear any relation to the creation of a realistic representation of the external world' (Palmer, 2013: 68). This is particularly apparent in the realisation of Barker's works in production, since these propose untenable, irresolvable situations that grapple with the fundamental tension of staging the extremes of human experience in an open-ended, non-prescriptive manner.

The textual provocations of *The Forty* are mostly, and even sometimes entirely, placeless (regarding the identification of a concrete 'where'); nonetheless in production they require an actualisation in space. In a circumstance where spatial flexibility was key, scene changes fluid, and budget negligible at best, the productions of *The Forty* depended on the other scenographic elements (costume, sound, light) to take on some of the properties usually fulfilled by set: to provide a (crucially ambiguous) sense of place and time. In the 2014 productions, the rich jewel tones of select costume pieces (e.g. a tea length, deep fuchsia satin gown worn by the character of the Woman in playlet 8) – providing points of interest among the more subdued colour palette of the majority of costumes (focussed largely on black and white, muted browns, beiges, and greys) – offered themselves as canvas for Weaver's side-lighting, visually grabbing the audience's attention and sculpting the performing bodies on stage through contrast (of colours, as well as light and shadow). The notions of a theatrical equivalent of filmic zoom and perspectival cuts from one person to another were facilitated by lighting, 'seeking to expand and strengthen the visual dimension of the performance and the experience of spectatorship beyond textual reference' (Abulafia, 2016: 43, on Appia).

Working in such extreme lighting conditions, it became apparent that darkness is to light as silence is to sound: they are 'degrees of the same phenomenon' (Crisafulli, 2013: 11) and play together to achieve their full effects. The select areas of light offered further opportunities for fluid transitions between different playlets while offering visually fragmented spaces that complemented the snapshot nature of the different plays: moving swiftly from inside to outside, from the domestic to the political, the grandiose to the mundane, all the while delving deep into the driving passions of human interaction and the tensions they create. In both productions, Weaver worked with corridors of light achieved through steep angles (mostly from the sides) at heights ranging from just above the floor to head-height. Thus, performers could appear and disappear suddenly, affording a great range of dramatic entrances, exits, and also partial emergence: positioned in such a way that only a hand, or half of a performer's face, was lit, the lighting design in the productions of *The Forty* strove to visually carve out the moments of emotional intensity that each playlet is predicated upon.

The *Ganzfeld* effect and the limits of perception

At this point, it should be clear to the reader that the scenographic tradition of affective atmospheres generated by light, and the approach to lighting as active, evocative, and kinetic, is central to Barker's works. The intangibility and malleability of light, in conjunction with its fundamentally individualised perception (especially regarding colour) by spectators, works precisely along the lines of 'what consciousness cannot formulate' (Lyotard, 1989: 197). The experiential emphasis of lighting and its perception demands a '[l]etting-go of all grasping intelligence' (Ibid.), instead foregrounding the simple truth of its occurrence. It is therefore not improbable to consider light as a central scenographic device at the heart of the theatrical debates (begun in the late 19th and early 20th century) of how to stage that which cannot be represented, namely the sublime (cf. Abulafia, 2016: 44 and Welton, 2017: 506).

The oscillations between phenomenological impact and semiotic significance that suffuse the experience of light make it both/and rather than either/or. The overabundance of potential associations generated evokes the sublime through offering spectators both too much and too little as the same time (cf. Ibid.: 497). This questions not only the work being seen but also the role of spectatorship, and beyond that, a personal understanding of self-hood. This questioning process, and its philosophical connections to visibility as equated to truth and knowledge in Western Enlightenment thinking (as the movement's name implies), is thematically at the heart of many different Barker plays, such as *The Twelfth Battle of Isonzo*, *Gertrude – The Cry*, and of course *I Saw Myself*. The notion of the secret and its dependency on darkness (cf. Barker, 1997, 2005a) are crucial to Barker's playwriting and subsequently his scenography. Where Brecht sought 'to harshly expose the course of actions on stage and lead to an immediate impression concerning the artificiality of the presentation' (Abulafia on Brecht, 2016: 31) through light, Barker's approach, though no less concerned with realism,[4] instead privileges darkness, not-seeing, and the secret over Brecht's desired exposition and critical engagement, which results in an elevation and pursuit of individualised, personal, private experience (cf. also Abulafia, 2016: 32–33). The Western philosophical alignment of seeing with knowledge equally then aligns not-seeing with not-knowing, but perhaps also with being unknowable, which in turn leads back to the ecstasy and horror of the sublime experience that is beyond rational understanding and articulable thought. The implications generated by the subconscious cultural perception of light as good/desirable/honest (cf. also Sloterdijk in Keller, 2010: 27), the absence of light, and abundance of darkness in Barker's scenographic realisation of lighting are unquestionably essential to his anti-Enlightenment stance.

The formlessness of light per se illustrates its fundamental interrelationship to space: it is only in offering contrast (through shadow and darkness) and by offering light objects and bodies to hit and flow around that it is expressed, not unlike the body of an instrument that creates a resonating space for sound to become expressible and malleable (cf. Tkatch, 2010: 11; Welton, 2017: 503–504). The politics of visibility and looking are inextricably bound up with lighting: the choices of what is revealed versus what is concealed are crucial to the creation of tension on stage; light and shadow alternately offer or deny parts of the onstage space (cf. Johnson, 2012a; Graham, 2016: 74). In Barker's works, this potential malleability, its association with infinity, and the politically charged nature of exposure and concealment as realised through light all become crucial in the generation of associatively rich spaces on stage. Tkatch writes (on the artist James Turrell) of creating an 'artistic frame for the sublime'[5] (2010: 8; my translation) which 'attempts to make it "presentable" by reaching into abstraction, even dematerialisation, of the artwork and a shift of the art event into the spectator's perception'[6] (Ibid.: 9; my translation). In other words, the materials of light and darkness require the active imaginative engagement of individual spectators, which foregrounds experiential, affective, and importantly inconclusive encounters with the work. Both the independent contributions to meaning that light makes (cf. Graham, 2016: 74) and the materiality of darkness (cf. Welton, 2017) actively contribute to this multiplication.

Barker's work offers its audiences a dematerialisation of concrete spatio-temporal and culturally fixed semiotic signifiers through fragmentation, suggestion, and multiplication of content that audiences register as significant. The extremes of light and darkness that dominate his stage spaces and the resultant fragmentation not only of the stage space, but also frequently of the bodies that occupy it, refuse to be reducible to single meanings or conclusive answers. In their ambiguity they demand that a spectator make a choice, not only of what to watch but also of what to consider as significant to the individual, offering a plethora of possible ways of watching. The sense of instability, mutability, even unreliability that pervades Barker's stage spaces – which is in no small part a result of the lighting – is in line with historical developments of 'postmodern explorations regarding representation of the human condition' (Abulafia on Svoboda, 2016: 35). As such, Barker's theatrical endeavour follows a long line of 20th century theatre makers for whom the mere representation of everyday surface reality fell short of the deeper capacities of the theatre.

Barker's work has been referred to as both pictorial (e.g. Morley in interview in Kipp, 2016; Lamb in Rabey and Goldingay, 2013) and compared to installation art (cf. Morley again). The formlessness[7] and suggestive nature of light lends itself to this process, and may be found in the ways in which Barker writes light – directly and indirectly – in his play texts, but also in the lighting solutions that appear in production. Ultimately, it is in the imaginative processes of the audience's mind that the totality of Barker's scenography comes to life, though always crucially incomplete, frustrated, and unresolved. As this chapter demonstrates, the different scenographic elements work together, weaving 'landscapes of ideas' (Abulafia, 2016: 2) in which the imagination is free to roam, to recombine aspects, and experience differently, repeatedly, and anew. Though theatre lighting unquestionable fulfils communicative functions (cf. Keller, 2010: 13), in Barker's scenography, as in his playwriting, there are no messages, no ultimate truth, no resolution. Consequently, lighting in his works guides attention, draws focus, allows for actors to appear and disappear into the shadows around the edges of the stage, yet always privileges expressive content over communication.

The realisation of deeply poetic texts, provocative and passionate characters, and sculptural, iconic costuming come together on stage, and are brought together by light and sound, which transgress the boundary of the proscenium arch and infiltrate the spectators' bodies (physically as much as figuratively). Where Turrell tricks his spectators' perception in spaces often flooded with richly coloured lights, Barker's selective highlighting, subtle colour palette, and abundance of darkness appear diametrically opposed. However, the principles of suggestiveness, artful perceptual seduction to the point of optical illusion, and visual sensory overload (by bright abundance in Turrell, by strenuous darkness in Barker) actually work on the audience's senses in a similar manner. In both practitioners' work, light is used to 'assist in creating an illusion of depth and a sense of passing time' (Abulafia,

2016: 44): both Barker and Turrell play with spatial and temporal perception in a manner that is ambiguous, individualised, and not immediately or rationally comprehensible. If we therefore consider 'light-space as space in the *process of becoming*' (Böhme in Abulafia, 2016: 58; original emphasis), the perpetual generation of new meanings over the course of Barker's plays is not only founded on the introduction of new information through text, but also in the altogether less tangible process of re-shaping space through light over time.

In this, the phenomenology of the stage image outweighs or perhaps overwhelms the semiotic content in Barker, due to the multiplicity of sensory input it offers. This holds true even when this input is constrained or highly selective, as is often the case in Barker, due to low-level lightings and a proportional overabundance of shadows. These work in conjunction with the highly theatrical costuming as well as the heightened and densely packed language to create a plethora of audio-visual stimuli. It is precisely the lack on which Barker's lighting centres that makes it so rich in potential associations, after all '[i]nsubstantial light is substantially effective and affective' (Hannah in Crisafulli, 2013: 13). Barker's selective lighting, with deep shadows and stark highlights, not only draws on the imaginative capabilities of the individual spectator, but also situates the stage images in a definitively European art history context: Barker and his lighting designers explicitly reference *chiaroscuro* techniques (Morley in Kipp, 2016: 258, 261 and Appendix 1: 181). As long-standing Wrestling School Associate and lighting designer Ace McCarron puts it: 'A strong lighting moment on stage is usually achieved by judicious use of darkness' (in Reynolds and Smith, 2015: 69). As Welton discusses (2017), theatrical darkness is not merely an absence of light, but very much a thing in itself that demands spectators' attention as much as its conceptual and physical counterpart.

I want to propose the notion of the *Ganzfeld* effect (cf. Abulafia, 2016: 55; Karasek, 2010: 88; Weibel, 2006: 116) with regard to Barker's staging practices and frequent low-level lighting, as well as side-lighting. The *Ganzfeld* effect denies spectators precise information regarding the dimensions of the stage resulting in 'a state of disorientation caused by a confusion of the senses in response to continuous, uniform stimulation' (Lauson in Abulafia, 2016: 55). Karasek specifies that the 'borders [of the *Ganzfeld* lie] outside the field of vision'[8] (2010: 88; my translation). Arguably, the frame of the proscenium arch that Barker works with therefore undermines a pure or complete *Ganzfeld* effect. However, I maintain that his lighting design nonetheless draws on related principles of playing with the limits of human perception.

In Barker's theatre, the actors' bodies, fragmented by thin beams of light become the natural focal point for the eyes, as the stage spaces generally offer no, or only little in the way of concretising objects. The lighting techniques employed by Barker's associates in their designs for different plays incorporate the staging principles of ambiguity, multiplication, and fragmentation – conceptual and physical – in ways that imbue the stage image with painterly qualities at the same time as they reveal the three-dimensionality of the human body. The sparse use of lighting in Wrestling School productions demand of the audience states of perception that function through deception, destabilisation, or subtraction (cf. Tkatch, 2010: 29): what is not visible, or only partially visible, attains equal, if not higher, significance to that which is unequivocally illuminated. The frequent use of side-lighting produces additionally ambiguous states that cast objects, bodies, and crucially also faces into alternating states of light and dark. These sculpt their three-dimensionality and never offer full visibility (cf. Morley in Kipp, 2016 and McCarron in Appendix 1, and 2015 in Reynolds and Smith). Helen Morley elaborates on these principles:

> Shadow is really important; it is the other side of light. You cannot have one without the other. You can think of shadow as the absence of light, but sometimes it is more useful to think of it as something in its own right; so that you are creating shapes with shadows instead of light. [...] The object is the shadow, not the light. It is what makes spaces interesting; it is what gives faces interesting shapes. It is what surrounds the stage. Shadow around the edges is where the imagination happens.
>
> (in Kipp, 2016: 262)

If it is light's role to 'unify the entire scene and to emphasize the plasticity of the performers and their space, but also to change the way in which spectators perceive every object in the performance' (Abulafia, 2016: 20), I would argue that while light as a suggestive framework for directing attention in Barker's work, the severe contrasts between lit areas and darkness create multiple, inexhaustible, and unfathomable spaces. In addition, the intangibility of spatial boundaries upsets the audience's sense of temporality, skewing the flow of time. Further, the *chiaroscuro* effects enhance a performer's plasticity by sculpting their three-dimensional bodies through contrasting areas of light and shade (cf. Barker, Morley and Bull's comments in Morley in Kipp, 2016: 260 and Appendix 1: 155–157, 181, and McCarron in Reynolds and Smith, 2015: 71). Ace McCarron refers to this process as 'enhanced presence' (Appendix 1: 155–157 and in Reynolds and Smith, 2015: 70 ff.) in which the spectators' spatial perception, particularly in terms of their distance to the actors, is deliberately skewed in order to foreground the expressive performing body, especially the face. Additionally, the low lighting levels contribute to a sense of monochrome (cf. Leising, 2006: 58), already pervasive in set design and costume, through which the performed language on stage is elevated (cf. Barker in Brown, 2011: 190). The monochromatic appearance of the stage image engages in a process of denaturalisation in which painterly qualities are foregrounded.

Lighting and darkness in Barker's scenography undermine the concept of a stable, unified subject identity and produce fluid, fundamentally unstable spaces. The Aristotelian unities[9] of time, place, and action are deliberately overturned, fragmented, and recombined to create a scenography that is excessive and overwhelming on multiple sensory and conceptual levels. If one considers visibility in terms of modernity, and the Enlightenment movement, in which it signifies reason, order, and knowledge, it is not a far stretch to engage with deliberate invisibility, or obscured, partial visibility as is presented in Barker's theatre, as a manifestation of postmodern criticisms of the Enlightenment akin to those raised in Romanticism. The importance attached to emotion and experience over reason and knowledge is reflected in the relative domination of Barker's stages by darkness, punctuated by selective highlighting that brings into focus but does not resolve (the strangeness of the characters, the multiplicity or absence of narratives, etc.). In this, lighting works in tandem with set, which conjures up somewhat familiar, yet ultimately strange indefinite places through which each play's figures move in passionate explorations of identity and the limits of imagination.

After all, it is only through light that space comes into being (cf. Zyman, 2006: 466); it does so dynamically, and in conjunction with the spectators' perception wherefore it is never fixed, but always subjective and fluid (cf. Ibid.: 467). It is consequently not a great conceptual leap to liken the dark expanse of the stage's invasive fringes to the image of the abyss that keeps appearing in discourse on Barker's playwriting, and in discourse on the sublime: in our still significantly oculocentric Western thinking, not-seeing or rather not being able to see is rife with implications of potentiality, and undoubtedly one that is unsettling, disturbing but also seductive and intriguing. The proliferation of imaginative possibilities to which the dark stage literally and figuratively gives space, emphasises an experiential encounter with the work that cannot be alleviated or overcome by reason. In opposition to the traditional Western philosophical association of light with knowledge, the abundance of darkness and shadows, and the severe, deliberate limitations of light within the scenographic realisations of Barker's plays (that so often call for darkness and ambiguity in their stage directions) offer a contrasting philosophy that is founded on the embrace of a profound unknowing (cf. Barker, 2005a). This dark abyss invites imagination to expand and multiply in terms that defy generalisation.

Notes

1 This was echoed in Tenna's costume: white wedding dress and black glasses, and in the contrast of her clothing to Isonzo's dark suit.

2 *The Fence* by Howard Barker, available at https://youtu.be/NSQHegJhhlY, accessed on 03.11.2015.

3 One should note here the clearly bounded cloth that was used to delineate the playing area and distinguish the onstage world from that outside the theatre (cf. Morley in Kipp, 2016: 261); its matte absorption of top-down lights softened some effects, such as in the scene with the babies. It also reduced reflection more than a painted floor of equivalent colour would, allowing for deepened shadows to be created with side-lights.

4 I must note Barker's repeated rejection of 'social realism' (cf. 1997, 2007, 2014b). Instead I propose a 'paradoxical realism' that accounts for the internal coherence of Barker's stage worlds without imposing external, everyday logic upon them. This addresses the fundamental separation of events on stage from life outside the theatre, without losing a sense of the fact, that within the parameters of the play, the events of the plot are real, i.e. not imagined by characters.

5 'einen künstlerischen Rahmen für das Erhabene'.

6 'versucht es "darstellbar" zu machen, indem er zur Abstraktion, gar zur Entmaterialisierung des Kunstwerks und der Verschiebung des Kunstereignisses in die Betrachterwahrnehmung eingreift'.

7 I want to highlight here the continued importance of formlessness to the concept of the sublime, from Kant's dynamically sublime (2007: 84/85) to Lyotard (1989: 202; 1991a: 33), and also emphasised by Aretoulakis (1996).

8 'dessen Grenzen außerhalb des Gesichtsfeldes liegen'.

9 These unities were frequently suspended in Elizabethan times, but narrative was rarely so utterly fragmented, and the audience left to make meaning for themselves.

3   Costume and styling

Barker's engagement as director and designer with his own play texts warrants an investigation into the methods and styles he has developed for his drama's realisation since the first Tomas Leipzig set for the 1998 Wrestling School production of *Ursula*. As stated previously, the interrelationships between different aspects of scenography are crucial to the overall effect of a dramatic realisation in production; they never function in isolation. However, the separation as presented in each chapter is necessary to afford an appropriate focus for each element before drawing overarching conclusions. The ephemerality of costuming, animated as it is through the living body of the actor (cf. Monks, 2010 and Maclaurin and Monks, 2015), offers a very particular set of scenographic functions to theatrical production: it creates bodies and – by extension – relations on stage; it attests to geographical location (including details such as weather and climate) and historical period as well as to the status of its wearer. In addition to such semiotic markers, it functions phenomenologically, through colour, texture, and materiality (cf. Blau, 1999: 20–21).

This chapter explores the ways in which Barker's costumes are crucial in the generation of semiotically and phenomenologically rich and internally coherent stage worlds and how these relate to the other scenographic elements. The chapter also considers the role of costuming in the generation of character and how Barker's work in this area remains evocative, yet resolutely ambiguous regarding conventional markers of time period and social status. It explores the connections between the body and its environment with particular attention to Kristeva's writing on the abject and the sublime (1982), and the principle of seduction (cf. Lingis, 2000; Lamb, 2005; Rabey, 2009) in the context of Barker's work. Rather than detailing Barker's engagement with costume and styling chronologically, the chapter explores several core themes: first, I discuss Barker's use of shape, colour, and materials through his many recurring brides and widows. Then, I engage with the processes of dressing and undressing, and nakedness, with some attention to servants and familiars. I then bring together the findings of both sections to propose the notion of grades of likeness, revisit the principle of both/and, and establish theatricality and denaturalisation as key principles of Barker's scenography.

Material matters

Considering the ways in which costume invariably shapes the body and thereby furthers its performative qualities, it is unsurprising that it does this even more so when costume and body are inscribed with a socially recognisable role. In Barker's theatre, there are several recurring motifs regarding characters' functions – though they continually refuse to become archetypal in their behaviours – such as the servant and the aristocrat. One of the strongest recurring motifs of Barker's women, apart from different aristocratic levels, is that of marital status: brides and widows abound in his work. Their status as such is often crucially configured, but also subverted through their costumes. Below follows an analysis of shape, colour, and materials in Barker's costumes through his many brides and widows. I draw on a range of plays, beginning with *Ursula*.

The 1998 Wrestling School production of *Ursula* offers the earliest example of Barker's scenographic work, though costumes appear to have remained largely the province of Lucy Weller (where credits are recorded) until Billie Kaiser's[1] first appearance in 2000 with *He Stumbled*. However, the particularity of *Ursula*'s set of characters, dominated by the nine identically attired 'virgins' (Barker, 2008a: 85) and the climactic scene featuring Placida's unusual wedding gown, is an early example of Barker's visual imagination, and the motif of brides, recurrent throughout his work, dramatically and theoretically (cf. Barker, 2005b, 2007; Kipp, 2017).

The uniformity of the nuns in different shades of white and off-white in the 1998 production,[2] with a carapace-like top layer, high-necked, and without immediately visible fastenings, suggested from the outset their ordered everyday life through its formality. The different shades of white (bright on the long sleeves, slightly off on the ankle-length sheath skirts, and a noticeably darker, cream colour on the sleeveless vests) and the contrasting structure of the upper half to the unadorned bottom result in a sense of constriction, precision, and subordination to rules. However, by being close-cut to the body, the nuns' garments also hint at what lies beneath, suggesting from the very beginning the thematic challenges to order, purity and sexual abstinence that the play explores.

Without high-quality video materials that show the garments in movement, it is difficult to discern their particular materiality.[3] However, photographic records (cf. Reynolds and Smith, 2015; Kipp, 2017) seem to suggest a thicker and stiffer material for the off-white vests in contrast to the softer, flowing materials of sleeves and skirts. Perhaps the nuns' attire actually consisted of a shift dress with a sheath silhouette over which the structured vests were worn. The vertical shoulder seams and stiff-looking high collars are reminiscent of fencing vests (with a slightly padded appearance and visible vertical parallel seams). Consequently, the virgins' appearance in the Wrestling School's production also incorporated a more martial aspect in addition to the immediate association of white with purity and innocence in a Western context. There is no suggestion in the play text that Placida, the Mother Superior, is necessarily differently attired at this point, though photographic and filmic evidence suggests a different colour and collar shape.[4] The arrival of 'a vagrant' (Barker, 2008a: 85), Leonora, in 'ragged dresses' (Ibid.: 92) disturbs the neatly attired ranks of the virgins.

The notion of nuns as Christ's brides that is referenced and maintained in the play (cf. Barker, 2008a: 104, 120, 163) is also reflected in the colours of their attire. All the more in contrast then the 'bridal gown of scarlet' (Ibid.: 163) that Placida wears at the end of the play, colour-coded for passion, blood, perhaps even guilt, resolutely refusing the myth of the virgin bride (Ibid.: 162), and instead embracing and openly displaying her sexuality. The beginnings of this are already apparent in the frivolity of Placida's 'little hat' (Ibid.: 148) that singles her out among the nuns. Notably though, the Wrestling School's production appears to have outfitted all the nuns with simple hats and capes.[5] However, Placida's hat, a small curvette (brimless, close-fitting to the head), clearly served more as a fashion statement than practical head covering, indicating a deviation and possible attachment to worldly values of attractiveness. The suggested worldliness of a hat, specifically Placida's, is dependent on contrast to the unadorned modesty of the virgins' loose hair (Ibid.: 137) and, in production, their large, rather shapeless, wide-brimmed hats. In Placida's case, concealment or cover of the head speaks of a conscious construction of self-image and consequently of vanity (cf. Ibid.: 153). This was also apparent in production through Placida's change of costume at the start of the journey down the river into a New Look style dress of tea-length with three-quarter sleeves, a high v-neckline, and an expansive A-line skirt in what appears on record as muted, matte aubergine purple, with a split-front skirt exposing a lighter (peach/pink) coloured satin underskirt, perhaps a foreshadowing of her unconventional scarlet bridal attire.

Placida's bridal gown in the 1998 production appears to have consisted of a tight corset of a shining material, perhaps leather, and a sleek sheath skirt, low on the hips. In combination with a high choker with straps on her neck, this attire highlighted and shaped actress Victoria Wicks' bodily contours (cf. Bech and Hann, 2014: 4). With exposed shoulders and arms (a marked contrast from the nuns' modest attire), the costume conjured associations of fetish-wear – particularly the combination of choker and corset, and the skirt's slippage to reveal the curvature of Wicks' hips – and unabashed sexuality, founded in a tight encasing of the desirable female body (cf. Figure 2 in Reynolds and Smith, 2015). This process becomes, in the words of Trigg (discussing her work on costume and gender), a process of '[u]nfolding the body, as if pulling back velvet curtains to expose a stage' (2014: 128). Placida stages herself and her newfound sexuality in the exposure of her body 'beyond the line of hope' (Barker, 2008a: 153), harnessing 'the seductive power of the image' in which the 'construction of the image is, at the same time, the construction of the body' (Calefato in Trigg, 2014: 130). Here, this body is sexual, female, and fecund, a repudiation of the values of the convent. The figure of the bride in *Ursula* is therefore a challenge to traditional conceptions of the role and accompanying associations of ideal matrimony. Placida stages her bridal self as self-determined, sensual, and sexual. She may lift the sword to kill the virgins where Lucas may not (Barker, 2008a: 163) and he stumbles (cf. Ibid.: 166) in the wake of her radical literal and figurative self-fashioning (cf. Ibid.: 162) as a terrible and seductive bride.

My next example, *The Twelfth Battle of Isonzo*, highlights the performativity of socially recognisable dress, namely bridalwear. The titular character in this case is the eleven-time widowed, ancient, and (possibly) blind man Isonzo who meets his latest bride-to-be. The opening stage directions simply specify 'a blind bride seated' (Barker, 2012a: 55). Tenna's definition as a bride is thus in all likelihood achieved through costuming.

In the 2001 production, her status was established through a Billie Kaiser design: a cream-coloured vinyl corset top with twisted straps and a full tea-length skirt of multiple tulle layers (some translucent), short white gloves, and accompanied by a round white hat with a white satin band, perched on a large chignon at the back of her head.[6] From the front, this positioning of the hat framed actress Antoinette Walsh's face like a halo and contrasted starkly with the dark glasses worn to indicate blindness.[7] Immediately, the colour symbolisms of bridal attire – purity, virginity, innocence – were at play, despite the distinct lack of other common Western markers of bridal attire, such as a veil. Furthermore, the contrasting textures of the corseted top (stiff, largely unyielding, sleek and certainly not a common fabric in bridal attire, with the boning structures visibly stitched in) and the tulle skirt (soft, light, buoyant, commonly and commercially used in bridal wear) enabled an interesting tension: though recognisably a bride, Tenna was also immediately identified as an unusual one.

Additionally, the particularities of Tenna's appearance refused a conclusive identification of geographical location and time period, whether historical or contemporary. Before the entrance of Isonzo, Tenna speculates about the function of her own matrimonial state: 'THE BRIDE WHAT IS SHE SOME WOULD SAY THE GROTESQUE RELIC OF ARCHAIC PRACTICES A TESTAMENT TO MANKIND'S REVERENCE FOR SYMBOLS' (Ibid.: 56). She embraces this symbolism, though the characters' appearance is arguably for the benefit of the audience, as both she and Isonzo are blind and consequently 'make no distinction any more between the surface and the depths' (Ibid.: 58). Notably, in production the choice of set materials (with jagged metal edges at the back and a raised metal grille upon which the chair was positioned) offered a particularly stark contrast to the softness and vulnerability of Tenna's attire, and later her naked body (as discussed below, and in Chapter 1).

The materiality of Tenna's costume featured not just visually, but textually and aurally, too. She masterfully conjures the sensation of tactile engagement with her clothes, for example when she describes her quest for the perfect under-garment: 'The Heaven of Unworn Underwear/[...] pools of petals/Scented/

Cool/[…] I sifted for you one solitary and weightless pair' (Ibid.: 72). These allusions to physical sensations, even to a sense of smell, expand the visual appearance of the characters. Their costumes become markers that attest to these other, invisible, qualities. Isonzo repeatedly makes olfactory references, asserting that 'blindness made [him] a connoisseur' (Ibid.: 65) and describes her skirts in sensual detail as 'seething finery/the foam of/surf of/breaking and cascading seas' (Ibid.: 84). Despite this explicit relegation of visuals, Isonzo insists on the importance of Tenna's undergarments' appearance, in particular regarding colour: 'Shell pink/Shell pink/SHELL PINK/OR/IVORY [...] GOD HELP YOU IF THEY'RE BLUE' (Ibid.: 73). This 'unexpected/[...]/unpredicted/[...] agony of colour' (Ibid.: 76) may be considered with regard to the intricate and more importantly intimate relationships between clothing and its body and by extension between body and subject identity. Hann and Bech consider it thus: 'costume as *object* is complicit within the body as *event*. The two constitute a reciprocal performance' (2014: 5; original emphases). In order for Tenna and Isonzo's impending wedding to fully constitute that specific rite of passage, their appearance must be in accordance with the expectations it engenders regarding their respective performances as bride and groom.

Barker once again subverts the audience's expectations: before the consummation of the wedding (already curiously lacking in any witnesses), Isonzo appears to die (Barker, 2012a: 105) before briefly and eerily reviving (Ibid.: 106),[8] yet ultimately remains prone and still (Ibid.: 109) as Tenna sobs: 'Oh, I so require to be …' (Ibid.) witnessed (as a bride, in the moment of consummation). Though identifiable through her clothes, she recognises that it is only in the public performance of the role through costume that she truly becomes a bride. Though at this point in the play text, Tenna is naked but for her shoes and stockings, in production, she had taken off the hat, loosened her hair, and picked up a light black scarf that covered her front that had dropped from the ceiling during the moment of Isonzo's collapse (Barker, 2012a: 105). In its style (semi-translucent, with a fringe) this scarf could be considered reminiscent of mourning attire, another suggested doubling of the roles of widow and bride. Her attire upon exiting (stockings, loose hair, one shoe, a hastily thrown-on scarf) might then also be read as a bride's appearance after consummation, marked by traces of the original immaculacy (of bridal dress, and supposedly virginal self).

In *The Twelfth Battle of Isonzo*, Tenna's recognisable appearance as bride through the iconic white dress highlights 'the experience of the costume as a provocative sign-object' (Fensham, 2014: 57): it carries with it expectations of behaviour on her part, as well as that of Isonzo, and relatedly of plot developments. Both of these are subverted in Barker's play. The costumed body of the bride is therefore a visual red herring that generates the potential for surprising and unexpected actions to take place on stage. In the words of Hannah, costume appears as a 'spatial body-object, disrupting and charging social environments to reveal their "evental" nature: calling up monumental moments [and] productive aesthetic encounters' (2014: 15). This is also apparent at the very end of *The Twelfth Battle of Isonzo*, in which Tenna, an unwed bride, simultaneously appears as already widowed in a strange doubling of roles.

This convergence of contrasting roles such as widow and bride also features in *Gertrude – The Cry*. The titular character's attire is crucial (as is her nakedness, the general theme of which is discussed later in this chapter): it is openly referenced by other characters, but Gertrude also engages with it consciously. A notable feature are her blue shoes (Barker, 2006: 86, 114), which may be considered in terms of Western colour symbolism (blue as the colour of harmony, honesty, loyalty, and fidelity; Gage, 2000: 13), the qualities which Gertrude repudiates over the course of the play. Similarly, the shoes may serve as an allusion to the famous rhyme about bridal attire ('Something old, something new, something borrowed, something blue') in which the blue serves both as a manifestation of the bride's faithfulness and to ward off evil. The irony of this colour symbolism regarding Gertrude's actions heightens the contradictions between her appearance – seemingly in keeping with social norms – and her subversive nature.

Her particular clothes are not specified at the beginning of the play, but since she tears them off after a few lines (Barker, 2006: 83), it is her nakedness that becomes crucial before she is 'enclosed in the gown' (Ibid.: 89) that her servant Cascan brings. The next time we see her, she is 'in mourning' (Ibid.: 88), though the severity (Ibid.: 89) of her appearance is not entirely within social propriety. After all, her 'skirt says everything to those who can read skirts' (Ibid.: 92). The script suggests a skirt at below knee-length (Ibid.: 92); however, cut and fabric may draw attention to bodily contours and highlight sensuality through material. David Ian Rabey recalls actress Victoria Wicks changing into a sheer dress[9] for this scene, from the preceding graveyard one, which rendered Hamlet's reservations about the skirt length absurdly comical. Perhaps his articulation of Gertrude's impropriety (as it took shape in the Wrestling School production) takes this form as he is overwhelmed with the (biblically sinful) visibility of his mother's obviously near-naked body which he can neither acknowledge nor let pass without comment.

Barker uses recognisable items of clothing, like veils, high heels, or (Western) mourning attire to establish expectations of appropriate behaviours visually. Through costume, the characters of a scene are set, their bodies readable to the audience. Consequently, their words and actions subvert and transgress convention, highlighting the performative nature of clothing. This is also apparent in Hamlet's assertion that Gertrude's skirt is 'too short' (Ibid.: 97). Immediately thereafter Isola identifies the potentially confusing relationship between performing body and the clothing that adorns it. She states what Hamlet cannot: 'IT'S HER THAT HAS THE SEX […]/He thinks the skirt is sex' (Ibid.: 98). As Monks discusses (2010), the distinction between the body and its costume is one that is ambiguous: after all, it is the body that animates the clothes, but it is the clothes that shape the body (visually and also physically, by affecting movement).

Gertrude consciously engages with her status as newly married widow (though in Barker's text Claudius and Gertrude do not appear to officially marry); however, she refuses to uphold sartorial markers of her positions – as either widow or bride – and instead plays with the performativity of attire. This is particularly noticeable when she takes off the laddered stockings (cf. Barker, 2006: 111–113) and demands a 'PROSTITUTE'S COAT' (Ibid.: 114). Later, she calls for her 'BLACKEST AND MOST/[...]/[HER] WORST BLACK' (Ibid.: 154) after Cascan's death, adopting an aesthetic of mourning for her loyal servant that she previously refused her first husband.

Gertrude's clothing, whether on her body (cf. Ibid.: 110) or not (cf. Ibid.: 115), attains a fetishistic quality in which the men around her equate her clothing with her body and attractiveness. She, however, asserts that 'Desire's/In/The/Brain' (Ibid.: 104) and therefore not to be possessed. It is this elusiveness that drives Claudius' increasingly violent interactions (cf. Ibid.: 131) as well as the foundation of Albert's obsession with her (Ibid.: 124–125). The play expertly invites speculation about the relationship of the naked body to clothing, too, as I discuss later. In *Gertrude – The Cry* the titular protagonist presents the audience with an ambiguous doubling of roles: the widow is a bride, twice; however, it is not for either husband that she is 'impeccable, funereal' (Ibid.: 163) but for her servant and her son.

The play concludes with the wedding of Albert and Gertrude (Ibid.: 173) and though the newlywed queen is 'hatted, suited, gloved for her honeymoon' (Ibid.) the perfection of her appearance is counterpointed by her 'ruined face' (Ibid.: 175), grief-stricken over the loss of Claudius. The visual inconclusiveness of elegant, formal travelling attire and Gertrude's ruined make-up highlight the transgressive potential of her body and emotions. In this case, they literally spill over into her final cry (Ibid.: 174) and upset the fragile equilibrium of her proper attire. Notably, her honeymoon attire in its mustard yellow (a colour recurring, for example, in Burgteata's gown in the Wrestling School's production of *Found in the Ground*) was a significant counterpoint to the predominant monochromes in the Wrestling School's production (cf. Barker in Brown, 2011: 125). The duality of yellow in Western colour symbolism – on the one hand signifying happiness, optimism, and enlightenment, on the other betrayal and cowardice (Gage, 2000: 15, 23, 30) – and its historical association with prostitution in Europe (Connor, 2004: 167) layer on multiple and contradictory associations that contrast Gertrude's status as a newly married woman. In a perfect inversion of the beginning, the ecstatic widow leaves as a grieving bride. This trajectory is accompanied, illustrated, and highlighted through different costumes throughout the play. Gertrude's deliberate and subversive engagement with the performative qualities of clothing in relation to social position and life's events expose the arbitrary and artificial nature of these unwritten rules. Her conscious choices regarding colour, shape, and material thus expose the semiotic resonance all three possess as part of costume.

The doubling of widows as brides is a recurring motif in Barker: for example, it lies at the heart of the next play I discuss, *I Saw Myself*. Its protagonist, the widow Sleev, openly addresses the performative qualities of her status as widow, particularly in relation to her supposed duties to her deceased husband as expected by society. However, she asserts that '[t]he widow is of all people the least qualified to describe her husband arguably the grief the rage and in many cases let us admit it the sheer ecstasy' (Barker, 2008b: 11). As such, she immediately demonstrates a keen awareness of the performative nature of her position at the opening of the play. Though not explicitly described in the play text, her attire in the 2008 Wrestling School production (black pillbox hat with a short black veil at the back and a black, floor-length, narrow skirt and high-waisted, long-sleeved formfitting jacket;[10] Figure 3.5) appeared on the one hand as suitably severe mourning attire, on the other hand its close contouring of the body and its low v-shaped neckline foregrounded Sleev's sensuality (cf. Koda, 2001) and thereby hinted at her disregard for social expectations regarding her behaviour. Through her costume, audiences garner a visual sense of her attitude before she speaks, as costumes 'always precede action' (Hannah, 2014: 18). In her skilful yet subversive imitation of appropriate mourning, Sleev's costume becomes a stark illustration of the fact that in Barker, as in other productions such as the one Hannah discusses, 'what is on the outside surface as appearance is juxtaposed with what is beneath as potential disruption' (2014: 23; describing *Tongues of Stone*).

This principle of a fundamental tension between the surface and the depths, the outward impression and the contrasting actuality of characters in Barker's work, is supported by the mutability of their appearance in costumes that facilitate their play with and subversion of social norms and expectations. Notably, Sleev's daughter (Figure 3.6), married with a young child, appeared in a gown that might seem more suited to modesty, despite its more open neckline: loose around her body, with full, wide sleeves and a black hat with attached long veil in matching colour that completely covered her hair, Sheeth was visually more removed from her body. The square neckline, though relatively low, in conjunction with the flowing quality of the garment, shrouded her body. By contrast, her widowed mother's attire was much more structured, tight, and with raised and padded shoulders and a deep v-neckline; it attested to a consciousness regarding appearance: Sleev's mourning is a performance, and a flattering one at that. The neckline draws the eye along her slim frame (cf. Koda, 2001: 23), her hat is more fashion statement than modest covering. This is also apparent in her frequent turns to the mirror on the wardrobe. Her first action after standing up at the opening of the play is to examine herself (Barker, 2008b: 11) and 'adjus[t] the tilt of her hat' (Ibid.); later, she 'drifts to the wardrobe mirror' again and 'plucks a shoulder of her dress' (Ibid.: 20). Sleev consciously weaves her own life's story in defiance of society;

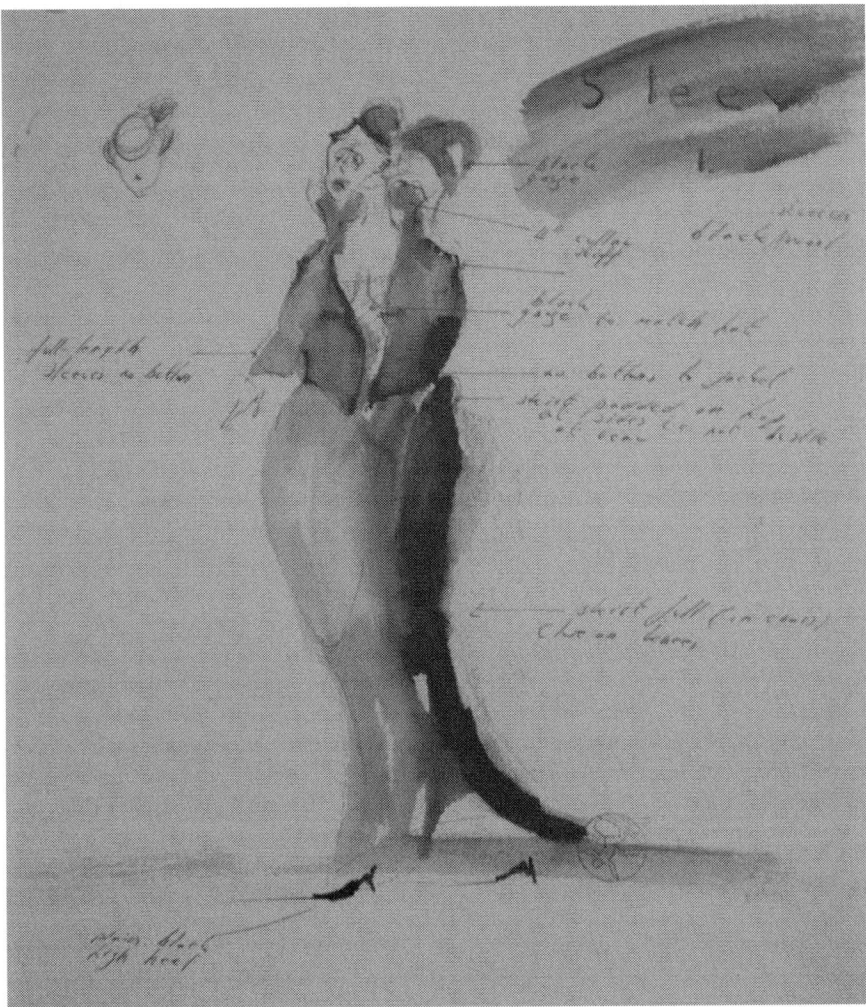

Figure 3.5 Costume design for Sleev. © Howard Barker

this attitude is already suggested from the very opening of the piece in the structured, artificial, and performative qualities of her costume.

In the 2008 production, just prior to the final stitch (about two-thirds into Act 2), Sleev appeared in another black dress, this one much shorter, though still below the knee, with a full skirt and loosely draped top; this was accompanied by a simple black cap without veil that covered most of her hair. This change, not indicated in the play text, highlights Bugg's observation that 'clothing cannot be passive as it will always be active in some way in the development of the [piece]' (2014: 70). Interestingly, this scene is supposedly

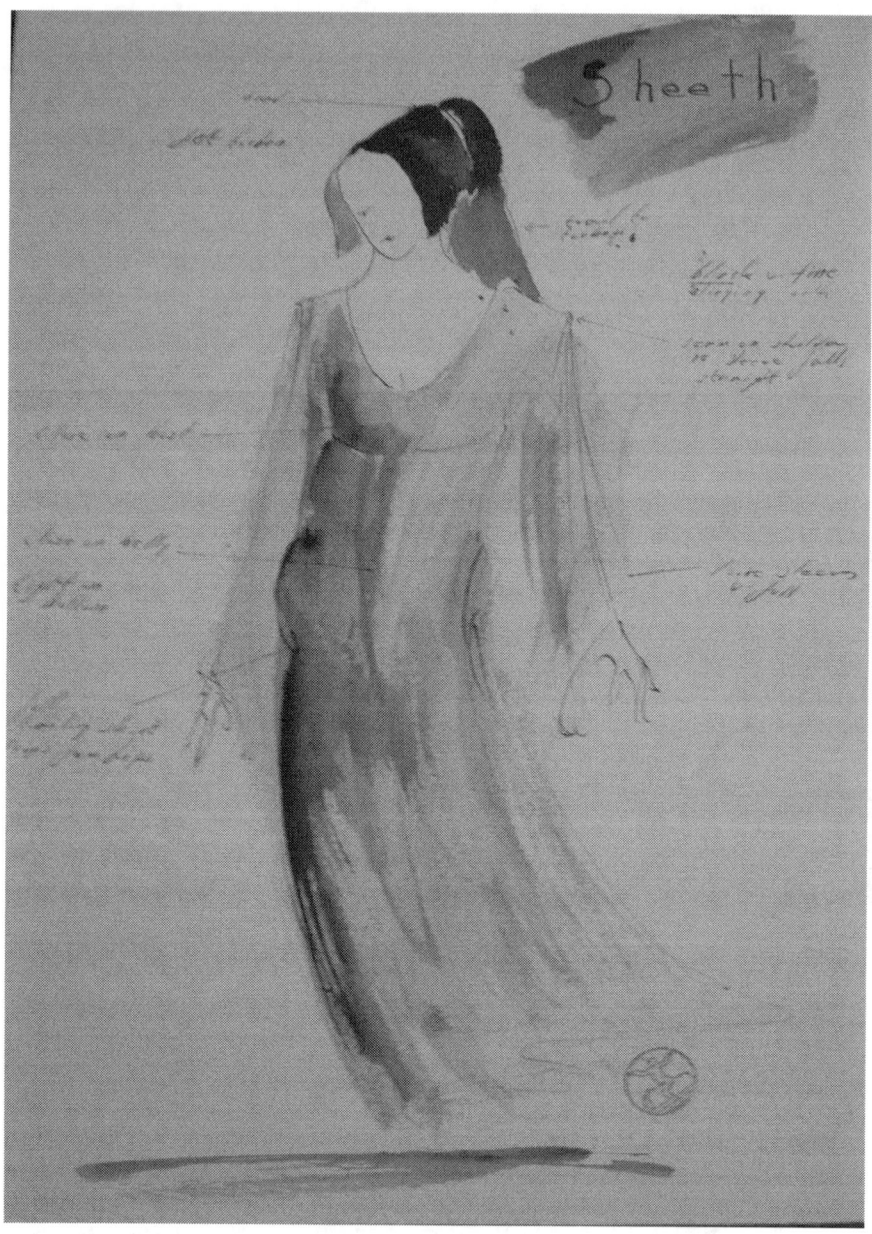

Figure 3.6 Costume design for Sheeth. © Howard Barker

the conclusion of Sleev's widowhood, as she promises Club marriage only when the tapestry is done 'and not before' (Barker, 2008b: 37). This particular attire was much more modest in its loose covering of her body; the length appeared more practical as it precluded tripping of the by-then blinded protagonist. This costume, shrouding the body's contours, subsequently functioned as Sleev's bridal attire. However, her marriage to Club is neither formally confirmed ('CLUB: The priest is also me the real one fled'; Ibid.: 67) nor subsequently consummated ('CLUB: I cannot now/I cannot'; Ibid.: 70). Sleev therefore remains poised somewhere in-between: she resolutely refuses her role as widow through the relentless examination of her own self and life outside matrimonial constraints and social norms by way of weaving the tapestry, and remains promised yet unwed. Supposedly she is widowed again (and thereby echoes Gertrude's position as twice widowed, twice wed) at the very end: 'Go out now and be killed' (Ibid.: 69) Modicum advises Club.

Sleev's costumes, whether formal and seductive at the beginning or apparently comfortable and practical towards the end, stood in contrast with her servants' lightly-coloured formal attire, colour-complemented her daughter's though diverging sharply in style, and juxtaposed her clearly against the different men in her life: Guardaloop's open front cream-coloured shirt poses as much of a contrast to her mourning garbs as Modicum's naked skin or Club's mustard yellow clothes. The conscious and subversive performance of Sleev's widowhood evolves over the course of the play, from a supposed adherence to formality at the beginning that already hints at her transgressive behaviours, towards a conceptual construction of self through the embodied act of weaving at the end of Act 2. Throughout the play, Sleev's attire invites speculation on subjective identity and its (social) construction through clothing. The recurring doubling of social states presents meeting points for the respective expectations such roles place upon women in terms of social standing, implicit and explicit restrictions of their behaviour, and their perceived social power. By layering multiple rites of passage on to the same body, Barker draws attention to its socially constructed nature, as bridehood and widowhood are exposed as complementary. Yet, Barker's female characters achieve self-definition beyond those roles.

Found in the Ground, like the plays discussed above, again sees a doubling of roles in which rites of passage – specifically marriage and mourning – are layered on top of one another. In it, the nymphomaniac daughter of the crippled former Nuremberg judge Toonelhuis, Burgteata, has an ongoing affair with the 19-year-old librarian Denmark (Barker, 2008b: 135) and manipulates him into contemplating marriage (Ibid.: 134). Though he initially considers it a 'fatuous condition' (Ibid.), Burgteata later appears as 'a bride [...] emerging from the dark with long, slow strides' (Ibid.: 183), carrying a baby. The wedding ceremony per se is neither shown nor discussed. Just prior to Burgteata's appearance as bride, Denmark is onstage, threatening her father; nonetheless, she refers to the librarian as her husband (Ibid.: 190).

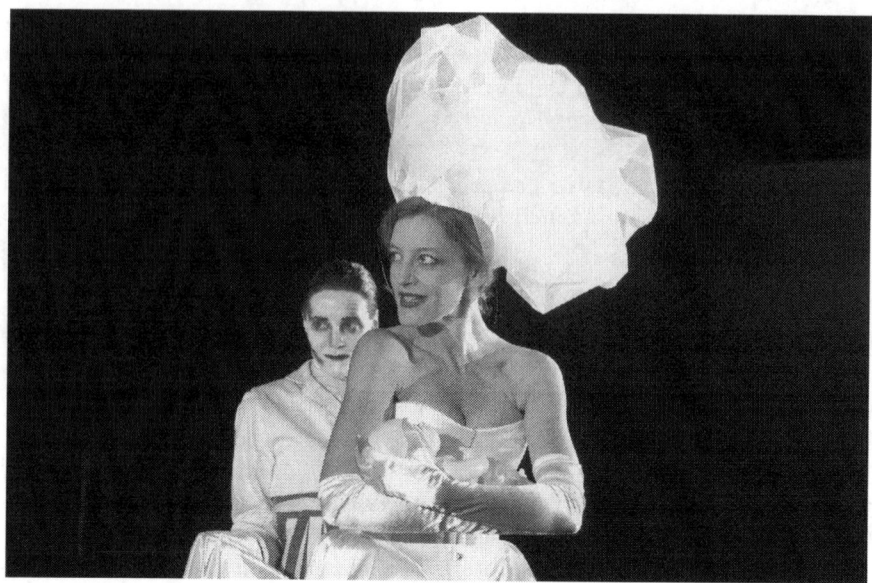

Figure 3.7 Suzy Cooper as Burgteata. © Donald Cooper, Photostage UK

In the 2009 Wrestling School production, her bridal attire consisted of a white half-bust corset with a low, pointed busk front reminiscent of Elizabethan fashions, with a matching white skirt with a substantial train and panniers that echoed – albeit on a reasonably small scale – the shape of a *robe à la française*. In addition, Burgteata's wedding attire included white opera gloves and a large headpiece of white tulle (attached to a small pillbox hat of the same colour) hovering like a cloud over actress Suzy Cooper's head (Figure 3.7). Her costume clearly identifies her as a bride (at least in Western aesthetics), while combining formality (the gloves, length, and shape of the skirt) and sensuality (the half-bust corset with exposed shoulders, visible boning structure, and connotations of lingerie). The collagist nature of her appearance is decidedly anti-historical by combining elements from various periods into a newly whole that cannot be assigned to any specific place and time. The appearance of Burgteata as a bride coincides with her appearance as a mother, as she bears infant Hitler[11] with her (Ibid.: 183); just three scenes later, she is on the brink of widowhood and being orphaned (Ibid.: 190): still in her wedding dress, she mourns her 'Dying husband/[and]/Dying dad' (Ibid.).

The multiplicity of roles that converge in Burgteata at this point are juxtaposed by her costume and simultaneously exposed as performative through the almost ridiculous theatricality of her wedding attire. In this context, theatricality should not be considered as 'in opposition with the concepts of the natural, true, sincere and authentic, [but instead] it connotes a merging of the political and social within the power of an image that is aware of spectatorship and stagecraft' (Hannah, 2014: 16, following Davis and Postelwait, 2003: 29). This holds true for characters across Barker's works, in particular his many brides and widows. Notably, these roles appear as bound to the women's relationships with men: future or past husbands. However, the conscious and often playfully subversive engagement of the women with these roles, their relationships to men (dead or living husbands of all tenses) and their conscious performativity within the frameworks largely drawn up by their costume expose the artifice of their respective social situations, which they confidently transgress in their radical reassessments of subject identity.

If indeed costume serves as 'the means through which an imagined historical authenticity can be accessed' (Monks in Maclaurin and Monks, 2015: 3), in Barker's case, this consists of an exclusively constructed authenticity and offers a material groundedness that is part of the 'visual coherence within a scenographical logic' (Ibid.: 3) and, in the context of the play, becomes truthful (cf. Sleev's assertion that '[her] tapestry is true', Barker, 2008b: 56). The work of costume (in conjunction with the actor's body) to 'create a cultural and historical world for the audience' (Maclaurin in Maclaurin and Monks, 2015: 37) is always decidedly fictional in Barker's work, yet closely enough related (aesthetically) to offstage historical events as to evoke their presence within the world of the play, placing it 'in the midst of in-between-ness' (Gregg and Seigworth, 2010: 1). This is particularly apparent in the ambiguous doublings that surround Barker's brides and widows that are often combined within one person. One might consider these women as archetypes, and therefore somewhat reductive. However, the unquestionable complexity of their characters, often as protagonists, destabilises the expected narratives their immediately recognisable and therefore potentially archetypical attire may initially suggest.

Whether it is Placida's loving sacrifice of the virgins, Gertrude's insatiable and destructive seductiveness, Sleev's passionate rewriting of history into her story, Tenna's ultimate refusal to perform her role as bride to Isonzo's expectations, Sopron's remodelling of grief after her own fashion, or Burgteata's terrible and often self-destructive pursuits, these women exceed and redefine their roles beyond their relationships with men, and beyond socially imposed rules of appropriate behaviour in 'closed correspondences between external appearance and social order' (Calefato, 2004: 2). Instead their performances of self become a 'gesture of profound joy and delight, of pleasure in masquerade, and sensual enjoyment. A synaesthetic game' (Ibid.). This game takes place through heavily, yet incongruently[12] coded visuals (at least in terms of conventional semiotics) in costuming that resonate with the decidedly ambiguous stage spaces. They are painstakingly specific as well as generally recognisable, yet importantly indeterminate. In this, the costuming serves to further the effects of the set and lighting designs (cf. Chapters 1 and 2). Furthermore, the performative nature of costume is foregrounded by characters' tactile engagement with their attire, which they use to subvert and redefine their social roles and selves. By drawing attention to the materiality of their clothing, the characters' conscious engagement with shape, colour, and material invites the audience to consider the presentational aspects of a piece (what it is) alongside the representational content (what it refers to). This enables a multiplication of significant content (what it means) through highlighting the sensory nature of theatrical experience.

The body (un)dressed

In a similar vein to the instantly recognisable and socially inscribed clothes of brides and widows, another recurring figure in Barker's works is that of the servant, who may also take the form of a familiar. Such figures may be offstage, as in *Und,* but more frequently drift in and out of the action on stage, shadowing or counterpointing protagonists. Additionally, these figures frequently engage in the acts of dressing or undressing those that they serve, rendering them even more crucial in the discussion of the functions of costume and the act of costuming in Barker. I emphasise this aspect of their role here, though undoubtedly, uniforms are fundamental examples of the symbolic qualities of dress and its social functions of 'disciplining mind and body' (Calefato, 2004: 19). Servants and familiars in Barker's works comply with, but also often complicate notions of status. Simultaneously, their (suitably attired) presence highlights the performative nature of costume both through their own self-effacing clothing and through dressing and undressing those that they serve. I analyse the relationship between those two aspects – servants and familiars, and processes of (un)dressing – below through a range of plays.

In *Gertrude – The Cry*, we first encounter Cascan, 'a servant to Gertrude' (Barker, 2006: 83) at the pivotal moment of Claudius' murder of the king (Ibid.: 84). He 'enters, holding a garment, and attends' (Ibid.). Immediately, the self-effacing qualities of his profession come into play as he 'extends the gown' (Ibid.) for the naked queen: not only does Cascan simply observe the old king's murder, he also bears witness to the queen's adultery. Nonetheless, his loyalty is relentless. He even goes so far as to compliment her: 'your nakedness is so perfect' (Ibid.: 85), he states before enclosing her in the gown. In the act of dressing the transgressive queen, now newly grieving widow, the servant becomes complicit in the dark and 'rare acts' (Ibid.) of her convictions. Rather than re-establish social order through concealing her naked body, thereby constricting or imposing order on her subversiveness, the act of dressing Gertrude generates the potential for secrets (cf. Barker, 1997: 182 ff.). As well as dressing Gertrude, Cascan also fashions the alibi for Gertrude and Claudius: 'I'll call dinner/When he doesn't come I'll look for him/First in the stables/After the stables I'll come here' (Ibid.: 86). He thereby provides two types of cover: one, in the form of clothing, and the other in terms of concealing Gertrude's actions.

In a similar manner, Gertrude's twice mother-in-law, Isola, acts as a familiar to Gertrude, who engages directly and repeatedly with the queen's costume, exploring the ways in which items of clothing offer layers of meaning that go beyond the immediate associations. For example, she recalls meeting the young Gertrude: 'I saw you as a child once on a wall/Sitting on your hands/ Little socks/Swinging your legs' (Ibid.: 94). The 'little white socks' (Ibid.: 95) are a recurring motif in Barker's writing, for example in *Found in the Ground* where they similarly appear as a marker of girlhood (Barker, 2008b: 199) and innocence that Burgteata claims in her private life (Ibid.: 142). They are a fundamental token of identity beyond her vocation to sleep with the dying (Ibid.: 128–129) so much so that she is horrified when realising she wore them whilst copulating with the Workman (Ibid.: 180). In *Gertrude – The Cry* the white socks similarly denote childish innocence, but also attest to a burgeoning sexuality and mischief that Isola could detect in the adolescent Gertrude (Barker, 2006: 95). The change from child to adult and girl to woman is echoed in the move from little white socks to stockings (Ibid.: 110) that show off Gertrude's legs. Furthermore, the destruction of the stockings, once Isola has pointed out that they are faulty (Ibid.: 113), and the queen's subsequent decision to be bare-legged (Ibid.: 114) bring into play notions of proper attire once more. The (lack of) stockings simultaneously emphasise their materiality and highlight the sensuality of bare skin. At the suggestion of her mother-in-law Isola, Gertrude prioritises personal desire over social structure, a choice which is echoed in the exposure of the private body that overshadows the (properly attired, covered) body politic of the queen.

As the play develops, Gertrude approaches once more a radically free nakedness (in an echo of her appearance at the opening of the play), the catastrophe of which 'contains the potential not only to destroy the city but to set things off in unfamiliar directions' (Hannah, 2014: 20; cf. also Obis on the disruptive power of nakedness in Barker's work, 2013: 74). The processes of dressing and undressing, facilitated and instigated by both Cascan and Isola, allow for a repeated manipulation of the social *status quo* and juxtapose notions of propriety and transgression. Consequently, these performative reconstructions of self highlight the crucial importance of costume in the creation of bodies and status in Barker's theatre.

This principle is also at work in *The Fence in Its Thousandth Year*, where the newly widowed and subsequently newly married duchess Algeria appears 'elegant [...], hatted and veiled' (Barker, 2005b: 7), '[h]eaven with red lips' (Ibid.: 8). She, too, has a manservant, Kidney, and a familiar, Istoria. In addition, her nephew Photo, who is actually her son (Ibid.: 14), acts as another familiar as well as lover, brushing her hair (Ibid.: 22) and offering to bathe the duchess. In his presence, it is Algeria who undresses herself (Ibid.), her nakedness more than that of Doorway's previous wife, for whom it was 'simply being without clothes' (Ibid.: 25). Her attire is a marker of her status, for example she exposes herself in the zoo by inviting the public to 'finger the labels of [her] clothes' (Ibid.). The brand names ('Fortini of Milan' and 'KATHLEEN PASSOWITZ OF NEW YORK', Ibid.) act as a legitimising of identity; only people of a certain status would have access to such renowned

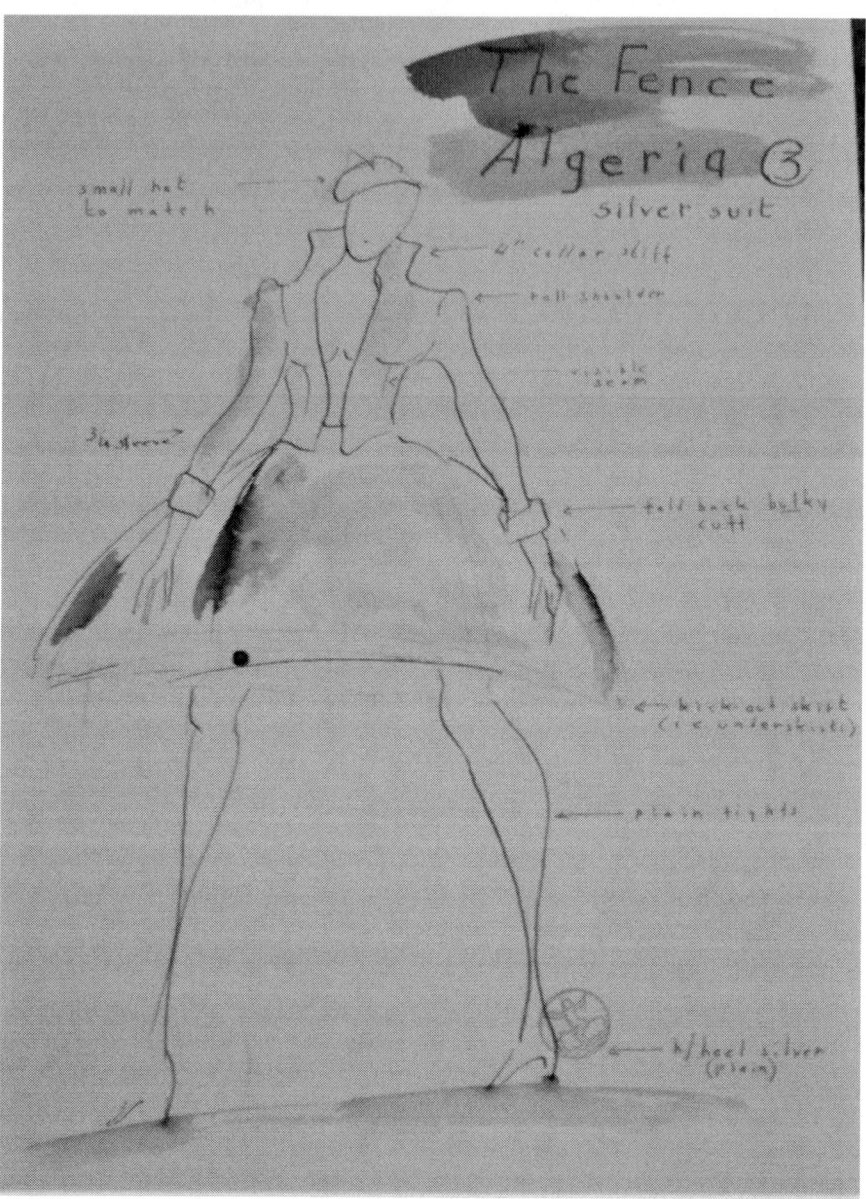

Figure 3.8 Costume design for Algeria. © Howard Barker

and international (though fictional) goods. It is through her attire that the duchess becomes herself (Figures 3.8 and 3.9).

Similarly, it is through the exposure of her physical body that the body politic is undermined, despite Kidney's later protestations that a 'duchess

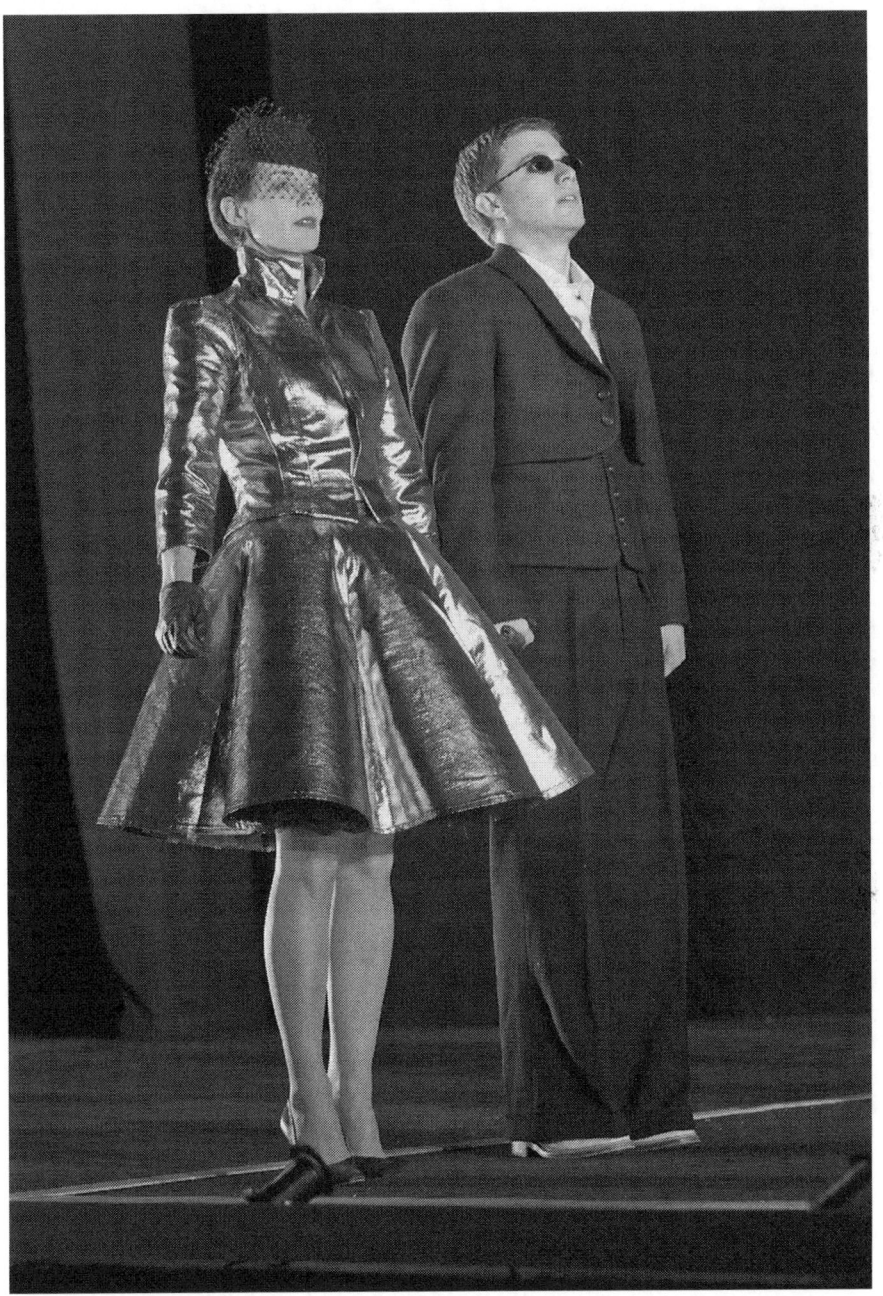

Figure 3.9 The Fence in Its Thousandth Year, l-r, Victoria Wicks (Algeria), Philip Cumbus (Photo). © Donald Cooper, Photostage UK

can't be naked [...] always is she clothed in dignity' (Ibid.: 57). Unlike Cascan's unending loyalty and absolute knowledge of the queen's actions, Kidney appears to be somewhat more distant from Algeria, 'ill with anxiety' (Ibid.: 29) when he discovers her nightly transgressions at the fence. Photo on the other hand, upon discovering the incestuous relationship with his mother, demands she 'DESCRIBE THE BIRTH/[...]/THE AGONY UNDRESS THE AWFUL CRIES/UNDRESS UNDRESS' (Ibid.: 50). As the layers of lies are stripped away, so should the costumes be that uphold the notions of propriety; in the next scene Algeria indeed appears naked (Ibid.: 51), though, in a surprising inversion[13] of her previous transgressions, this time she actually copulates with her husband, Doorway (Ibid.: 52).

In a notable difference from *Gertrude – The Cry*, it is the familiar in this play, and not the servant, who unfailingly supports the duchess' personal desires and resulting transgressions. Whilst Kidney urges the incarcerated Algeria to put some clothes on (Ibid.: 57), Istoria later undresses the recuperating duchess 'with infinite care' (Ibid.: 72) and gazes at her naked form 'lovingly' (Ibid.) at the very end of the play. The servant in this instance is responsible for dressing the transgressive body, and simultaneously dressing up the public image of the duchess. Though he insists repeatedly that he is not deserting her (Ibid.: 57, 66) and even kills Youterus (Ibid.: 66) in what might be read as an act of socially cleansing retribution, it is Istoria who remains with Algeria at the very end. Thereby, Istoria uncovers her 'thin and bruised friend['s]' (Ibid.: 71) personal dignity that stands 'immobile' (Ibid.: 72) in the face of the perpetual rise and fall of seemingly stable social norms. Though she urges Algeria to 'WEAR A HAT/[...]/AND PROPER SHOES' (Ibid.: 69) in an attempt to assist her in regaining her former health and seductive beauty, she also recognises that the deposed duchess cannot be reintegrated into the circular structures of social order and clear boundaries, even as a new perimeter fence is being set up (Ibid.: 71). In the act of dressing and undressing, the body personal and body politic of Algeria are – as she correctly identifies at the very beginning (cf. Ibid.: 9) – a battlefield of personal desire, subjective identity, and social pressure to conform. Through costume, she is by turns transformed from seeming compliance to open transgression and back. Ultimately, the performative semblance of costume (which structures the body politic and body personal throughout the play) is exposed as a set of stylised, repeated actions and images that generate those meanings (cf. Butler, 1999), as Algeria is stripped off her clothes.

This theme is also central to *I Saw Myself*. The three maids, Ladder, Keshkemmity, and Hawelka, all serve the protagonist Sleev in some way, though the nature of their respective relationships is rather different. Notably, it is only Hawelka who is described as 'a maid' (Barker, 2008b: 9) in the character listing of the play, the other two feature as weavers (Ibid.). It is Hawelka, the least intelligent but perhaps also the kindest of Sleev's servants, who dresses her 'in the morning [...] undress[es] [her] at night' (Ibid.: 23) and therefore shares a particular physical intimacy with the protagonist. Though the act of dressing and undressing does not feature on stage in the action of the play, Sleev's attire is discussed frequently, and references to the act of undressing her feature in the dialogue. Sleev first raises the subject when she demands Modicum 'strip [her] now' (Ibid.: 12); he fails to oblige and her subsequent encounter with her son-in-law Guardaloop merely involves Sleev dragging up her clothes rather than undressing. She adjusts her clothes just moments before the arrival of her daughter.

Once more, dress serves as a signifier of propriety and its boundaries, but also of social repression of personal desire. The act of undressing, or disordering proper dress, becomes a transgressive engagement with the performative qualities of clothing: their signifying properties are literally and figuratively disturbed by the unruly bodies they clothe (cf. Warwick and Cavallaro, 1998: xviii; Brownie, 2017). This appears to have been the case throughout Sleev's life as she remembers one of her adulterous encounters: 'naked I said he had no time for nakedness he dragged my dress high' (Barker, 2008b: 18). The processes of dressing and undressing are apparently too formal and scheduled to fit into the tempestuous sexual encounters that Sleev has not only throughout her life, but also the play. This is highlighted again when Ladder suggests Sleev roll up the tapestry and 'wear it underneath [her] skirt' (Ibid.: 26) to which the protagonist candidly replies '[u]nderneath my skirt and that is a safe place according to you [...] I assure you Ladder wars or no wars there is no sanctuary in skirt' (Ibid.). The social order that is partially performed through the appropriate attire, which in turn is intended to complement and generate appropriate behaviours, is performative, imaginary (in that it only exists by general consensus and obedience; cf. Barker, 2008b: 41), and fatally fragile: the will to self-discovery of one woman is enough to overthrow it.

In a similar fashion, *Found in the Ground* offers its audience three starkly contrasting types of servant figures that attend to their employers' bodily needs. The Workman, perpetually heaping more wheelbarrow loads of books onto the fire, or otherwise tending to the burning process throughout the play, offers a rough-around-the-edges, lower class example of a servant. Not only is this apparent in the play text through his repetitive and simplified speech (Ibid.: 131) and deference to 'Lord Toonelhuis' (Ibid.: 192), but, in the 2009 Wrestling School production, it was highlighted through his heavy working boots, dirty beige, loose-fitting trousers, and open-collared off-white shirt. Paired with a wide-brimmed straw-hat, the Workman evoked associations of gardening (furthered by the wheelbarrow), and hard physical labour outdoors. By contrast, the other servant figures, namely the Nurses and Lobe, were all much more formally attired, and thus the Workman conjured a sense of animalistic danger, setting him apart from the rest of the cast. Notably, it is the Workman who strips Burgteata of her bizarre attire when she appears wrapped in the bandages of a recently deceased man she slept with (Ibid.: 158–159). This process of undressing, or more precisely, unwrapping, precedes their later copulation (Ibid.: 169). This unravelling of bandages is immediately followed by Denmark 'draw[ing] on her little socks' (Ibid.: 159), markers of privacy that hark back to an innocence Burgteata lost very early on in her life. Simultaneously, as noted previously, the little socks denote a performativity of innocence, a semblance of purity and propriety that she ostensibly aspires to, first appearing on stage 'classically attired, gloved, hatted' (Ibid.: 123). The socks therefore become a symbol of cleanliness, youth, and health, starkly contrasting her decaying surroundings and the smell of death and sickness that clings to Burgteata's body (Ibid.: 132–133).

The colour-coding of the Workman's attire (discoloured and dusty with use and age) furthermore contrasts with that of Lobe, 'a valet formerly a POW' (Ibid.: 121). The role of valet notably includes responsibilities regarding the appearance of one's employer. However, in *Found in the Ground* Lobe appears in stark contrast to Toonelhuis. In production, the former lawyer appeared topless and hunched over under a washed-out purple robe, with too-short, dirty white trousers and worn-out brown slippers. His valet on the other hand, was 'white-coated' (Ibid.: 125). Paired with a black tie, black trousers, and matching patent leather shoes, Lobe was the very picture of the immaculate servant. This appearance of propriety was starkly contrasted by some of his language, and later actions, too, such as when he slaps Burgteata (Ibid.: 171) and at the end of the play slits the dogs' throats (Ibid.: 211). He, too, affects a manner of respect and deference towards 'Lord Toonelhuis' (Ibid.: 200) and his employer's apparent sophistication. Unlike the Workman's roughness, Lobe's proper appearance (in costume and movement) contrasts the underlying violence of the character, who sexually abused Burgteata 30 years ago (Ibid.: 200).

Over the course of the play, he increasingly neglects his duties regarding Toonelhuis' strange attempts at consuming the earthly remains of Nazis he condemned to hanging: initially attendant, carefully pouring the water onto the heaps of earth (Ibid.: 125) and proffering a 'clean napkin' (Ibid.: 126) afterwards, later attending to his crippled employer 'with supreme detachment' (Ibid.: 178) and leaving him to exclaim: 'But I haven't eaten yet/[…]/ I HAVEN'T EATEN YET' (Ibid.: 180). Lobe does not engage in the activities of actively dressing or undressing either Toonelhuis or Burgteata, though his services are similarly personal and related to the body. This culminates in a repetition of the decades-old transgression of his employer's authority when he 'takes [Burgteata] from behind' (Ibid.: 199) shortly after he 'delivers a powerful backhanded blow' (Ibid.: 196) to the newly deceased Toonelhuis.

The five different nurses offer a third, complementary image of servitude. In production, they were uniformed in white apron dresses that came just above the knee, nursing caps, and black high heels. Though their attire changed upon returning from a funeral (Ibid.: 160) or later when sunbathing (Ibid.: 173), the variation of their costumes was never drastic enough to think of them as individuals. Rather, they attained characteristics of a Greek chorus, an impression furthered by repeatedly speaking in unison (Ibid.: 127, 143, etc.) whilst retaining the visual qualities of 'an ancient Egyptian frieze' (Ibid.: 123): distanced, abstracted, de-individuated, but mesmerising.

The potentially fetishistic approach to their attire and body was heightened in production by their red lipstick. Textually, it is exacerbated by the ways in which they discuss their own bodies (Ibid.: 173) and through Lobe's objectifying comments on their physical attributes 'from a Hellenistic point of view' (Ibid.: 162). The uniforms of the nurses functioned in multiple ways regarding the creation of bodies on stage for the audience to observe: firstly, the physical limitations of their attire (length of skirt, style of shoes) dictated constrained movements. Secondly, they denoted their position very much in a hierarchical sense – as well as identifiers of 'role' within the play. Thirdly, the colouring of their nursing uniforms stood in stark contrast to the dirtied and washed-out clothing of Toonelhuis and the Workman, whilst they complemented Lobe's overcoat: immediately, they were more closely aligned with the valet. Additionally, it set them apart from the only other female body on stage, that of Burgteata, initially sombre in dark colours, then a bright splash of colour and desire in a silken mustard yellow robe, and ultimately dramatic in her anachronistic and stylistically bricolage wedding gown (Figure 3.10).

The various servant figures in *Found in the Ground* offer a cast of recognisable occupations that are historically pervasive in Western culture (the handyman, the manservant, the nurse). Their immediate associative potential is thoroughly bound up with their appearance, whilst their behaviours (dangerously violent, yet strangely gentle and educated in the Workman; disparaging and cruel, yet devoted and passionate in Lobe; callous, patronising, yet emotionally highly expressive in the nurses) present their fallible, complex, and unfixed humanity that goes far beyond the potential stereotyping their clothing might initially trigger. Though generally not involved in the processes of dressing and undressing those they serve, unlike other examples discussed here, these servants are still involved in the (dis)ordering of their employers' transgressive and subversive physical bodies.

Before I relate Barker's use of costume to the overarching scenographic principles that underlie his work, I briefly analyse nakedness as a form of costuming (cf. Monks, 2010) in Barker's scenography. Immediately, one has to draw the distinction between nudity (which on the one hand simply denotes an unclothed body, but also refers to the controlled depiction of it in canonical Western art) and nakedness, which to Barker hinges on vulnerability and an 'element of the uncanny' (Barker in Brown, 2011: 136; cf. also Obis, 2013). In this, his terminology is diametrically opposed to that of Monks, who asserts 'the purely naked body is self-contained and impermeable, whereas the nude body surrounded by objects, reaches out into the world, and destabilises its borders' (Monks, 2010: 105). I will privilege Barker's terminology here, contrasting nakedness to the 'carefully contained and safely nude body' (Ibid.: 104) of classical art. Similarly, the intersubjectivity of nakedness has to be acknowledged: 'it could not exist without the gaze of the other' (Barcan, 2004: 23). Barcan furthermore identifies the naked body as 'a site of ambivalence' (Ibid.: 3) that exists as part of a continuum between the states of being clothed and naked (cf. Ibid.: 17; cf. Brownie, 2017), terms that inform

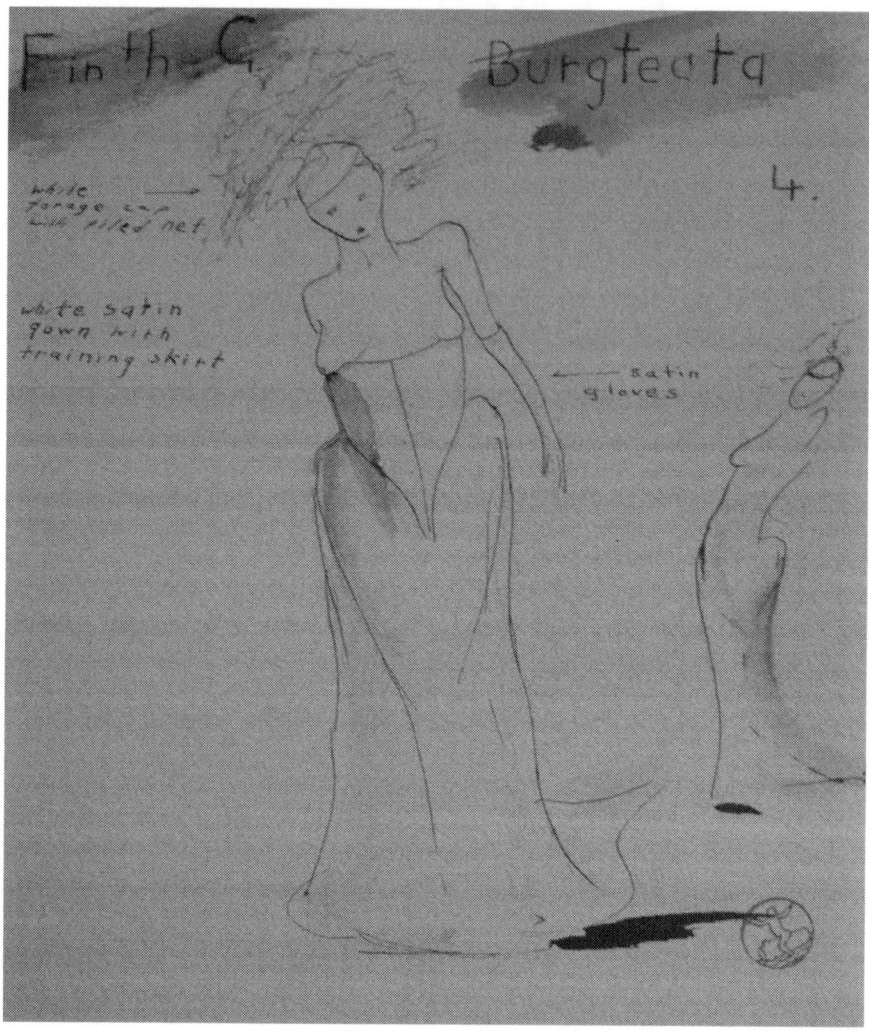

Figure 3.10 Costume design for Burgteata. © Howard Barker

and structure our perception of each in turn (cf. Barcan, 2004: 25). The raw and confrontational reality of the naked body is never just that in Barker, as I detail below.

Both *Ursula* and *I Saw Myself* offer rare examples of full male nakedness in Barker's theatre (though it also appears, in a miniature version relatable to *I Saw Myself* in playlet 28 of *The Forty*[14]), with starkly different effects. In *Ursula*, Lucas' nakedness – the audience's first encounter with him, no less – is a mark of his madness (Barker, 2008a: 99), which here may be reconsidered as an overabundance of irrational desires, and a stark contrast to the properly and identically attired nuns that precede him on stage. The confrontational nature of Lucas' first appearance sets him up as antagonist to the principles and aims of the convent. The 'naked, wet' (Ibid.) reality of his active, aggressive, male body stands in contrast to the subjugated and controlled female bodies of the virgins. Simultaneously, Lucas' nakedness offers itself as vulnerability (through the suggested exposure to unkind elements) and a foreshadowing of the havoc his desire will wreak on the unity of the nuns. Though briefly covered by a gown lent to him by the peasant women who discover him at the estuary (Ibid.: 100), he is left naked and still (Ibid. 101) to become the voice of Christ (Ibid.: 103). The conflation of Lucas' naked male body and that of Christ erases the boundary between the mundane and the sacred, and offers conflicting yet overlapping motivations for the women's journey at the heart of the play that leads Placida to her radical redefinition of self and the virgins to their deaths.

By contrast, the naked male body of Modicum in *I Saw Myself* (like the one of the unnamed naked man in the queen's wardrobe in *The Forty*; Barker, 2014a: 325) is initially an object of desire to a powerful woman (cf. Dahl, 2013: 129), her secret passion exposed in the face of forbidding social conventions. Though in both plays the fragile boundary of the desired man inside and the desiring woman outside is not visibly violated on stage (despite repeated textual references to it in *I Saw Myself*). The positioning of the naked male behind each of the women's mirrors might trigger associations of a completion of self that is (unsuccessfully) sought in sexual encounters with the other (gender, sex, person). Additionally, both desiring men and mirrors may serve as a (in one case literal) reflection of the women's subversive beauty and resultant transgressive potential.

The strangeness of Modicum's appearance 'in a plain dressing gown' (Barker, 2008b: 22) positions his naked body in terms of previously established object-hood (cf. Monks, 2010: 103), which is not just challenged by his speaking, but in this case perhaps more importantly through costuming: putting on clothes renders Modicum's body 'normal', though not quite in the acceptable spectrum of the play's depicted *status quo*. In the play text, when Modicum reappears towards the end of the play, he is naked, 'revealed, an image of immobility and patience, as before, but altered' (Barker, 2008b: 69). This presents a notable difference to the patent leather combat boots and black riding trousers with braces that actor Nick Barber wore in the 2008 production. However, some element of the unruly naked body prevailed through the still-bare chest in this instance. In *I Saw Myself*, Modicum's nakedness does not just become a manifestation of Sleev's transgressive sexual desires but surprisingly also, at the end of the play, where it is a choice rather than compliance with his mistress' demands, functions as a reassertion of radical, unapologetic, and catastrophic subjectivity. In the context of these plays, the naked male body is highly performative, meaning that its nakedness draws attention to its appearance in unusual circumstances (in terms of its supposed physical location: on an estuary bank in winter; living in the wardrobe of an aristocratic woman). This heightens the spectators' awareness of meaning-making processes that are attached to the body and all it signifies. The contrast between traditional Western conceptions of masculinity that emphasise strength and reason and the undeniable vulnerability of these desirable and desiring bodies as they are presented in the plays further emphasises this performativity.

On the other hand, naked female bodies are a more frequent occurrence in Barker's work. In both *Gertrude – The Cry* and *The Twelfth Battle of Isonzo*, women strip off their clothes for men. Gertrude offers Claudius 'the reason [he is] killing' (Barker, 2006: 83), which he also refers to as 'what [he] has stolen/[...]/What now belongs to [him]/THE THING' (Ibid.). This immediate objectification of Gertrude's naked body in the opening scene of the play is unsettled through the 'music of extremes' (Ibid.: 84) that is produced in the simultaneous death of the king with the copulation of Gertrude and Claudius. Though Claudius believes himself to be in possession of Gertrude, her 'perfect and pathetic' (Ibid.: 107) nakedness, her body and her sex, the uncontrolled sonic overspill of her cry already foreshadows his later demise. Gertrude and her cry cannot be possessed, nor controlled; her late husband 'could not meet her' (Ibid.: 86), and neither can Claudius, despite his protestations to the contrary (Ibid.: 87). Cascan advises her to keep her nakedness 'for the dark or these rare acts' (Ibid.: 85), imbuing it with a sense of transgressive power that reorders the world around it. As duchess Algeria's in *The Fence in Its Thousandth Year*, Gertrude's radical nakedness asserts the body personal over the (clothed, though according to Hamlet insufficiently; Ibid.: 97) body politic.

The historical importance of regulating and controlling the fecundity of women in general, but royal women in particular, to assert the validity of patrilineal inheritance surfaces once more when Gertrude dresses up in her 'PROSTITUTE'S COAT' (Ibid.: 114) that she keeps 'belted/To draw a line at violation/So whilst I'm owned in one part I'm not owned/everywhere' (Ibid.). In this instance, the choice of garment, with its associations of prostitution as extolled by Gertrude herself (Ibid.: 114–115) becomes an instrument of self-control. However, it is the prospect of undressing and the potentially devastating results of this process (Ibid.: 137–138) that are even more important. Though she 'pulls [the] coat tight over her body' (Ibid.: 138), offering Albert only a short, frustrated glimpse at her nakedness, this is enough to thwart Claudius' killing: 'FORGIVE ME WHEN I LOOKED AT HIM I SAW MYSELF/[...]/YOUR NAKEDNESS WAS MORE INCREDIBLE TO HIM THAN IF GOD STOOD AND PRESSED THE FIRMAMENT AGAINST HIS LIPS' (Ibid.: 140). The utter awe that he describes aligns itself with traditional descriptions of the sublime: Gertrude's naked, monstrous, uncontrollable female body[15] is sublime, gouging 'LACERATIONS ALL THE LENGTH OF [Albert]' (Ibid.: 125) and driving Claudius to ever more extreme measures in his quest for the cry.

Her body's contaminating potential is once more presented after the birth of her daughter (Ibid.: 148) and then again when – after Hamlet's murder of Cascan – she confronts her son: '*GERTRUDE is defiant. With a gesture of self-assertion she slips the gown from her shoulders [...]. She is naked before HAMLET*' (Ibid.: 156). Interestingly, this defiant gesture follows her son's urging that she dispense with her high heels, the 'UNMATERNAL/ CLUTTER/CLINGING/TO/[HER]/FEET' (Ibid.). This emphasis on Gertrude's function as mother to Hamlet and the new born Jane exposes the perceived danger of a woman who not only owns her own body and sexuality, but also does not constitute her sense of self through the biological functions that society traditionally and routinely privileges over her own desires. Gertrude's stripping to nakedness, yet retaining the high heels (with their sexual connotations of altered walking style and accentuation of the rear; cf. Barker in Brown, 2011: 198–199) is a refusal of Hamlet's and society's attempts at controlling her. As Barker asserts for Algeria, whose 'nakedness is a supreme rebuke to the forces that overthrew her regime' (Ibid.: 127), Gertrude's nakedness, incomprehensible to the men around her in its assertion of intensely passionate self-avowal, 'mocks pornography [...] by being authentically secret' (Ibid.). The performance of self that Algeria and Gertrude generate in their conscious self-presentation as naked women (frequently elevated by retaining their footwear, thereby acknowledging the performative frame[16]) offers the performing body on stage as a radical visual strategy that powerfully affects the space in which it is deployed.

Interestingly, in *The Twelfth Battle of Isonzo*, the man for whom Tenna strips is ostensibly blind (Barker, 2012a: 57), rendering the visual spectacle as one that is perhaps intended to affect the audience, whom it frames as voyeurs, since neither character on stage can ostensibly look back at them. Nonetheless, her nakedness retains 'the power to be discovered *differently*' (Barker in Brown, 2011: 127) as Isonzo's repeated focus on her insides and emphasis on depths (Barker, 2012a: 58, 78, 84) suggests that the surface value of visual spectacle does not provide the resolution or satisfaction that it might suggest. Tenna identifies the performativity of dressing (up, for a wedding) and undressing at the very end of the play where she exclaims that 'A BRIDE MUST BE OBSERVED' (Ibid.: 109). It is in the active presentation of actions that have been instilled with social significance through repetition (e.g. putting on a white dress, speaking vows) that an identity is forged.

Tenna's existence as bride is dependent on others' recognition of her performance in this role (cf. Butler, 1999). This realisation is triggered by 'the distant sound of a wedding carillon, brought on a wind' (Ibid). Her response to this recognisable facet of traditional (Western, British) wedding ceremonies clearly illustrates that she is conscious of the performativity of nakedness (heightened in her case through the hat, stockings, and shoes she retains: Tenna is naked, and yet not), despite her earlier claim that nakedness is simply 'being without/(Pause.)/Clothes' (Barker, 2012a: 101). On the contrary, nakedness is equally shaped by social expectation and normative morality (which both usually demand nakedness to be hidden, confined to absolute privacy) which cannot accept a freely thinking and speaking body that owns itself. Though it is at Isonzo's demand that she strips, Tenna nonetheless makes her naked-ness her own: 'Now/I'm/Perfect/And/A/Bride' (Ibid.: 104). Over the course of the play, Tenna discovers not only the power of her sexuality that manifests itself in an expertly orchestrated seduction (always promised, never fulfilled, 'You a promise/Me a rumour/Immaculate suspension'; Ibid.: 100), but also overcomes the objectification of being 'Gazed upon/A landscape/A picture in a gallery' (Ibid.: 95). Instead, she seizes her roles as bride and woman, which she performs – ultimately – of her own volition and in her own way, though this comes at a cost: 'Nose bleeding' (Ibid.: 109) she flees the room.[17]

The radical and subversive potential of the naked female body is also explored in Barker's play *Dead Hands*, where the grieving body of Sopron stands juxtaposed to the corpse of her dead lover. As with the other female examples cited here, she appears not entirely naked, but rather 'naked under a coat' (Ibid.: 11), which only slips from her shoulders to expose her body when she 'leans across [the coffin] as if stricken with grief' (Ibid.). Sopron directly acknowledges the performative nature of her appearance: 'All my gestures/ [...]/Hang in the air' (Ibid.: 12). The possibly exhibitionist drive of her actions (cf. Ibid.: 13, 26, 30, 50) further illustrates her conscious engagement with their effects. One might associate her nakedness with biblical extremes of mourning and penitence (figuratively being in sackcloth and ashes over her – later discovered – infidelity to the deceased). But, the fact that in production she remained in high heels, poised before wailing and sobbing, and immedi-ately controlled again thereafter, undermines any reading of her nakedness as a genuine, uncontrolled expression of grief.[18] Instead it foregrounds the pro-vocative, transgressive, and seductive qualities of these entrances.

These displays of unsettling mourning contrast her otherwise perfectly attired appearances in which she repeatedly extolls the virtues of (dress) conventions (Ibid.: 19, 37, 51); this juxtaposition, alternating in quick succession, highlights the artifice of each state of dress or undress (mourning garb/nakedness) in turn. Sopron's half-dressed appearances furthermore hinge on the crucial moment of revelation, which is always triggered by her contrasting performance of grief, sobbing over the dead body. The close prox-imity of the naked female body and the (in production immaculately suited) corpse further unsettles boundaries of propriety (cf. also Barker on the sexu-ality of the corpse, 2010a). This abject encounter is potentially as disturbing to audiences as the material contrasts between the naked women in *The Fence in Its Thousandth Year*, *The Twelfth Battle of Isonzo*, and *Found in the Ground*, and the forbidding stage spaces these plays presented in production, in which cold, hard, and occasionally sharp metals were juxtaposed to the actresses' vulnerable bodies.

In *Found in the Ground*, this discomfort (with its implications of voyeurism, gender relations, normative conceptions of morality and propriety, etc.) is furthered by the fact that the naked woman who traverses the catastrophic wasteland of the stage is in fact headless (Barker, 2008b: 123). It should be noted that in the 2009 production, Macedonia was not entirely naked, but rather wore a pale, possibly beige garter belt in addition to her high heels. Again, the notion of a nakedness enhanced by the traces of dress (often sexualised in their connotations such as the high heels or partial lingerie) features centrally in the construction of powerful but also powerfully disturbing female bodies. Similarly, Burgteata appears not naked, but 'in an unfastened dressing gown' (Ibid.: 128) and later 'entirely bandaged' (Ibid.: 155): once again the impression of transgressive nakedness is enhanced by the presence of incomplete and even improper attire. This is also furthered by contrasting these strange and half-dressed entrances to Burgteata's first one in which she is 'classically attired, gloved, hatted' (Ibid.: 123; Figure 3.11). The formality of the audience's first encounter with her sets out a set of expectations (regarding her – unseen – body and a sense of appropriate attire within the world of the play) that she subsequently repeatedly subverts, as much through costume as through action. In the case of Burgteata's bandage-swathed appearance, the otherwise implicit muddling of boundaries (naked/dressed, proper/improper, living/dead) is made explicit as her living, desiring body (cf. Ibid.: 158) is in immediate contact with the material remnants of death, unifying sex, and death drive in one person, and one body. The transgressive potential of her appearance is thereby doubled.

These unsettling appearances are twinned with equally non-conformist and potentially disturbing behaviours, such as her vocation to 'sleep with the dying' (Ibid.: 128) and later breastfeeding her dying father (Ibid.: 193). The close proximity of the living and the dead, the implicit and explicit exchanges of bodily fluids, and the crossing of (social and moral) boundaries confront the figures of play as well as the audience with 'what life withstands, hardly and with difficulty, on the part of death' (Kristeva, 1982: 3). It sharply confronts them with the abject, which according to Kristeva nestles side by side with the sublime, as an inextricable lining (Ibid.: 11): on the other side of horror may lie an overwhelming awe, a terrible beauty beyond moral categorisation. The naked female bodies of Burgteata and Macedonia in *Found in the Ground* serve as markers of this unstable demarcation that throws into question that which is normally perceived as stable: the flow of time, social convention, and the moral *status quo*, and even the conditions of being alive versus being dead, to name but a few examples.

The enhancing of nakedness through the careful and deliberate use of clothing is also apparent in playlet 40 of *The Forty*, in which 'a naked woman of considerable beauty' (Barker, 2014a: 341) performs a strange, reverse strip-tease for a 'sighted male, whose unmoving eyes imitate authentic blindness' (Ibid.). The added witnesses of 'a throng of people' (Ibid.) cover their eyes. First she 'strides across what might have been their line of sight' (Ibid.), then 'runs back, now wearing a hat and matching gloves' (Ibid.). Finally, she reappears 'fully clothed in matching garments' (Ibid.). This third appearance is furthermore described as a 'provocation' (Ibid.), which in this case might be considered to lie in the reverse process of dressing, rather than undressing, which nonetheless serves as a teasing seduction as the male is 'haunted, tortured by imagination' (Ibid.) from the fleeting image of her nakedness.

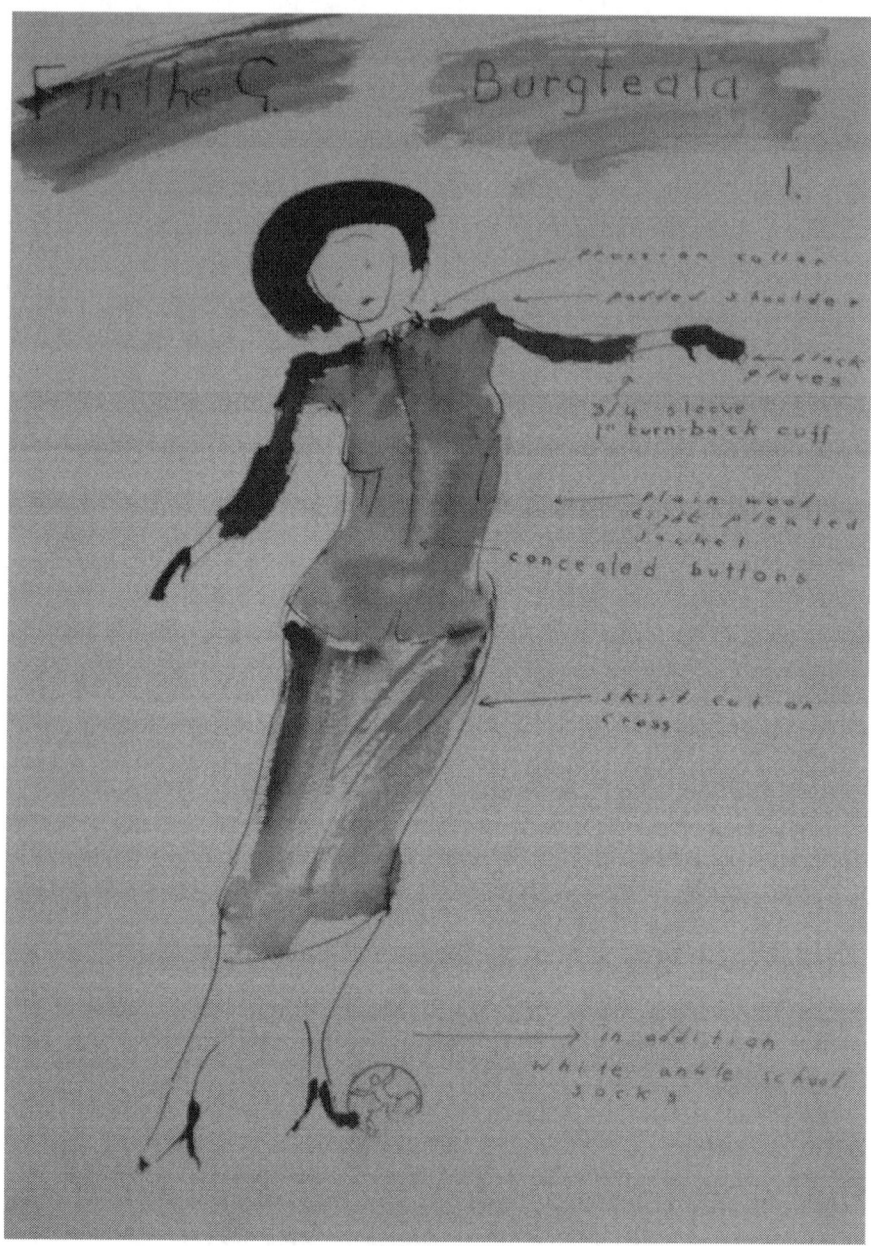

Figure 3.11 Costume design for Burgteata. © Howard Barker

Notably, once more the woman is not entirely naked: as she first passes, the text specifies 'her shoes making a characteristic sound' (Ibid.), identifying them as high heels. The seductive sonic potential of high heels (cf. Barker in Brown, 2011: 198–99) is juxtaposed with the potentially confrontational reality of a living, breathing, naked body that nonetheless performs its appearance in a particular, socially recognisable manner, forced into particular movement patterns by the footwear, but also simply by virtue of being staged.

Aoife Monks observes the ways in which a naked woman challenges notions of objecthood that might traditionally be associated with the classical nude: 'Not only does this naked performer move: she might also speak, and speech potentially imbues the naked body with subjectivity' (2010: 104). The potentiality of asserting subjectivity (cf. Obis, 2013: 74) is enough to deny the audience refuge in voyeurism. In the final playlet of *The Forty* this is exacerbated by the simultaneous presentation of the unseeing mass of people on stage, and the lone male figure that looks, but cannot see: in this configuration, the pleasure of looking at the naked woman in her different stages of dress is complicated on the one hand by being confronted with the voyeuristic connotations of the act as performed by the man on stage and on the other by the naked woman's potential to look back. After all, her reverse striptease (cf. also Monks discussion of an early 20th century trend of such performances, 2010: 102) is framed as a conscious performance, not only through the gradual addition of (formal) items of clothing (such as the 'hat and matching gloves'; Barker, 2014a: 341), but also through the sense of this process as a 'provocation' (Ibid.) through the act of dressing:

> dressing or undressing establishes a 'normal' body (naked or clothed) and taking off or putting on clothes then crosses the boundary of that normal body. It is less the loss of clothing [or in this case, the addition] that matters, as much as the shift in boundaries of the body that makes the striptease erotic.
>
> (Monks, 2010: 102; cf. also Warwick and Cavallaro, 1998: xv–xviii; Barcan, 2004: 19; and Brownie, 2017)

Simultaneously, the shift in bodily and conceptual boundaries is what makes the naked bodies in Barker's work unsettling, too (cf. Obis, 2013: 77–78). In conjunction with their radical striving for self-determination, their presentation in stage spaces that are equally porous and indeterminate regarding boundaries results in ever-shifting places filled with characters whose conscious performances of fashionable (in both senses of the word) selves is fundamentally tied up with their costuming, whether that be archetypical in design or founded upon the performative nature of nakedness on stage.

If indeed we follow Kristeva's logic and assert that 'the abject is edged with the sublime. It is not the same moment on the journey, but the same subject and speech bring them into being' (Kristeva, 1982: 11), it is the latter part that features more heavily in Barker's uses of nakedness on stage as a scenographic device that creates uncanny subjects[19] that perpetually perform and reinvent themselves. In this, Barker's costuming engages a fluidity of boundaries that Lyotard and Kristeva see as constitutive of the sublime, and which Johnson identifies as a postmodern condition of 'becoming-unbounded' (2012: 122) in which 'new and unfamiliar forms' (Ibid.) are perpetually sought out. Though Johnson specifically addresses avant-garde art in this particular passage, I would argue that the principles hold true in terms of the ongoing and repeated reinvention that Barker's figures present to the audience. Even in cases where speech is incoherent (e.g. Macedonia in *Found in the Ground*) or utterly absent (e.g. the Woman in playlet 40 of *The Forty*), it is the potential of self-expressive utterance and the conscious performance of body on stage through movement that renders these figures subjective. Their nakedness subsequently serves to subvert processes of objectification, since it is as performative as any other costume. This is heightened further in Barker's work, as naked figures usually retain some element of clothing (cf. Barker, 2012a: 84) and thus equally, and perhaps in this absence of clothing even more unsettlingly, foreground the processual and perpetually unfinished attempts at establishing the body's boundaries (cf. Warwick and Cavallaro, 1998: 3).

Grades of likeness

The resolutely ambiguous nature of Barker's plays distances the action from everyday reality for the audience. However, the recognisability of certain articles of clothing that function as identity markers (e.g. a crown for a queen, a black veil for a widow, an apron for a servant or maid) offer a seductive limbo of 'grades of likeness': this time is somewhat like the 1930s or 1940s, this place is somewhat like Beachy Head, and so on. Costume consequently functions as a visual anchor that provides a sense of location that nonetheless never exceeds the realm of semblance: always seemingly familiar, never truly fixed or comprehensible in its entirety. This layering of a social, collective memory as construed by dominant historical discourses with individual memory gives a sense of incomplete recognition, inviting the spectator to identify the known, yet thwarting the completion of that process. Costumes give the actors a body, even (or perhaps especially) when there is otherwise no discernible traditional character, in terms of their history, personal connections and motivations. The audience recognise this body as an amalgamation of multiple collective and individual histories that enables original figures to emerge while preserving the unfixed state of their spatio-temporal situation.

The fundamentally 'performative qualities inherent within the remodelling of the body's sculptural form' (Bech and Hann, 2014: 7) that takes place through costuming reveal it as a 'spatial body-object, disrupting and charging social environments to reveal their "evental" nature: calling up monumental moments [and] productive aesthetic encounters' (Hannah, 2014: 15). It is important to note that it is not just the animation of costuming through the moving body that brings forth this 'uncanny status of costume as a material object that works to produce apparently immaterial effects' (Monks in Maclaurin and Monks,

2015: 5) regarding the play's world and the characters' socio-economic status, for example. Part of the perpetual regeneration of bodies in space and reinvention of self takes place through characters putting on and taking off different guises, each expressive of different parts of self, whether they are the externally imposed markers of widowhood on Gertrude in the play of the same name or the cascades of bridal tulle for Tenna in *The Twelfth Battle of Isonzo*.

When Kristeva considers the sublime as a 'cluster of meaning, of colors, of words, of caresses, there are light touches, scents, sighs, cadences' (Kristeva, 1982: 12), this description also brings to mind the many resonances of costume, the materiality of which works along similar lines, whether it is on its own, ghosted by the bodies it points towards, or in the complex interrelationships that arise between the performing body and its clothes. Costume always extends beyond the simple materiality of its existence (cf. Blau, 1999: 22). It is more than fabrics of a certain colour and weight: 'as intrinsically corporeal objects, they contain hidden implications that dynamically charge social settings as well as the stage itself' (Hannah, 2014: 16). Costume is imbued with memories, collective and individual, cultural associations of cuts and colours that can be harnessed into reconstituted and mutable meanings that offer audiences seductive glimpses of something familiar that suddenly becomes more, strange, and exciting. This is particularly tangible with iconic garments, such as a wedding dress or mourning attire which invariably evoke 'multiple readings particular to other times and places. Simultaneously iconic and banal they abound with abstraction and specificity, looking to both the past and the future: their meanings constantly morph through societal memory and unrealized potential' (Ibid.: 17). The processes of dressing and undressing are central to the realisation of these multitudes of potential, as the disturbance of what was framed as a 'normal' body 'thrusts a small hiatus into the time of our everyday work' (Lingis, 2000: 131). This 'aesthetic density' (Barker in Brown, 2011: 125) of layered content results in a state of both/and that refuses clear demarcation and stable boundaries.

Costuming thus offers audiences 'layers of signification that surrounds [sic] [performers'] bodies like ghosts at a grave' (Trigg, 2014: 128). This may ultimately result in the 'raptures of a bottomless memory' (Kristeva, 1982: 12) of multiple times and places that all converge on the costumed performing body, naked or dressed. Barker reflects on this relationship as well as on that of costume to nakedness thus:

> The Barker/Kaiser designs are part of an overall vision of the stage, part of the denaturalizing imagery. [...] the costumes are beautiful and [...] owe a great deal to classic haute couture of the 1930s, 1940s and 1950s, not least in their hats. [...] They have a profound relationship with the naked body because, in some sense, they almost command their own desecration, the unveiling of the female characters. [...] The use of the narrow range of shades in the clothing of the performers asserts the non-naturalism of the production [...].
>
> (Barker in Brown, 2011: 124–25)

The contrast of monochromatic formal attire to occasional bursts of colour, but more frequently also to the naked body of a performer, exposed in the 'pure chance of its shape and colour' (Lingis, 2000: 131) results in an overwhelming flood of sensory and conceptual content from onstage may be described as a veritable frenzy that 'sweeps its vertiginous way over barriers' (Lingis, 2000: 149) – of language, of coherent thought, of socially accepted standards of beauty and propriety (cf. here also Lamb on Barker, 2005: 46–47, 50–51). In the 'decomposition of the world of work and reason, transgressive and ruinous passions [spectators may] catch sight of the sacred' (Lingis, 2000: 157). In Barker's scenography, this is in no small part achieved through the sensuous seduction of the audience's imagination by way of costuming that is seemingly recognisable: always decidedly historical, always drawing on collective cultural memory, yet never offering a full resolution in the terms that have been tantalisingly, yet also frustratingly only partially, set out. Costuming in Barker's work offers a more subtle destabilisation of traditional expectations of the theatre, as unlike the stage spaces, it is complete (in that they are actual clothes, not abstractions in the line of the Bauhaus), yet the world that it points towards is anachronistic on the one hand, and decidedly fictional in its re-conception of style on the other hand. By being decidedly theatrical in Hannah's sense (cf. 2014), Barker's costume refuses the limitations imposed by cultural, historical, and geographical specificity. Instead, to use Barker's word, it denaturalises the performing body, elevates it, and sets it apart from everyday life. It is both recognisable and strange, it performs the artificiality of the body on stage, aware of the politics and power of its image (cf. Hannah, 2014: 16).

In this, Lamb's consideration of seduction (following Baudrillard, 1979; expanded upon by Rabey, 2009) as a strategy in opposition to production and rationalism (cf. Lamb, 2005: 46) comes to bear the material reality of costume, and of the performing bodies it adorns exceeds the associative social content ascribed to it (regarding social status, function, age, and gender). Simultaneously, the explicit performativity of characters that is in part generated by their attire – and frequently discussed in terms of it, by themselves or others – attests to the flawed idea of a true self (cf. Lamb, 2005: 43–44), a stable subject identity. In Barker, self, as costuming, is 'a process: a series of practices that are ongoing [sic]' (Monks, 2010: 20). The challenge this presents and the accompanying 'sense of a vast opening-up of possibilities' (Lamb, 2005: 53) closely resemble Kristeva's discussion of the sublime as

> [n]ot at all short of but always with and through perception and words, the sublime is a *something added* that expands us, overstrains us, and causes us to be both *here*, as dejects, and *there*, as others and sparkling. A divergence, an impossible bounding.
>
> (Kristeva, 1982: 12; original emphases)

My argument therefore is that the initially seemingly comprehensible worlds that Barker's costumes attest to actually possess such an overwhelming multiplicity of potential meanings, that their initial appeal as something real, tangible, and recognisable is exploded into fragments of likeness (Burgteata's wedding dress is like a *robe à la française*, but also not, Sleev's mourning attire is both appropriate and yet again not, etc.). These offer a complementary seduction to Barker's stage spaces as sites of infinite possibility. In Barker's work the costumed body very clearly works as 'a scenic or environmental element [rather] than an individual signifier of character' (Maclaurin in Maclaurin and Monks, 2015: 141). On the one hand, this is due to the often-times archetypical status of the costumes (brides, widows, servants) that gesture beyond the particular character to a more generalised and historical idea of characters 'like that'. On the other hand, it is the decisive non-specificity of the costumes that denies a reduction of these radically self-inventive and performing subjects to simple archetypes (cf. also Ibid.: 109).

The cohesive presentation of costume as part of an overall style that is governed by distancing, structure, and self-conscious performativity lends Barker's figures on stage a distinctive appearance in accordance with their elevated verbal expressiveness. Furthermore, the visual composition of the stage spaces which includes the costumed performing bodies (cf. Ibid.: 157) of the actors enables costume to 'transform from the sartorial to the scenic and vice versa' (Ibid.: 158), once again emphasising its unfixed performativity: it may work in conjunction with a character's actions, or serve to contrast their behaviour to their social environment (e.g. body politic versus body personal, as discussed above; cf. also Reynolds, 2015: 158). The shifts between these functions are fluid, and often ambiguous. Through its connection with the performing body, costume is less abstract than set. Nonetheless it refuses full understanding (in terms of accurate time period or geographical location), while at the same time presenting a seductive and crucially internally coherent stage world to the audience. As Barker's stage spaces gesture beyond – in terms of the visible onstage to the invisible offstage, but also regarding the layering of imaginary places within the mutable, indeterminate space of the stage – so the costumes (which as elaborated above, include nakedness) draw on a multitude of recognisable, yet non-reconcilable, socio-historical and cultural associations that perpetually elude complete comprehension.

Notes

1 A pseudonym of Barker's, alongside Tomas Leipzig, Caroline Shentang, and Eduardo Houth.
2 www.thewrestlingschool.co.uk/ursula.html, accessed on 15.09.2015 and artvideotv 'Howard Barker: Ursula' available at https://youtu.be/BFDlbreNIYU at 1:35, accessed on 15.09.2019.
3 One should note that Barker very consciously engages with the materiality of costuming: his choices are motivated by a garments' capability to move as well as cost (see Appendix 1: 175).
4 cf. www.thewrestlingschool.co.uk/ursula.html, accessed on 15.09.2019.
5 cf. www.thewrestlingschool.co.uk/ursula.html, accessed on 15.09.2015.

6 Many thanks to David Ian Rabey, who generously lent me his DVD of the piece, filmed in Aberystwyth.

7 She also used a walking stick to find her seat, which she subsequently broke in half across her knee and discarded just before the play proper began.

8 Though possibly undead and speaking posthumously, as suggested by Barker in rehearsal, actor David Ian Rabey recalls.

9 On record, it appears as a short 1920s flapper style dress in charcoal grey or black with a deep v-neck and back, a side slit, with a high-low hem (at the back almost to ankle-length). It seems to be light, transparent chiffon, with approximately inch-wide shoulder straps featuring black floral decoration on one side. As such, the dress itself might be considered scandalous and inappropriate mourning garb, irrespective of its length.

10 Barker's costume designs frequently feature intentional gaps that sit in unexpected places, or proportions that are unlike any specific period's dress. The promise of opening contained therein is important to him (cf. Appendix: 184; cf. also Brownie, 2017: 43).

11 Her suggested pregnancy and the child's parentage are not discussed, and further the already complex and strange ways in which time operates in the play.

12 Incongruent in terms of traditional readings of stage space and costume as an immediately comprehensible visual sign-system, in which the different elements serve to support the audience's understanding of it.

13 Nonetheless, the confrontational nature of this act, in front of Youterus and Photo, father of her child and her son-and-lover, frame the encounter as another kind of transgression in its pseudo-exhibitionist cruelty – neither of them can observe the act, as they are both blind.

14 Further examples – outside the remit of this book include – *That Good Between Us, Downchild, The Bite of the Night*, and *The Brilliance of the Servant*.

15 Or as Kristeva puts it in her paraphrasing of Celine: 'those females who can wreck the infinite' (1982: 157).

16 Also exemplified by Isonzo's insistence 'shoes last' (Barker, 2012a: 84) regarding Tenna's performance of undressing.

17 This was in production only, which actor and Barker scholar David Ian Rabey recalls was at the insistence of the playwright-director; the text merely specifies that she 'blindly collides with one thing after another in her attempt to leave the room' (Barker, 2012a: 109).

18 This is not to suggest that her expression of grief is not real, but rather that Sopron is acutely aware of the performativity.

19 Compare here also Barcan's discussion of hair as a 'form of "dirt"' at the borderline 'between flesh and clothing' (2004: 30); this resonates strongly with Kristeva's notion of the abject, and recalls the graphic descriptions of pubic hair in Barker's *Dead Hands* (2004) as a salient example of the complicated nature of nakedness on stage, but moreover as a cultural concept bound up with morality, shame, anxiety, and desire.

4   Sound and silence

In dramatic theatre generally, but Barker's works in particular, sound is central to the generation of a cohesive and expressive scenography in performance. The seeming absence of sonic stage directions in his work imbues those few that are present with special significance: they offer a textual scenographic proposal regarding a play's imagined aurality. Additionally, the expressive potential of the human voice in the densely packed, highly structured speeches of Barker's characters forms a complimentary aspect to the sonic scenography. The poetry of Barker's writing has been the subject of much detailed analysis (e.g. Rabey, 2009; Gritzner 2012; Rabey and Goldingay, 2013; Roberts, 2014), yet its function as part of a larger aurality – the sonic 'counterpart and complement of visuality' (Pavis in Kendrick and Roesner, 2011a: x) – within the scenography of a piece has so far received little attention, let alone been subjected to sustained analysis. This chapter therefore offers an analytical reading of the scenographic role of sound in Barker's theatre. Before delving into the analysis of play texts and productions, I outline the contextual research and terminology that shapes my thinking on the subject of sonic scenography.

There has been a spate of scholarly writings on sound in the theatre recently, such as Home-Cook's *Theatre and Aural Attention* (2015), Kendrick's *Theatre Aurality* (2017), Bennett's *Theory for Theatre Studies: Sound* (2019), and Brown's *Sound Effect: The Theatre We Hear* (2020), among others. Further, Curtin's 2012 article on Barker as sound designer offers a useful analysis of some of the sonic scenographic principles at work in select Wrestling School productions. Curtin develops analytical approaches to theatre sound further in his 2014 monograph *Avant-Garde Theatre Sound*. In relation to this book, his monograph's in-depth engagement with the 'acoustic imaginary' (Curtin, 2014: 21 ff.) and its relation to perception, its limits, and the potential disruptions it offers to stable conceptions of self (predicated on distinction between self and other) draws close to theories of the sublime in relation to scenography, as I explore in terms of sound below.

Though specifically focussed on an everyday context, Augoyard and Torgue's *Sonic Experience* (2005; first English edition) presents an outstanding glossary of terminology that enables a well-contextualised discussion of sound in Barker's scenography. Two terms in particular stand out in relation to Barker's sonic scenography: ubiquity (Augoyard and Torgue, 2005: 130–131 and 187 ff.) and 'sharawadji' (Ibid.: 117 ff.). The former addresses the 'effect linked to spatio-temporal conditions that expresses the difficulty or impossibility of locating a sound source' (Ibid.: 130), often manifested as 'drone' (Ibid.: 131). The authors identify the *failure* of identification (of a sound's origin) as crucial to the ubiquity effect (Ibid.). The immediate spatiality of sound thus highlighted leads me to consider it as a sonic analogue to the *Ganzfeld* effect (cf. Chapter 3). The two concepts work in tandem to destabilise spatial boundaries: both engage the audiences' limits of perception and present an overwhelming scenography that is both 'too little' (in terms of concrete, comprehensible audio-visual content) and 'too much' (in terms of sensory and conceptual stimulation of the imagination).

Sharawadji on the other hand refers to a sense of beauty arising from a lack of discernible order (Ibid.: 117) that stimulates the imagination precisely by the absence of design. Augoyard and Torgue explain that this effect results in a movement 'beyond the strict representation of things' (Ibid.) that engenders a 'brutally present confusion' (Ibid.) resulting in the loss of 'both our senses and our sense' (Ibid.). The affinity of this concept, introduced to Europe in the 17th century by travellers returning from China (Ibid.), to that of the sublime is immediately apparent. Augoyard and Torgue place sharawadji 'at the frontier of art itself' (Ibid.: 118) and identify an 'internal tension' (Ibid.) that 'maintains the contradictory poles of this beauty' (Ibid.) – not sought, but accidental, unplanned, unstructured, and fundamentally disruptive – 'in the consciousness of their limits and the surpassing of these limits' (Ibid.). In terms of sonic experience, in a moment of sharawadji 'sound material loses its sense [the surprise of which is such] that it seizes the mind and no sense can supplement this loss; a circumstantial effect of […] going beyond sense' (Ibid.: 119). Crucially, they designate it as distinct from the sublime (Ibid.) in that it occurs 'without splendour or theatricality' (Ibid.) and is founded in the everyday (Ibid.): 'sounds become sharawadji less by their excessiveness than by their implausibility' (Ibid.: xvi). Whilst the ubiquity effect directly features in the analysis of sound in Barker's scenography, the term 'sharawadji' ('the sublime of the everyday'; Ibid.) does not. Nonetheless, its existence (or rather, accidental occurrence) specifically in the context of everyday aesthetic perception reinforces my conviction that there is an explicit need to generate a terminology that fulfils this function in a theatrical context (in which one would assume a deliberate orchestration of most effects, though accidents persist, of course). The recognition of the concept (sharawadji) in an everyday context – though not specifically tied to sound – therefore may open up possibilities of exploring a complementary concept (similarly not specifically bound to a particular mode of perception), which I call the scenographic sublime, that functions similarly (arising in 'a situation of rupture, where perceptive confusion gives way to an inexplicable aesthetic pleasure'; Ibid.: xv) though specifically in a theatrical context, and by theatrical means.

Home-Cook's monograph *Theatre and Aural Attention* offers the concept of the *acousmêtric* (following on from Chion, 1994) which exists neither inside nor outside the image (cf. Home-Cook, 2015: 91) and becomes a sonic descriptor complementing the recurring both/and principle[1] at work in Barker's scenography. One of the predecessors whom Home-Cook directly acknowledges is Ross Brown (2005: 180), whose essay 'The Theatre Soundscape and the End of Noise' (2005, *Performance Research*, Vol. 10, No. 4) offers a compelling argument for the inherent connection of postmodern theatre to the notion of 'soundscape' (cf. Brown, 2005: 105). Brown offers a provocative and convincing argument of the postmodern shift from visual emphasis to aural content as a conceptual echo to cultural and conceptual disenfranchisement with Enlightenment values (and their preoccupation with absolute knowledge; Brown, 2005: 109–112; see also Ovadija, 2013: 7) in the arts in the wake of the two World Wars. This conceptual development that Brown traces has immediate conceptual connections to the theatrical aims of Howard Barker (e.g. Barker, 1997, 2005a). In addition, Brown's consideration of the soundscape in relation to the concept of landscape clearly articulates the fundamentally environmental (cf. Brown, 2005: 109), spatial nature of sound (in the theatre, specifically; cf. also Ovadija, 2013: 4 and Voegelin, 2010: 124, 130).

The above scholarship informs my analysis of Barker's soundscapes both theoretically (regarding the imagined aurality as proposed by the play texts) and in the analysis of production recordings. The chapter takes Pavis' proposal of the term 'aurality' (2011: x) as a complementary expression to visuality in order to denote the overall sonic appearance of a play, which may also be referred to as 'sonic scenography' and 'soundscape', though the latter is likely to refer more specifically to non[2]- or extra-diegetic sonic content, and largely excludes spoken text (though not other vocalisations, such as cries or breaths) whereas the former two consider more exclusively the totality of sound within a piece. The term 'aurality' serves to address the fundamentally constitutive nature of sound in performance that is often literally overlooked in favour of visuality. Sound is defined as the 'tangible spatial event' (Kendrick and Roesner, 2011a: xxviii) of any perceptible aural content; its lack is silence.[3] The crucial role of silence within the aurality of Barker's plays is addressed within the overall analysis of his sonic scenography below. The difficulty of finding appropriate, suitably detailed, and to a reasonable extent commonly understood terminology regarding the discussion of any scenography, but especially the intangible aspects of light and sound is already apparent. Some overlap between terms is therefore not only possible, but highly likely. However, they are subsequently no less suitable for the discussion of the subject matter.

Furthermore, the chapter considers the relation of sound to music, again drawing on Pavis' identification of the former as 'impure music' (Ibid.: xi), but expanding it to consider music as subcategory of sound that is recognisably rhythmical and structured as well as fundamentally melodious (specifically in terms of a Western tradition of music). This is neither to the exclusion of melodic qualities in non-musical sound, nor the exclusion of musicality in sound in general; however, some attempt at distinction has to be made, in particular regarding Barker's explicit rejection of music (cf. see Appendix 1: 181) within his plays' soundscapes, unless diegetically specified. Additionally, this chapter considers the importance of noise within Barker's sonic scenography. Noise, like music, presents itself as another subcategory of sound that is usually perceived as intrusive, even if it is only perceived subliminally (cf. Voegelin, 2010: 43 ff.). However, it is important to note that intrusiveness does not necessarily equal a negative perception, or auditory distress on the part of the listener, instead it refers to noise's ability to insert itself into the audience's consciousness either unnoticed or if noticed, in an acousmatic manner: without offering concrete clues as to its source (cf. Home-Cook, 2015: 44, citing Schaeffer, 1977). The plays discussed in this chapter are *Ursula, Und, Gertrude – The Cry, Found in the Ground*, and *Blok/Eko*, expanded upon by other salient examples where appropriate. The aim is to chart and establish recurring fundamental principles of sound design within the scenography of Howard Barker and their development over time in the frame identified (1989–2011). The analysis is chronological and interweaves analysis of the spoken texts as constituent components of an overall sonic scenography with analysis of other sound that is textually founded or as it appeared in production by the Wrestling School.

(In)human voices and de-naturalised sounds

The prominence of sound within Barker's work is apparent from the very beginning of his scenographic engagement with his own dramatic works. This is already apparent in the emphasis on heightened language and poetic verbal expression by characters that predate the selection of plays this book focuses on. Just as we find conceptual doubling in the roles that characters fulfil, notably brides and widows, as discussed in Chapter 3, the performance of the play texts by actors also presents a doubling in the ways in which the human voice can be perceived by audiences. Lagaay formulates this as the difference between voice and language, the distinction of which presents a continuous oscillation:

> the moment I begin listening to what a voice is saying I tend to lose focus of the sounding materiality of the medium, and inversely, when I focus on the fleshy, melodious noise of the words [...] I tend to lose track of their meaning.

(2011: 63)

Meaning here refers to the semantic and semiotic content of the words, as the expressiveness of the human voice also goes beyond language (Ibid.: 64). In the analysis of spoken text as part of Barker's sonic scenography, I foreground the embodied aspects of the text, though they are necessarily intimately connected to its semantic and semiotic content.

The play *Ursula*, a darkly erotic speculation on the legend of St. Ursula and the 11000 virgins, explores not only the expressive potential and manipulative power of the human voice (and, crucially, its failure), but also utilises its non-communicative functions in the creation of a deeply affective play about love, lust, loss, and betrayal. The 1989 Wrestling School production opened to fragmented but melodic extracts of piano music, with female vocal accompaniment. The repetitive vocal patterns, most frequently centring on small intervals of semitones – with maximum jumps of a fifth on what appears as a diatonic scale – that were reminiscent of early Christian plainchant and recognisably within the tradition of Western sacred music, created at once a historic distance between the action on stage and the contemporary audience. Furthermore, the uncertain familiarity of the singing in conjunction with the contrasting piano notes created a sense of uneasy archaic order before the play proper had begun.

Victoria Wicks' performance as Placida – notably described in the *dramatis personae* as 'a Perfect Liar' (Barker, 2008a: 85) – offered a quick flow of words, with intense vowels contrasted by extremely clear consonants, as the text invites: 'Marrying...!/[...]/AND WHY NOT IS URSULA NOT BEAUTIFUL IS SHE NOT FECUND IS HER FATHER NOT RICH' (Ibid.: 87), moving from open, lighter vowels ('mæriŋ in 'marrying') to heavier, darker tones (ænd waɪ nɒt in 'and why not'), a movement that is repeated multiple times in her opening speech (light–dark–light–dark from 'is Ursula': ɪz 'ɜːsjʊlə nɒt 'bjuːtəfʊl ɪz ʃiː nɒt 'fiːkənd ɪz hɜː 'faːðə nɒt rɪʧ), sometimes within single words (such as 'beautiful', which contains the movement twice, and 'fecund' which contains it once). This sets out a principle of consciously melodic speech that contains numerous emotional expressions simply by virtue of its vowel colours, even before an actor's expressive rendition brings the text to life on stage. The emphasis generated by capitalisation of the passage further offers Placida's speech as expressive beyond its communicative content.

I use the adjectives light and dark here in a German tradition that employs the term *Vokalfärbung*, literally 'vowel colouring' to describe the relative positioning of vowels as well as their consequent timbre (cf. Prégardien, 2006 and Kiese-Himmel, 2016). For the relative positioning of vowels see Figure 4.12 below. In the German *Vokalfärbung* the positioning from front to back corresponds roughly to an imagined movement from light to dark, with variations arising through guttural or nasal positioning and the openness of the vowel, among other things.

In the 1998 Wrestling School production of *Ursula*, '[t]he sound of chairs dragged over flagstones' (Ibid.), which on record appear as wooden chairs over a metal floor, contrasted the clarity of Wicks' voice. The song-like fluctuations of light and dark vowels sounds were cut across by the grating noise of the scraping chairs, adding a layer of distress to Placida's supposed – and expertly declared – delight (Ibid.: 88). Her struggle to express her reaction to the news of Ursula's impending marriage is furthered by Phyllis' interjections of

VOWELS

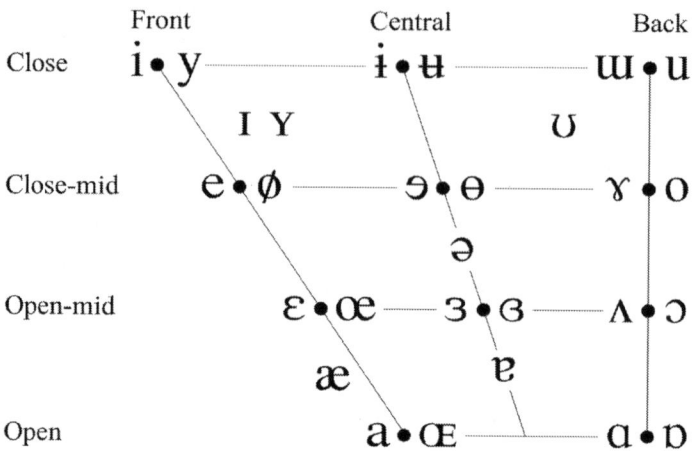

Where symbols appear in pairs, the one
to the right represents a rounded vowel.

Figure 4.12 IPA chart, available under a Creative Commons Attribution-Sharealike
3.0 Unported License. Copyright © 2015 International Phonetic
Association

'Shh…' (Ibid.: 87–88) that punctuate the Mother Superior's speech tonelessly,
yet also may be considered in their function as expressive breath: an exhale
that is commonly used to silence, but also to comfort. The rhythmical and
necessarily notably embodied nature of the interjection highlights the musicality of Placida's speech precisely through the absence of vocalised sound
in Phyllis' counterpointed expression. The rhythmical speeches of different
characters in the play, most notably Placida and the titular Ursula, play with
assonances, alliteration, and fricatives, such as Placida's declaration that the
proposition of any subject matter but Ursula would leave her 'STIFF/WITH/
HYPOCRISY' (Ibid.: 89), in which the repetition of the vowel 'ɪ' complements
the two, short monosyllabic emphases before opening up into 'hypocrisy',
which once again contains the same vowel sound (stɪf wɪð hɪˈpɒkrəsi). On
the other hand Ursula's pleas to the Mother Superior (Ibid.: 95) play with
repeated fricatives, especially in the repetition of 'please' (Ibid.).

The onomatopoetic possibilities of language are repeatedly tapped into by
various characters over the course of the play, such as when Lucas demands
'CHUCK US A BRIDE' (Ibid.: 99) in which the verb contains the movement it
describes: short, sharp, direct, and potentially violent or careless. Placida herself considers the relationship between semantic meaning and sonic quality in
language when she muses on her pupil's impending nuptials: 'MARRIAGE/
A beautiful word/Soft in every syllable/MARRIAGE' (Ibid.: 89). Perhaps

even more important to the consideration of sonic expressivity through spoken words are the repeated references to Placida's voice, which Leonora (who is ostensibly blind) describes as 'the most beautiful voice in the world' (Ibid.: 90) and even goes so far as to declare that 'EVERYTHING [Placida says] IS PERFECT' (Ibid.: 91). Ursula asserts that '[Placida's] silences are bricks' (Ibid.: 95) and Lucas declares her voice 'terrible/[...]/Because nothing it proposes can be denied' (Ibid.: 146).

The interruption and punctuation of speeches by other characters, often through laughter (cf. Ibid.: 91) but also through action, further highlight the rhythmical and lyrical qualities of Barker's writing that exist alongside the semantic content, and serve to strengthen, contrast, and counterpoint it in turns. This is most notably the case when Lucas 'overpowers' (Ibid.: 146) Placida, who at that very moment wonders what might happen if she 'lacked this voice' (Ibid.) and 'some accident befell [it]' (Ibid.). Subsequently, Ursula claims that Placida's voice has changed (Ibid.: 152–153) and adopts the Mother Superior's 'rhythm/Even the tone' (Ibid.: 156) for herself. In the repeated references to the power of Placida's voice, *Ursula* contains one of the most salient and self-referential examples of the way in which Barker utilises the spoken word as a musically expressive component in the sonic scenography of his pieces. The significance of the spoken word as poetic sound within Barker's work cannot be overstated, and is a recurring theme in this chapter.

Beyond the rich tapestry of spoken word, the soundscape of *Ursula* is furthermore constituted of a combination of live sounds that include the tapping of Leonora's stick, the giggles and gasps[4] of the virgins (Ibid.: 91, 93), their repeated singing (Ibid.: 133–134) – which serves as a tense attempt to retain some semblance of their normally ordered life when they arrive at Lucas' castle, a self-soothing through familiarity – and pre-recorded sounds such as the recurring cry of the curlew (Ibid.: 146, 148, 149, 163, 166) that accompanies the fateful encounter of Placida and Lucas and its tragic aftermath. In addition to offering an ambiguous yet undeniable sense of place[5] through using this natural sound, the sharp, shrill, and mournful notes of the bird call offer an uncanny echo of the virgins' distress and final demise, which Placida presages by her eerie description of what awaits Ursula at the beginning of the play: 'I shudder to think of the solitude of the estuary [...] imagine the sunsets on an afternoon in winter lapping water and one solitary curlew crying' (Ibid.: 87).

In addition to the non-directional curlew cry played over speakers, the production offered a multitude of ambient sounds that together formed an at times cacophonous environment through which the virgins moved towards their death and their Mother Superior to a painful ecstasy. Though often used as transitional impulses between scenes, many of the pre-recorded sounds in production could also feasibly be associated with recurring themes or images, such as the low piano or cello note, grating, combined with a short operatic scream, a sustained hum and the cry of a man that accompanied the revelation of Lucas' portrait and reappeared in variations whenever the portrait was at the centre of the action. Even more notable was the rough, far-off drone of a fog horn that was the sound cue audiences came to associate with Lucas and his castle at the estuary: imposing, yet invisible, drawing slowly nearer (conceptually at least; the sound cue played at the same volume and pitch throughout). The use of recorded vocalisations, often Stockhausen, that have long become a notable feature of any Wrestling School production under Barker, was already present in *Ursula*. The production used this polyphonic layering of sounds and noises to great effect in the de-realisation and estrangement of various characters, such as when Lucas encounters the peasant women (Ibid.: 99), which in production was accompanied by Stockhausenesque strings, brass, and operatic vocalisation that were used intermittently whenever Lucas attempted to interact with them and expanded with more notable emphasis on male vocalisation as he withdrew into the shadows at the back of the stage at the conclusion of the scene.

Overall, the boundaries between music, sounds, and noise overlapped significantly in this production, creating close cluster polyphonies and dissonances in order to facilitate an unsettling environment in which the action could unfold. Considering the almost-bare stage of the production (with lines cutting across a black, polished floor), the sonic scenography acted as place marker instead. The components of *Ursula*'s aural landscape can be loosely grouped into three categories that appear throughout Barker's sonic scenography: on the one hand, he uses abstract sounds that mostly serve an ambient effect[6] of offering a sense of place, decidedly unfixed and often deliberately counteracting or undermining the physical reality of the stage space (dimensions, materials, etc.). However, such de-realising sounds may also reveal themselves as an emotional punctuation that only becomes apparent over the course of a piece (e.g. the titular cry in *Gertrude – The Cry*). Secondly, these are complemented and contrasted by locational sounds (such as various bird songs) that, though arguably natural and thereby grounded in the real world, destabilise the place of the play even further, by offering something supposedly realistic that nonetheless openly owns its own artifice (through volume, precise repetition, etc.). The usage of recorded sound effects is consciously and notably theatrical in Barker's work: it does not attempt to disguise itself as actuality. Lastly, the soundscapes contain a category of sounds that falls between the two: denaturalised[7] sounds. These may be either recorded or performed live, but offer a separation of the expected from the surprising in audio content.

In *Ursula*, the virgins' singing may serve such an ambivalent purpose: though stemming from an identifiable source during the live performance, the quality of sounds produced – in the 1998 Wrestling School production – was harsh, occasionally contained an undeniable echo[8] and in its collectivity transcended the bond with the individual actresses' bodies. Notably, the performance replaced some of the singing stipulated in the text by other sound cues (e.g. during Lucas' and Ursula's conversation in Act 3, Scene 1; Ibid.: 138). The collective outbursts of singing, which at times moved from lyrical song into

Sprechgesang[9] or shouting, not only estranged the sound from its (visible) source of origin, but also presented a good example of Barker's use of non-communicative yet expressive vocalisations. Most notable in this regard was Lamentia's 'psalm' (Ibid: 134), whose singing was followed by the rough, far-off drone of the foghorn (Lucas' cue). When she broke into song again, it was markedly more high-pitched, intense in its anxiety, and shifted into a minor key, as well as performed more breathily, a last defense against Lucas' rage. Another example of denaturalised aural content was provided by recorded sounds such as voices in the distance and distant clanging noises, and throughout the play different water-related sounds: repeatedly the production used recordings from underwater (as if a microphone had been submerged just under the surface of a moving body of water, or recorded through the hull of a boat), loud and imposing, with a rhythmical beating like buoys against a hull, or waves against mooring timber pillars. Though recognisable to an extent, the volume of these sounds in combination with a collage of other sounds emerging alongside (both live on stage in speech and other vocalisation, and recorded sounds, ambient and locational) appear to audiences as disembodied, estranged, and consequently unsettling: the potential for understanding the source of a sound does not alleviate the anxiety it instills by the strangeness of its appearance.

The Wrestling School's production of *Ursula* illustrates several things regarding sonic scenography: one the one hand it demonstrates the three-fold split of aural content (spoken text, live, and recorded sounds), which within themselves fulfil different functions (locational, ambient, and expressive). These different potential uses of sound are already to an extent implied in the play text that uses them as scenic punctuation and transitions, and for the creation of locale and ambience. In terms of scenography, the plurality of sound in Barker's work suggests a conscious and deliberate multiplication of content for audiences that acts on their perception both noticeably (e.g. in the intense emotion of the final scene of the virgins' death, where their pleas are counterpointed by their dying screams[10]) and unconsciously (e.g. through the common low drones that wax and wane throughout the piece, and may only be noticed in the absence of other sounds, or when they cut out suddenly). The notion of locational (mis)information and a resulting tense dynamic of places with ambiguous spatial properties is one that recurs in Barker's work, and is repeatedly constructed scenographically through sound. The next play discussed here, *Und*, serves as a prime example of this method.

The play takes place within a single location of uncertain spatio-temporal dimensions and location (see Chapter 2 for details). Its titular protagonist 'waits for a man' (Barker, 2012a: 9). As her identity and world slowly unravel, the scenography of the piece accompanies and aggravates this process both spatially and sonically. The simplicity of *Und's* staging premise – a singular location, supposedly inside – is very quickly complicated by the protagonist's demand 'Go away/I did not ring/Out/Out/Servants oh' (Barker, 2012a: 10) that imply an invisible presence of said personnel. Since they are spatially absent, the logical conclusion would be to infer their presence by sound.[11] Whether this was indeed the case in production in 1999 cannot be confirmed here, as archival production materials are limited to a handful of private photographs only. Nonetheless, the presence or absence of a sound that might imply Und's servants draws the audience's attention to the sonic environment, and its expansion beyond the visible limitations of the onstage space. More addresses to the invisible staff follow, such as when she bids them 'REMOVE THE TEA TRAY' (Barker, 2012a: 11) only to contradict herself moments later 'DON'T REMOVE IT' (Ibid.). The visual and potentially (at least in the script, if not in production) sonic absence of concretising indicators of her servants leads the audience to question whether they exist only in Und's imagination.

Just as an audience may ponder the potential insanity of the woman on stage, a 'faint ring' (Barker, 2012a: 14) (possibly directional in production, likely pre-recorded and certainly not located on stage) suggests that perhaps there are other people beyond the visible and audible reach of the auditorium, now brought into existence by the sound cue and Und's exclamation 'THAT'S HIM THERE'S THE BELL' (Ibid.). What follows might be considered in terms of a duet: her monologue is punctuated by the repeated ringing of the bell (Ibid.: 14–16) and suggests an increasing urgency in the sound, which Und describes as 'the slightest irritation in the pulling of the rope' (Ibid.: 14), subsequently 'NOW THAT IS TEMPER' (Ibid.: 15) and finally 'THAT IS NO WAY TO TREAT A BELL' (Ibid.). If indeed the sound cue changed in production,[12] it would have deepened the sense of an offstage presence of someone, perhaps the man Und is waiting for. If the bell remained the same, Und's increasingly agitated reactions to it might suggest hysteria, and further a sense of underlying tension that becomes apparent only in the direct inter-action of onstage performer and offstage/recorded sound. In addition, Und addresses her servants over the course of this aural to and fro – which she her-self identifies as 'A CONTEST' (Ibid.: 17) a mere page later – between sharp bell and cutting consonants ('Coke/Coal/Butchery'; Ibid.), first telling them not to go (Ibid.: 14), then contradicting herself again: 'WHY DON'T YOU GO' (Ibid.: 15) – to answer the door presumably. She then calls on another sound cue (or rather the absence thereof) that leads her to conclude it is not her expected visitor after all: 'I didn't hear a van/I didn't hear a lorry/But by the same token nor did I hear a car/IT IS NOT HIM IT IS A LOUT' (Ibid.). The layering of live performed sound (in production, actress Melanie Jessop's voice), recorded or offstage sound (the bell) and imagined sonic content (the absence of the sound of a motorised vehicle), demand complex auditory and imaginary labour (cf. Sellars in Brown, 2010: 46; Curtin, 2014: 21 ff.; cf. also Goebbels' usage of Finter's term 'imaginary interspace', 2015: 49) from an audience. The extension of sonic scenography beyond the actually physically perceptible to include the imperceptible (but supposedly nonetheless pre-sent in this case) counts on an audience's sound memory (of a van, or lorry, for example), which they may then subsequently strain to hear, whilst being confronted with a complex live soundscape that may or may not include what they believe to be listening out for (cf. Brown, 2010: 73). The immediate spatial implications of this process offer a subtle yet effective way of expanding the world of the performance beyond the perceptible stage space (both visual and aural).

After demanding the bell be disconnected (Barker, 2012a: 17), Und's solitary musings are interrupted by '[a] shattering of glass' (Ibid.: 18), in response to which '[o]nly her eyes register her alarm' (Ibid.). This sound cue – in order to be recognisable as the breaking of glass – must be both clearly audible and of such a quality (either performed off stage, or recorded) that the audience are invited to imagine the physical process of destruction that manifests itself within the onstage space as sound, yet in the imagination of the audience will likely conjure visual stimuli, too.[13] After a second and third shattering of glass, which punctuate Und's speech like the bell beforehand, she demands of her invisible servants to 'CONNECT THE BELL AGAIN' (Ibid.: 19). This passage of Barker's writing exemplifies the spatial capacities of sound: it appears as action (ringing of a bell, disconnecting of a bell, breaking of glass) that, whilst not tangibly manifest, nonetheless has a distinct physical impact on the performer on stage – who responds in words and action – and the audience, who by perceiving it, are invited to imagine the ambiguous locational information[14] provided by audio cues. The punctuation[15] of Und's monologue by intrusive sounds is heightened just after halfway into the play text when she is interrupted by the 'shattering blow of a hammer on a door' (Ibid.: 26), which after repeating itself is replaced by the bell again (Ibid.) in very quick intervals. This precedes the appearance of the 'tray bearing paper, pen and ink' (Ibid.: 29) that begins the succession of increasingly strange suspended objects that slowly fill the space.

The sound cues of bell, glass, and hammering all serve to make – and perhaps also unmake in turns – the audience's assumptions about the dimensions of Und's residence, which are only once explicitly yet indirectly referenced within the play text when she 'erupts into profound weeping' (Ibid.: 30) after struggling to find the right singular word to write (Ibid.: 29–30): 'Her howl echoes through the house' (Ibid.: 30). The implication therefore is that of a large space, and likely a fairly empty one, with sparse furnishings and bare walls. The physical properties of any space can be supposedly quite precisely deduced from the quality that sounds within it take on. However, the particularity of theatre sounds offers scenographic ways of destabilising space, as they may be recorded in a space with properties different from the stage space, or manipulated to emulate the sonic qualities of other spaces. Similarly, live sounds on stage may be manipulated with regard to their implicit reflection of physical spatial properties. The aurality of a theatrical production may therefore be counterpointed, or even at odds with its visuality, demanding audiences to assign both importance and meaning to it, alongside or in spite of other scenographic content.

The sonic content of *Und*, onstage and offstage, is complicated beyond the supposedly real – which develops after the sonic attacks on the protagonist's residence to include the 'sound of weeping' (Ibid.: 36) – by the direction '[t]he sound of distances and plains' (Ibid.) that contains very clear spatial implications to be rendered sonically (cf. the echo of Und's howling earlier) and contrasts with the supposedly domestic setting of the play. This is exacerbated when, at the revelation of the yellow[16] flowers (Ibid.: 42), '[a] taut sound is emitted from a string' (Ibid.: 43) that disappears once she 'emerges' (Ibid.) from the flowers. This extradiegetic sound cue in the script suggests an overall soundscape that – true to Barker's theatrical aims – repudiates stage realism and instead offers multiplicities of potentially meaningful content. Arguably, this is also taken up by a supposedly diegetic sound, the hammering, which returns at the end of the play, 'terrible' (Ibid.: 47), and 'acquires a certain rhythm, a pulse, a music' (Ibid.: 47–48) that starts and stops, punctuating the final moments of the play before morphing into '[a] new sound of dragging and friction' (Ibid.: 48). In combination with the steady, heavy rain (Ibid.) that concludes the play (another sonic layer, either through the actual sound of falling drops, or rendered sonically), the soundscape of *Und* offers its audiences a cacophonous, invisible yet no less affective threat to the stage space and its occupant.

Gertrude – The Cry renders the sonic spatial relations of onstage and offstage rather differently, by complicating the dichotomy of inside and outside with specific focus on the protagonist. This is still a spatial relation, yet one that is fundamentally more troubling (cf. Kristeva, 1982). Like the previous examples, *Gertrude – The Cry* also makes use of the multiple potential meanings of sound, as well as the ambiguity of sound in performance to its source and the resultant destabilisation of ontological aural content: not only is it unclear where these sounds are coming from, it increasingly becomes unclear what they are. In the 2002 Wrestling School production of the play, the opening scene already offered such disembodied, ambient sound, which included dissonant strings that preceded and then accompanied the poisoning of the old king (cf. Barker's description of these sounds as 'anxious'; see Appendix 1: 180). In counterpoint to the strange and unsettling ambient score, the ecstasy of Gertrude and Claudius, and the dying man's cry combine into 'a music of extremes' (Barker, 2006: 84). The ambivalent nature of Gertrude's cry is implicated in the stage direction '[she] seems to vomit in her ecstasy' (Ibid.), which Cascan describes moments later: 'what magnificence your cry […] its depth its resonance' (Ibid.: 85). At this point in time, the titular cry is something of Gertrude's[17] that nonetheless appears to threaten to overwhelm her. This poses a challenge to any actress performing the role, as she has to find a vocal expression that contains both the ecstatic and the disturbing qualities that Cascan considers 'unrepeatable surely' (Ibid.), and be able to repeat and intensify this over the course of the play.

In the 2002 Wrestling School production, it consisted of a low chest voice vocalisation by Victoria Wicks as Gertrude that was successively layered with recorded[18] versions of her cry over the course of the play. As in *Ursula*, the performance of language[19] lies at the heart of *Gertrude – The Cry*, too. The abundance of assonances particularly in Gertrude's lines ('shoe blue shoe ALL MY SHOES ARE BLUE NOW YOU INSIST ON IT'; Ibid.: 86) offers a recurring intensity of vowels, often dark in tone (oe- and ue-diphthongs, here especially the recurring uː), though contrapuntal lighter vowels (particularly the multiple use of ɪ in 'INSIST ON IT'; Ibid.) do come into the speech, intensifying each word by contrast to the next, and by sonic difference to the overall colour of a line, dark in this particular example (ʃuː bluː ʃuː ɔːl maɪ ʃuːz ɑː bluː naʊ juː ɪnˈsɪst ɒn ɪt). These echo the sighing and moaning of the murder scene through vocalised language steeped in emotive content (cf. here also 'O HOW I LOVED MY HUSBAND', which offers pulses of lighter vowels against an abundance of dark: əʊ haʊ aɪ lʌvd maɪ ˈhʌzbənd; Ibid.: 85).

Though clear consonants are always a rhythmical structure in Barker's writing, it becomes more pronounced in certain characters' speech patterns; in *Gertrude – The Cry* it is Hamlet who possesses some of the sharpest, most cutting exclamations that add to his agitation and generally mischievous (cf. Appendix 1: 176) and stroppy demeanour: 'SHIFT/FIDGET/AND FLAP THEIR HANDS' (Barker, 2006: 90) appears alongside repetitions of 'bitch' (Ibid.: 87) and 'shocking' (Ibid: 88–90), the pronunciation of which requires strong impulses from an actors thoracic diaphragm and reads like a conscious performance of petulant adolescent outbursts. These strong, central vocal performances were accompanied by recorded vocalisations (breathing in particular), which may have stemmed from rehearsal, or been used from another source; the distinctions between inside and outside the actors' bodies, and the movement of sound from one to the other as usually understood was to some extent muddled. This is crucial in considering the violently affective nature of Barker's scenography, in this case the contamination of spaces (imagined and real) by sonic content that does not belong: 'when the boundary between subject and object is shaken, and when even the limit between inside and outside becomes uncertain, the narrative is what is challenged first' (1982: 141) writes Kristeva. With regard to the aurality of *Gertrude – The Cry* this refers to the cognitive rupture caused by (dis)embodied sound that upsets the conception of the actress as subject and the sound as intangible object that she issues forth (cf. Fakhrkonandeh, 2014: 242); ultimately, 'her great cry comes, not from herself, but from the land' (Barker, 2006: 174–175) and yet it is hers.

In the violation, perhaps even suspension, of conventional conceptual rulesets regarding the audience's presumed ability to locate sound (on, or offstage, coming forth from an actor, or a recording), the soundscape of Barker's playwriting not only advocates a necessary rethinking of rules, but challenges its listeners to accept its internal dissonance, both in terms of its sonic tensions and its conceptual disparities. As with the multiplanar spaces generated through set and light (and text), Barker's sonic scenography demands a struggle with both/and,[20] rather than offer a choice of either/or (cf.

Schneider's notion of 'binary terrorism' that engages the 'strategic implosion of binaried [sic] distinctions'; 1997: 18). In this, the works overwhelm, conceptually as much as in the physical actuality of the sensory stimuli – though they may appear deceptively minimalist; it is in the fundamental and ambiguous plurality of what is given and the forced absence of conventional meaning-making strategies[21] that Barker's scenography offers resonating bodies[22] to its audiences' imaginations.

The overwhelming nature of that which the audience is presented with in production – a premonition of which haunts the scenographic proposals contained in the play texts by way of their poetic ineffability – not only exceeds the rationally comprehensible but also strains the limits of imagination (cf. Johnson, 2012: 121); this 'becoming-unbounded of the imagination' (Ibid.: 122) is where a sublime experience may lie, the extremity of which 'negatively presents the idea of a reality absolutely different from our own' (Ibid.: 123). The duality of sound as intangible and physically intrusive (cf. Eke, 2014: 31), as formless and seductively reminiscent of the known, render it a crucial element in the generation of these landscapes that '[abolish] limits' (Lyotard, 1991: 182). In this contention with the reality of the theatrical world – even with its open acknowledgement of artifice – the turn to Lingis is not far-fetched: 'to seek contact with reality is to expose ourselves not only to the hard-edged resistance of things, but also to being pained and exhausted by them' (2000: 79). Though Lingis specifically refers to things, which here might include the physical reality of the scenography with all its elements, I would extend it to the reality of ideas in Barker that the audience has to contend with, consciously and unconsciously, willingly and forcibly, simply by exposure to the thing that is the play.

Ubiquity and the end of meaning

These principles of a seductive offering of all-too-much and the simultaneous denial of resolution are at the forefront not only of the soundscape, but rather central to the overall scenography of the next play in this discussion, *Found in the Ground*. This 'play about dead people'[23] offers an immense multitude of simultaneous content, visually and aurally as much as conceptually. The exordium and play open as follows (here focussed more closely on sonic direction):

> *The repetitive sound of an industrial process. A naked woman, headless, perambulates in front of three kennels. [...] When the sound ceases, the woman stops.*
>   *Scene 1*
>   *The sound of infinite distance. [...] The ferocious barking of dogs. An old man travels downstage in a wheelchair and stops. The barking also ceases. The industrial sound resumes. [...] Suddenly three bandaged dogs erupt from the kennels and travel downstage on wheels. The roar of their barking stops as they reach the edge of the stage. A long silence ensues.*
>   (Barker, 2008b: 123)

In the 2009 production this 'industrial process' (Ibid.) consisted of clanging metal, occasional high-pitched electrical whirring, and an ongoing, echoing drone of unspecified origin that suggested not only a place unfit for human habitation, but also machinations that disregard the individual human. This already excessive soundscape was then further expanded by the loud, pre-recorded, and decidedly unlocalised 'ferocious barking of dogs' (Ibid.) before Toonelhuis' recurring line 'I hear a woman pissing' (Ibid.) broke into the ongoing din, adding live sound to the pre-recorded tapestry of sonic assault which the exordium set out. The 'long silence' (Ibid.) was not absolute (in terms of a sudden absence of sound); instead the effect of silence was conjured by a sudden, noticeable reduction from the overwhelming cacophony of noise. As the industrial sound slowly faded, but did not disappear, Gerrard McArthur's idiosyncratic raspy bass took over. The quality of his particular voice was then counterpointed by Suzy Cooper's more melodious tones.

The play's fragmented lines emphasise repetition and assonance, foregrounding the affective sonic qualities of the words over their semantic content to an even greater extent than the examples I discuss above. Particularly Toonelhuis' 'catchphrase' which once more displays the movement pattern from darker to lighter vowels, and vice versa: aɪ hɪər ə 'wʊmən 'pɪsɪŋ ('I hear a woman pissing'; Ibid.) and, aɪ hɪər ə 'wʊmən 'strɪpɪŋ ɒf hɜː braː ('I hear a woman stripping off her bra'; Ibid.). The performance by Gerrard McArthur displayed a great awareness of this tonality. In his unique, rough but musical tones, he explored the full range of expressiveness without obscuring the meaning of the words, utilising consonants to frame vowels and cut cleanly between words. His performance might be considered very much in the sense of Lyotard, in which 'the powers of sensing and phrasing [were] being probed on the limits of what is possible' (1989: 190). Notably, Barker has referred to the Wrestling School's ensemble as an orchestra of voices (in Reynolds, 2006: 65).

The cacophony of multilayered sound was constructed from pre-recorded audio materials both scenically grounded such as the barking dogs and abstract such as the ongoing, not clearly identifiable industrial noises and the 'sound of infinity' (Barker, 2008b: 123, 131, 138, etc.) that the stage directions demand at various points; these were complemented by the live sounds of performers' voices, steps, and objects such as the wheelbarrow, wheelchair, and high-heeled shoes as well as the distorted sound of Macedonia's amplified and live manipulated voice. Her key line, 'I am all the Ann Franks/All the Ann Franks me' (Ibid.: 149, 152, 155, 158, 173, 175–176), offers a repetition of open 'A's, which were digitally elongated into mournful exclamations in production.

Repetition of non-communicative lines such as Macedonia's speaks to the incessant need that Barker's characters have to verbalise, externalise, and analyse their emotions as much as their selves. Privileging expression over communication, these fragments of performed sound gain meanings far beyond their semantic content and instead become integrated into the overall sonic scenography. A particularly salient example is the Workman's repeated address to the dogs 'All right/All right/SHUT UP/SHUT UP' (Ibid.: 141, 147, 154, 157), in a call-and-response with the canine cacophony (this seemingly long established routine fails only once, resulting in the Workman's exclamation 'BARK THEN/BARK' after initially urging quiet; Ibid. 156). Nigel Hastings' performance exaggerated the open-closed vowels (ɔːl raɪt ɔːl raɪt) in a falling vocalisation from higher pitch to lower, which he subsequently echoed in the remaining words of the line with greater intensity. Even where communicative content is present, the sounding out of the words, and their repetition, bring their sonic qualities to the forefront and may even obscure the semantic content, such as in this exchange between Toonelhuis and the First Nurse:

FIRST NURSE:	Piss?
TOONELHUIS:	Not now
FIRST NURSE:	Not now?
TOONELHUIS:	Not you
FIRST NURSE:	Not me?
TOONELHUIS:	Not/Your/Piss/Now

(Ibid.: 126)

In addition to the intense vowels, *Found in the Ground* displays Barker's usual clean, hard consonants; the names of those Toonelhuis sentenced to death provide a salient example: 'Hoss/Funck/Dolbuch/Klysek/Rimm'[24] (Ibid.: 138).

Before moving on to discuss the aurality of the 2009 Wrestling School production in more detail, a more detailed engagement with the nurses should briefly round off the analysis of performed language as component of sonic scenography in this particular play. Whilst many different figures repeatedly perform what might be considered key phrases over the course of the play (as already outlined above for Toonelhuis and the Workman, but also for example Burgteata's variations on 'I call this visiting'; Ibid.: 124, 142, 180, and 'I can't stop'; Ibid.: 142, 170, 171), the different nurses perform a much more choral function. This takes several forms: on the one hand they echo lines (usually to Toonelhuis, and occasionally Lobe) in unison, on the other they provide external commentary on the main action (the burning of the library). The cutting and possibly highly sarcastic repetition by multiple voices when Toonelhuis enquires about the nature of his 'dinner' by the nurses (e.g. 'TOONELHUIS: Was/That/Hoss/ ALL NURSES: WAS/THAT/HOSS/HE/ SAYS/ TOONELHUIS: It/ ALL NURSES: Was/THAT/HOSS'; Ibid.: 127, and repeats in variations with different names throughout; cf. Ibid.: 143, 150) obscures the semantic meaning and brings to the forefront the sound and subsequently affective potential of the words, especially the names of the war criminals the judge sentenced to hang (see above). Furthermore, the contextualisation the nurses provide ('NURSE A: Just the one left/ NURSE B: Just the one/ NURSE C: The one we like the least/[...]/ NURSE A: Just the one left/ NURSE B: Just the one/ NURSE C: The one we like the least'; Ibid.: 141[25]) regarding the overall, and especially offstage, world of the play (only Burgteata makes comparable references to events elsewhere, e.g. Ibid.: 155, until the intrusive appearance of Hitler, Ibid.: 194) highlights a sense of isolation that the setting of the play in its repetitive, and often cyclical structure conjures; in production, the sense of placelessness generated through set (cf. Chapter 2) suspended the figures of the play and their actions in an inescapable limbo, where neither words nor deeds could change the ultimate descent into catastrophe.

All conventional signification is subsumed by the 'weight of meaninglessness, about which there is nothing insignificant, and which crushes me' (Kristeva on subjectivity and abjection, 1982: 2). Kristeva describes this position in terms that are immediately salient to *Found in the Ground*: 'On the edge of nonexistence and hallucination, of a reality that, if I acknowledge it, annihilates me' (Ibid.). The complexity of the soundscape generated by performed text in this play could be enough to trigger such a limit experience in which signification and the rational construction of one's subjectivity are subsumed by exposure to overwhelming sensory stimuli; however *Found in the Ground* also confronts its audiences with an immensity of additional, often extradiegetic, sound. The relationship of these stage directions to the text that is intended for performance and their realisation as soundscape in the 2009 production are discussed below.

Already detailed above, the opening (both exordium and play proper) of *Found in the Ground* confronts audiences with multilayered sonic content that – in its textual form – is strange and possibly unrecognisable, such as the 'sound of infinity' (Barker, 2008b: 123) and the 'sound of an industrial process' (Ibid.). Without further specification, these directions already contain the crucial ambiguity that Barker's soundscapes attain in production: it is cognisable as industrial process, but nothing more; it seduces audiences into repeatedly frustrated acts of listening, as our ears are invariably drawn to sound and our minds subsequently and invariably will attempt to make sense of it. Another example of such intrusive ambient sound would be the 'long cry of despair [that] travels over the landscape' (Ibid.: 125) that offers no hints regarding its origin, nor the comfort of contextual reappearance: where the industrial sound appears to some extent connected to Macedonia (cf. the sound stops, so does she, it picks up again, she continues; Ibid.: 123, 126, 128,130, 132, 135, etc.), the cry occurs both during Toonelhuis' bizarre eating ritual (Ibid.: 125, 142) but also independently (Ibid.: 135, 162, 183, 201) and has no precise descriptor beyond 'despair' (Ibid.: 125, 142) and 'terrible' (Ibid.: 183). It seems this cry, like the profound silences interpolating in the overall cacophony, serves as rhythmical punctuation of the play as much as it is ambient sound in the production of a multi-sensory scenographic environment. Even sounds that are supposedly familiar, such as the barking of dogs, are made strange by their displacement from the supposed source of the sound: in the 2009 production, the barking was played at a loud volume via loudspeakers on either side of the stage, and therefore existed in addition, rather than connection to, the mechanical dog automata that travelled across diagonally

from upstage right to downstage left. Though the two were linked by association, the disconnection between the visible and the aural cue demanded
additional imaginative labour on the part of the audience. Furthermore, by
disrupting the localisation of the sound cue to its corresponding conceptual
visual origin, the sound served to denaturalise and theatricalise the scene as
much as the obvious artifice of the dogs themselves.

The sound of running liquids, whether it was Macedonia's or the nurses'
urine (Ibid.: 137, 140, 158, and 207), the 'amplified sound of animals drinking'
(Ibid.: 190) or the blood draining from the dogs' cut throats at the end 'with
a characteristic sound' (Ibid.: 211), were all presented in the 2009 Wrestling
School production by the same recorded sound cue, re-contextualising it in
each instance, yet without erasing the previous association. By layering these
associations, the majority of which contend with social taboo and disgust
(with regard to the potential for pollution, cf. Kristeva, 1982: 69), the sound
was invariably contaminated, and laden with affective content in the production. That this confrontation of the audience is orchestrated sonically adds
to the transgression, as sound traverses bodily boundaries. Sound therefore
transgresses against conceptual boundaries (cf. Lingis, 2000: 17) that are in
place to force a semblance of stability, to put into place (literally and figuratively) self and other, here and there. The heightened emotions that result from
this violation at once bring into focus the event (cf. Ibid.: 69) and at the same
time highlight its incomprehensibility: exultation and terror clash in a sublime
experience of self that has been displaced, neither here nor there, but both
to some unspecified extent. Lyotard describes such a process thus: 'Losing
oneself in a world of sound. Hearing breaks down the defences of the harmonic and melodic ear, and becomes aware of TIMBRE alone' (1991: 183).
Arguably, in Barker, the harmonic and melodic ear both persist, and continue
their meaning-making endeavours, but timbre rises to the forefront, obscuring
and counterpointing the sense-making attempts of the other aspects.

Regarding Barker's œuvre, nowhere is this foregrounding of expressive
sound more present and consciously employed than in the play *Blok/Eko*.
In the 2011 production, this became apparent straightaway from the exordium, in which the white-robed chorus (of doctors, possibly) chanted 'kyrie
eleison', situating language between musical and spoken expression from
the off.[26] Jane Bertish's delivery of lines (as the titular Eko) throughout the
play was at times liturgical, sung on sustained notes, and interspersed with
moments of *Sprechgesang* (not unlike the virgins' vocalisations in *Ursula*), a
development to the extreme from Barker's usual poetic and expressive language. Thematically, the expressive potential of language, in the form of
poetry, lies at the heart of the play, which then presents and explores this
theme in multiple iterations: the singing despot who has banned medicine, the
tortured poet Tot whose suffering Eko orchestrates in order to spur him on
to heightened forms of expression, her ageing lover, and poet extraordinaire
Blok who cannot write his last and best poem, the portentous poet Pindar who
serves as rival to Tot, the interpreters Quota and Nausicaa – the latter with a

crucial stutter – and the chorus of the masses: all these offer meditations on the notion of poetry, expressive language, and by extension also performed language as sound, which I have analysed in detail throughout this chapter. In addition to this, the play text is rich in sonic stage directions, the contribution of which to the overall sonic scenography of the play I explain below.

The play text opens on '[a] vast floor, empty. The sound of a winch' (Barker, 2011: 7), which in production followed on from the chorally orchestrated exordium; however, in production the thrust stage[27] retained a tableau of figures in white coats slumped over chairs in various poses of unconsciousness, perhaps death, a likely alteration from the 'slatted crate containing the bodies of two surgeons' (Ibid.) which the text stipulates. The stage directions also detail '[t]he slow beat of a pendulum' (Ibid.) and '[t]he sound of a winch' (Ibid.) both of which were played as recorded sound cues in production, and accompanied by a low volume, multi-tonal drone that possessed some of the qualities of white[28] and pink[29] noise, with an uncomfortable, echoing grain playing alongside whispering noises across a spectrum of frequencies, with an underlying dominant hum on a low note waxing and waning throughout the exordium and into the play proper.

These disembodied, ambient noises stood in contrast to the metallic clicking of the invisible winch (yet may have been conceptually linked to the slow descent of doctor's coats), which in combination with the tableau of figures might have been a substitute for the crate and the amplified mechanical beating of a pendulum (bringing to mind a pendulum clock, rather than a metronome due to its particular timbre). Subsequently added to this ambient, recorded soundscape are the sharp, staccato steps of a 'smartly dressed' (Ibid.: 8) woman, her fall and the clattering and smashing of the tray and glass she carries, in response to which 'an old man inches on stage with a broom' (Ibid.), adding the 'sound of glass shards shifted' (Ibid.). All of these live sounds may be described as noises for their non-musical character (though the steps undoubtedly possess rhythmical qualities) and are therefore set as counterpoints to the melodic performance of language in the play that is most exemplified by Eko.

Whilst one might consider the distinguishing feature between voice and noise the potential communicative value of the former, Lagaay formulates the following thesis: 'what distinguishes voice from noise is its intrinsic relation to the possibility of silence [...] inasmuch as silence can be considered as a mode of vocal expression' (2011: 65). If indeed 'voice cannot be defined in clear opposition to silence (nor vice versa)' (Ibid.) the expressive potential of the play text is even more heightened; notably, Quota and Nausicaa interpret for Eko even when she does not sing (e.g. in the first scene, Barker, 2011: 10). Lagaay describes it thus: 'the voice that is withheld is in many ways just as telling [...] only when voice remains silent, can silence begin to speak' (2011: 67). Eko's existence between interpreted silence and song therefore hones the audience's attention in on her vocal performance,[30] including the moments when she does not vocalise. The old woman's silence – 'still as a sculpture' (Barker, 2011: 16) – is juxtaposed with the dual 'translation' by her interpreters, either in turns (Ibid.: 18) or unison (Ibid.: 19–20), that displaces her voice not once, but twice. In performance, the actresses playing Quota and Nausicaa spoke in unison to some extent, but not perfectly, displacing both their voices. Since the text was already once removed from its supposed original source (Eko), this second displacement highlighted the locational (mis) information of these voices, conceptually pulling them from the bodies that produced the sound to offer up a more free-floating soundscape of live sound, closer in its ambiguous nature to the ambient sounds than to clearly identifiable speech.

Nausicaa's speech impediment, usually stumbling on the syllable 'in-', further draws attention to the sonic qualities of her lines, as opposed to their semantic content; as she struggles to 'maste[r] her speech' (Ibid.: 9), the audience is left to struggle for meaning, anticipating and substituting likely words to follow, probably with little success. The dual nature of 'in-' as a prefix and preposition serves to obscure the path of each sentence even further, obliging audiences to pause until Nausicaa overcomes her stutter. Additionally, the repetitions of lines with little to no variations by various characters (e.g. Quota and Tot, Ibid.: 12) create an echoing of singular words or snippets of phrases, not unlike the stutter, as characters interrupt and speak over each other, thereby obfuscating what meaning the audience may have derived from the lines. Verstraete's understanding of vocality as 'a broader spectrum of utterance' (2011: 82) provides a useful approach to examining the plethoric text of *Blok/Eko*, as it presents multiplicities of vocalised expression: from the sung poetry of the ageing tyrant, her 'small, sweet old woman's laugh' (Barker, 2011: 13) that rings forth eerily (cf. Ibid.: 16), and her attendants' staggered, grappling[31] interpretations, to the 'desperate [cries]' (Ibid.: 14) of the doomed doctors and the 'terrible chanting' (Ibid.: 28) of the furious crowds, the play abounds with vocalised expressions far in excess of structured language. These suspend the 'inner and outer borders in which and through which the speaking subject is constituted' (Kristeva, 1982: 69) by unhinging the usual separation of language from 'mere' noise in a manner similar to the acousmatic sounds that surround the stage and offer no clearly identifiable points of origin; instead, a proliferation of possibilities demands the audience dispense with attempts at conventional meaning-making and subject themselves to a proliferation of signification 'beyond the realm of form' (Lyotard, 1991: 186) that is rationally cognisable. Furthermore, the character's language offers Barker's characteristic harsh consonants (e.g. 'THAT IS THAT/THEN'; 2011: 31) and sharp diaphragmatic impulses (e.g. Nausicaa's repetition of 'Ha' in increasing intensity; Ibid.: 24, and later Pindar's angry recurrent exclamation of 'THAT YOU ARE'; Ibid.: 27).

Adding to this cacophony are often repetitive situational sounds such as the sweeping broom (e.g. Barker, 2011: 8, 11, 12, 20, 23, 38, 40), the shattering glass and subsequent movement of shards on the floor (e.g. Ibid.: 8, 10, 11, 12, 19, 20, 23, 36), and the old man's squeaking shoe soles (e.g. Ibid.: 20, 23,

30, 34, 38, 41) as well as gun shots (Ibid.: 28, 29) and a clattering 'cascade of scalpels' (Ibid.: 29). Barker's playwriting displays an acute awareness of scenographic structuring by visual and aural means; for example Scene 29 opens on a crowd scene, the death of the last surgeon is imminent as he is wheeled in 'into the stillness [on] a medical trolley [with] squealing castors, a sound which counter-points the regular but laboured creaking of BLOK's soles' (Ibid.: 30). Not only does this stage direction conjure a very particular sense of the visuality of the scene, but it also already taps into its aurality: both of these together present a dense materiality to the scenography even before it is realised in production.

In the Wrestling School's 2011 realisation of the piece in Exeter, the counterpointing layers of live and recorded sounds, spoken and sung words exemplified the return of audible expression of pain and desire that Tot identifies as Eko's legacy (Ibid.: 77); beyond the rational and comprehensible aspects of sound through language and sounds of identifiable origin lies 'auditory distress [that] materialises itself foremost as an *excess* of intensities in the listener' (Verstraete, 2011: 83; original emphasis). One should note here Barker's conscious awareness of the suitability of particular aural content over other:

> The general sound picture I don't think I come to until I know I have got the show on and I am directing it. Then I will go down to my CD collection and then I'll pick notes, or half-phrases from five, maybe, European composers, whom I admire, but beyond that, are suitable for theatre. My favourite composer is Bartók. But you can't really use Bartók in theatre without it sounding like music, because it is intensely musical. Whereas if you use Stockhausen…there is an awful lot of noise in Stockhausen. Noises, not music.
>
> (See Appendix 1: 180)

This danger of music as something potentially too recognisable, too seductive, and comprehensibly structured for the theatrical endeavour also arises in Kristeva's writing (in relation to Celine, though still appropriate in this context): 'the precise point where emotion turns into sound, on that articulation between body and language, on the catastrophe-fold between the two, there looms up [music]' (1982: 190). However, she goes on to elaborate that

> that slippage of emotion toward music and dance actually opens out on the void. Ultimately, at the end of the journey, there stands revealed the complete trajectory of the mutation of language into style under the impulse of an unnameable otherness.
>
> (Ibid.: 191)

In terms of the musicality of Barker's language, and his simultaneous refusal of overtly or conclusively recognisable musical ambient sound, the focus should be put on the implicit movement of the listener's imagination from logically comprehensible language to the emotional understanding of music (in a specifically Western European context). However, and crucially, I would argue this movement is left incomplete: the audience remains suspended between these two points of cognition, avoiding the bathetic lapse of the incomprehensible into concrete, streamlined and generalised emotion.[32]

In this, Barker's scenographic use of sound (performed and ambient) parallels that of his stage spaces: invoking grades of likeness, the sonic environment evokes fragmented and individualised memories without resolving the imaginative struggle to clearly identify a sound, nor by removing sounds so far from the audience's cultural aural memory that they are completely alienating, and therefore dismissed. Through fragmentation (e.g. Nausicaa's impediment), repetition as well as multi-source (e.g. Quota/Nausicaa's simultaneous interpretation for Eko) and acousmatic (e.g. the 'susurrating winds', Barker, 2011: 53, but also the recurring pendulum) layering respectively, Barker's soundscapes achieve a physical and conceptual sonic displacement in which the theatrical object, the play, has to be encountered on its own terms. These deliberately yield no resolution, instead sound, especially the spoken text in Barker's work, particularly that of *Blok/Eko* (and its companion piece in the exploration of plethora and bare sufficiency, *Charles V*; Barker, 2012b) 'floats in a syntactic irresolution that opens a path to various logical and semantic connotations, in short, to daydreaming' (Kristeva, 1982: 199). Though this daydreaming may very well be nightmarish in the anxiety its complexity can induce (cf. Lyotard, 1989: 198), the process of '[l]etting-go of all grasping intelligence and of its power' (Ibid.: 199) in the face of the overwhelming thing that is the play (realised or not) might offer up new possibilities of experiencing and imagining existence. The fundamentally intangible, yet concretely transgressive nature of sound is central to opening up opportunities for this process to happen.

There are several conclusions that can be drawn from the analysis of these plays regarding the use of sound in Barker's plays and the underlying principles of his sonic scenography. In describing the overall effect of Barker's aurality, the turn to George Home-Cook's use of the *acousmêtric* (following on from Chion, 1994) lies close, which exists neither inside nor outside the image (cf. Home-Cook, 2015: 91), but stands alongside the acousmatic; whilst the acousmatic denies the audience its source, it remains attached to said unseen/ unknown source. The *acousmêtric* on the other hand might be considered as part of an aural principle complementing that of the visual *Ganzfeld* effect, the 'ubiquity effect' (Ibid.: 94) in which the sound is perceived to '[reside] ambiguously on the margins of intended meaning' (Ibid.: 92) without a properly identifiable source, position, or even direction. Subsequently, the audience is challenged to '[stretch] out through space in search of a sound source that remains out [of] grasp' (Ibid.: 94). In light of the plays discussed in this chapter, the deduction arises that one of the foundational principles of Barker's sound designs is the generation of *acousmêtric* instances that call into question the reliability of the audience's senses regarding the origin of sounds, in which 'marginal *and* thematic content momentarily […] co-exist in a state of acute equivocality' (Ibid.: 92; original emphasis). Similarly, the ubiquity effect may very well arise from the simultaneous presentation and resultant perception of numerous sounds that lie atop each other, mutually shaping audiences' perception of each one.

The aurality of Barker's plays, whether textually implied or physically realised in production, consciously and carefully contains both sound and silence, and as with visuality, what is not perceptible is heightened. Silence in particular possesses deeply rhythmical qualities in Barker's work. Home-Cook aptly notes that 'our experience of silence is phenomenally shaped by the material conditions and sonic context from and within which silence emerges' (Ibid.: 99). The complexity of the complete scenography that Barker presents frames silences not as a relief from an otherwise sensorially and conceptually overwhelming scenography, but instead as a means by which to intensify: after all, '[s]ilence, like a mirror, makes us attend to that which is otherwise attentionally marginal' (Ibid.: 101). In the interplay between different scenographic elements, the absence of one stimulus, for example sound, on the one hand offers an opportunity to shift focus (onto the visual), on the other it actually serves to heighten precisely that which it apparently removes: silence (notably never complete in the theatre) is present through the absence of sound. In the void of perceptual lack, the absence becomes magnified and demands recognition by the audience. Like darkness in terms of visuality, this generates the possibility of a 'sonic zoom': in a circumstance of near-constant aural content, silence sounds very loud indeed.

Barker's orchestration of the stage space is as much auditory as it is visual, and extends from the ambient sounds produced via speakers and the performed sounds of actors' voices to their footsteps and even the sounding of their costumes (shoes, most notably, often women's high heels, but also the rustling of fabrics such as tulle, satin, the creaking of leather or the dragging of long coats or dresses' trains). Long-standing Wrestling School associate and sound designer Paul Bull considers Barker's work as

> epic vocalised poems that would probably have as much rhythm if you closed your eyes and listened to the production because they have a rich lyrical quality that can – on the surface – feel very confusing, almost like Brechtian alienation, but actually when you look at it in detail there is just an epic flow of humanity which nobody else writes.
>
> (See Appendix 1: 170)

I would argue that this flow Bull describes is a complimentary image to that of Lyotard's landscape, which I have discussed in relation to Barker's visual scenography in the preceding chapters: 'It does not ask you for your opinion. […] A landscape leaves the mind DESOLATE' (1991: 186). This desolation of the mind calls out the false Cartesian dichotomy that splits mind and body, and instead brings into acute focus the 'intensive reality of the sensing body, [...] engulfed by a chaotic profusion of sensations at different levels and intensities' (Johnson, 2012: 125). Barker's soundscapes generate such effects by offering complex strands of sonic content that perpetually vie for the audience's attention alongside the visual scenography; additionally they harness the fact that '[m]ishearing, ambiguity and uncertainty are parts of theatre's subjective aural aesthetic' (Brown, 2010: 73). The acoustic circumstance of performance, though it may be tightly controlled in an indoor studio space, can never fully account for the subjective hearing of audience members, be it through their position in an auditorium, the ambient noise produced by a living, breathing, moving audience, or simply their hearing ability (cf. Ibid.: 75–78). As such, the fundamental ambiguities inscribed in the sound design of Wrestling School productions are further multiplied by individual perception (cf. Ibid.: 128; cf. also Curtin, 2014: 62), and attention.

In terms of sonic scenography, Barker's principles – though necessarily simplified – might be described to draw on three categories of sound, with vocal performance offering a fourth, and somewhat separate, category. Barker's soundscapes contain: firstly, abstract, non-diegetic, and often acousmatic sounds for ambience[33] that are combined with, secondly, locational sounds (often bird song or other animal noise), and thirdly, denaturalised sounds, deliberately made strange and consciously theatrical (usually by amplification) that may have a discernible origin (e.g. Gertrude's cry, or Tonnelhuis' dogs' barking), yet the sound is noticeably locationally displaced from its supposed source; these sounds combine with the live performed sounds, of which vocal performance is central to the overall aurality of the plays.

These different categories of sound come together to engage the audience by way of the following principles: the spatial principle of placelessness is furthered by sonic means, often 'subliminal, but still essential to the whole' (Bull in interview, see Appendix 1: 173). The sounds, like stage properties and costumes, draw on grades of likeness[34] that seduce audiences into repeated meaning-making attempts that are bound to be frustrated. Additionally, repeated instances of near-recognition invoke once again the principle of both/and, in which the scenography invites a multiplicity of possible associations that are all presented as equally valid. For example, the clattering and hammering of industrial equipment that reappears throughout Barker's sonic scenography not only brings to mind the Industrial Revolution and resultant dehumanisation of production processes, but is also steeped in the mechanisation of killing in the wake of the First, but more importantly the Second, World War in a European cultural context. At the same time, the inclusion of abstracted vocal performances (either live, or in recorded snippets of e.g. Stockhausen pieces) calls forth the development of art in general, but music in particular, in the 20th century in terms of an avant-gardist refusal of historically developed norms and aesthetics (cf. Curtin, 2014: 165). To recapitulate: Barker's sonic scenography draws on the principles of placelessness (advanced through the ubiquity effect), grades of likeness, as well as both/and, in which multiple instances of partial recognition are layered.

Positioning the audience amidst this plurality of associations, Barker's sonic scenography denies resolution: again and again the sounds have to be encountered, re-evaluated, and ultimately remain to be accepted on an individual basis without conclusive understanding. In terms of the aurality in Wrestling School productions, this process of continual struggle for meaning is intensified by a conscious self-referentiality in which sound designs reuse previous productions' materials, drawing on a library of expressive sound materials that become potentially imbued with layers of meanings as they are reused and recontextualised over time. This takes place within a particular production, such as *Found in the Ground*, in which the same sound cue is reused in different situations, inscribing a new set of associations alongside the previous one, as the cue is recognisably the same as the audience heard earlier. Additionally, this process may expand across several productions by the Wrestling School, as audience members attending multiple pieces become conversant with the library of sounds in use by the company (e.g. a particular Stockhausen cry used in the Wrestling School production of *Ursula* in 1998 that was reused in 2005 for *The Fence in its Thousandth Year*, *Found in the Ground* in 2009, and *Blok/Eko* in 2011).

The intensely rhythmical and musical nature of the (vocalised) play texts is complemented by an equally rhythmical (non-vocal) soundscape that is used as an aural form of punctuation regarding both action and visuality. Though the Wagnerian notion of the *Gesamtkunstwerk* might lie close as a conclusion, Barker's work contains one fundamental and crucial difference: whilst Wagner's aim was to present a unified vision in which all elements strove to illustrate one central idea (cf. Roberts, 2011: 9–10), Barker's plays – whilst originating in one imagination – refuse this simplicity, and instead his scenography evokes a proliferation of potential ideas that cannot be resolved. He harnesses the relationality of signification that is particularly central to sound (cf. Brown, 2010: 131) in constructing resonant environments that present audiences with terms of engagement that are fundamentally individualised, fragmented, and inconclusive. At the same time, the cohesion[35] of Barker's overall scenography and sound within it do not alienate audiences in such a way that any manner of engagement is disrupted. Instead they tap into human curiosity, individual experience, and the dominant cultural 'background radiation' that informs the process of listening as much as the struggle for meaning that becomes apparent in the incongruence of any semantic readings attempted.

Ultimately, Barker offers his audiences snatches of seemingly familiar content that, whilst not in one single, discernible way meaningful[36] are nonetheless deeply expressive and subjectively relevant to the experience of the play. The simultaneous seduction and challenge this poses to audiences may indeed result in an experience that could feasibly be described in terms of the postmodern sublime as Johnson identifies it (2012, notably drawing on Lyotard and Kristeva, among others). This is a result of the oscillation between near-recognition of materials and the repeated denial of expected resolutions which frustrate conventional meaning-making. More importantly however, the origin of these processes (seduction/challenge/frustration) in the deliberate audio-visual, spatio-temporal rendering of space points towards a scenographic sublime.

Notes

1 Whether something is positively constituted by accumulation of possibilities (both/and) or negatively by demarcation from (neither/nor) ultimately results in the same dissolution of clear boundaries. The most notable distinction one might make between the two operative principles – which arguably present two sides of the same coin – is that the latter contains within it a sense of privation that has an immediate affinity to Lyotard's understanding of the sublime (1989, 1991a). The former might therefore become an attempt at describing that lack positively by cumulative layers, which are neither finite nor definite, yet address the necessary materiality of scenography as well as its conceptual content.

2 In terms of non-diegetic sonic content, the descriptor 'acousmatic' appears in close relation (cf. Chion, 1994 and Kane, 2014) though they are not interchangeable: whilst the former denotes sound that resides outside a play's plot, the latter, though without recognisable source, may very well have a perceived effect on the development on stage.

3 Which nonetheless possesses explicitly sonic qualities, particularly as it is never fully achieved in the theatre; if it were, the lack of sensory stimulus would likely lead to hallucination of sound, or introspection regarding tinnitus and other noises coming forth from the body.

4 In production, this was denaturalised and heightened in particular in Act 2, Scene 2 ('the deck at night'; Ibid.: 122) in which the sleeping virgins' breath was used in a rhythmical, almost percussive fashion that bore resemblance to certain throat singing techniques, alternating sighs, the toneless rushing of air, and the occasional roughened restriction of the airflow creating a harsher, less clean sound. The overall effect was deeply unsettling, especially as Ursula and Placida's conversation foreshadows the later murders in which Placida cuts the virgins' throats.

5 Sellars makes a crucial connection between sound and place: 'Sound evokes place, not space. That is to say, sound is where we locate ourselves, not physically, but mentally and spiritually' (quoted in Brown, 2010: 47; cf. also Voegelin, 2010: 123).

6 It is important to note that Barker empathically refuses 'mood music: I can't bear manipulating an audience like that. It's horrible. It's degrading. You degrade the audience, if you give it mood music'. (see Appendix 1: 181) Mood music is here understood as sonic content that is played with a particular emotional intention, simplifying and prescriptive; ambient sound in its wider sense on the other hand retains emotive ambiguity.

7 Barker speaks of 'denaturalizing imagery' (in Gritzner and Rabey, 2011: 124), which makes the extension of the principle to the sonic scenography all the more appropriate.

8 Though this may be a result of microphone placement during recording, long-standing Wrestling School Associate sound designer Paul Bull did occasionally use concealed microphones on stage to generate different effects (see Appendix 1: 168).

9 This term denotes an expressive use of voice between speaking and singing.

10 In production at least; the play text specifies a cacophony of fragmented singing and cries (Barker, 2008a: 165).

11 Especially since Und herself is still busy studying herself in the mirror (Barker, 2012a: 10) and therefore cannot be inferred to imply a just-offstage presence of staff in the wings by her actions.

12 A suggestion that is strengthened by the later directions of 'the same bell' (Ibid.: 39) and '[t]he gentle bell' (Ibid.: 42), which suggests an alteration of sound in the previous instance.

13 The connection with the brutal processes of the Reichskristallnacht pogrom in 1938 lies close, which saw the widespread destruction of the windows of Jewish properties, shops, and synagogues in Germany and Austria; thanks to Prof. David Ian Rabey for highlighting this connection.

14 Though a sound may very clearly originate from speakers in the theatre space, its impact on the action on stage and its contextual appearance may result in the audience locating it – in their imagination – off stage, beyond the visible playing area at the same time. In this, locational ambiguity may be the result; additionally, the particular sonic qualities of 'noises off' may straddle the bridge between recognisable and unfamiliar. As with place in Barker, sounds are characterised by grades of likeness.

15 Notably, Barker himself has described the use of sound in his plays as 'a kind of punctuation' (see Appendix 1: 181).

16 One might note the colour connotation here that has historic links with the yellow Star of David that Jews were required to wear during the Third Reich.

17 In this – initial – ascription of the cry to Gertrude, I position myself contra Fakhrkonandeh to better address the development of her erotic potential, personal desire, and uncontrollable subjectivity than a reduction of the cry to acousmatic noise outside of Gertrude can achieve (cf. Fakhrkonandeh, 2014).

18 Victoria Wicks recalls 'recording several cries one day which was rather a challenge because [...] there is a great deal of expectation in that cry' (in an email to the author); this also placed the onus on Wicks to re-perform the cry in a similar manner each time.

19 Naturally, the performance of language as a poetic vocal expression is central to Barker's work in general; however, it takes on an even more prominent role in these instances.

20 This also demands, arguably more disturbingly, and engagement with neither/nor (cf. Kristeva, 1982): recognition fails; yet the accumulation of potentially meaningful content across a number of scenographic components perhaps renders the expression of this principle as 'both/and' more appropriate in a material, rather than a purely conceptual context.

21 After all, these prove frustrating and inconclusive, confronting us with the 'dismemberment of our comfortable distinctions' (Schneider, 1997: 45).

22 This is achieved through his actors' bodies as much as the stages and plays themselves.

23 Barker, in conversation with the author in 2016.

24 Note there also the prevalence for short, even monosyllabic names, and the harsh voiceless velar fricative of 'ch' (χ).

25 Notably, in the 2009 production this last line was spoken in unison by all nurses.

26 By using a phrase that is likely to be recognisable in a Western-European cultural context, albeit one the literal translation may not be commonly known ('Lord,

have mercy'), and placing a Christian spiritual expression in the mouths of scientists, the production played with the supposed opposition of natural science and spirituality (the known and the unknown, or unknowable).

27 A notable change from Barker's usually classical proscenium arrangement.

28 White noise is characterised by containing many frequencies with equal intensities.

29 Pink noise is randomised, like white noise, yet contains equal parts per octave, and therefore contains more low-frequency components than white noise.

30 'if that parched/cracked/busted and encrusted/thing/is voice at all' (Barker, 2011: 10).

31 In terms of Nausicaa's speech impediment, but also the women's occasional strain to accurately interpret Eko's silence (cf. Barker, 2011: 20, 27, 42, 64).

32 Such simplified and generalised emotion and the implicit manipulation of audiences' perception by it, is precisely at the heart of Barker's objection to 'mood music' (cf. Appendix 1: 181).

33 Without the easy resolution of a clearly identifiable emotional content; 'unease' might be the only, and resoundingly ambiguous, common denominator.

34 This is achieved by using sounds that audiences may very well recognise in a different context, or manipulating recognisable sounds: 'That's how I treat sound: layer it, change the frequency, change the tonal balance, change the ambience it is in, turn it upside down, reverse it' (Paul Bull, see Appendix 1: 173).

35 This stems in no small part from the long-term working relationship Barker has with the realisers of his scenographic ideas, in this case Paul Bull, whose sound designs feature in the majority of plays discussed here.

36 In terms of referencing, attesting to, or expressing a particular idea or emotion, instead of a singular, rationally expressible communication (cf. Voegelin, 2010: 63).

Conclusion

This book explores the scenography of contemporary British playwright Howard Barker through detailed aesthetic analysis thereof in order to derive fundamental working principles of Barker's scenographic work. It evaluates the efficacy of the philosophical discourse of the sublime with regard to the analysis of Barker's scenographic work. Howard Barker's positioning as playwright–director–scenographer presents an exceptional example for analysis in terms of a unified theatrical imagination. Below follows an identification of his scenography's central working principles. I examine each of the fundamental tenets arising from this study in turn, and connect them to the theoretical framework established at the beginning in order to reassess the concept of the sublime in the context of scenography.

There are several interconnected principles at play throughout Barker's scenographic work. Let me note here once more that as with the different elements that constitute scenography, the different working principles are discussed in turn merely for clarity of argument and should not be considered as necessarily separate. Instead, they shape and inform each other, and often might better be considered as different aspects of an overall analytical perspective on Barker's scenographic work. These principles are: both/and, grades of likeness, denaturalisation and theatricalisation, play with the limits of perception (*Ganzfeld* effect, ubiquity effect), and ultimately, the scenographic sublime.

The principle of both/and is one that features centrally in the generation of ambiguous stage spaces, and consequently places on stage within Barker's playwriting. It arises from the simultaneous generation of multiple potentialities regarding space and place triggered by the presentation of often contradictory material as well as conceptual and associative content that are conceived of equal value, and offered to the audience without any particular weighting. This is exacerbated by the deliberate destabilisation or even absence of concrete spatial (and often also temporal) markers that would offer tangible or intangible locational clues.

Lighting plays a central role in achieving this effect, as it offers fluid boundaries to the physical stage space through deliberately deep shadows, contrasting the select brightly lit areas on stage. The technique of side-lighting further obscures the actual dimensions of the stage space, thereby offering audiences very little concrete spatial information; instead actors' bodies melt into and out of visibility in a deliberate echo of the *chiaroscuro* effect so often used in Renaissance painting. In addition, the materiality of the few select set pieces foregrounds their tangible, physical qualities, emphasising their texture, structure, and weight rather than attesting to any particular time period or geographical location. The interplay between set materiality and selective high- and low-lighting offers the audience a surprising tension between a very deliberately orchestrated emphasis on the here-and-now of that particular stage, its material reality, and its function as a theatre stage, and yet on the other offers them a wealth of potential socio-political contexts, historical, and geographical associations.

The deliberate and skilful obscuring of physical spatial dimensions and conceptual boundaries attests to the titular abyss that Aronson identifies (2005) in terms of scenography's capacity to render the stage a boundless void. This notion of the void offers a clear connection to postmodern conceptions of the sublime as they appear in the writings of Kristeva (1982) and Lyotard (1989, 1991) as well as more recently in the work of Zuckert, Guyer, and in more explicit detail Johnson (all 2012). Zuckert in particular makes salient connections between the experience of the sublime and its associative character (2012: 74) that arises not from any object, but from an affective encounter. As the preceding chapters demonstrate, Barker brings together scenography's different constitutive aspects in such a way that the pluralistic associations in conjunction with the absence of concretising (spatio-temporal but also conceptual) markers offer repeated opportunities for precisely such affective encounters. The layering that results from repeated instances of both/and offers an immense excess of sensory and conceptual content that demands an imaginative and experiential engagement on the audience's part.

This demand is further extended through the complex aurality of Barker's plays, which complement their visuality: though the stage spaces are deceptively simple, containing very few set pieces that are starkly and selectively lit, it is in the resonant spaces of the unseen, in the potentiality that an audience's imagination is challenged to explore, that an overabundance of affective scenographic content arises. The complex choreography of bodies in a liminal space is taken up by the detailed and complicated orchestration of live sounds (from performed language to footsteps, or rustling petticoats) with pre-recorded materials (diegetic and non-diegetic, often acousmatic). Engaging in a process of denaturalisation similar to that used in the generation of imagery in the plays (cf. Barker in Brown, 2011: 124), the fragility of locational information is further enhanced as audiences can trust neither their eyes nor their ears to provide them with conclusive materials. It is not either/or (here/there, now/then, etc.), it is both/and. This radical suspension of conceptual dichotomies (cf. Schneider, 1997) leads to an overload, aggravated by the complexity and overabundance[1] of sensory stimuli. By being both a sensually interesting theatre space and potential multiple places within the world of a play, the visual scenography of Barker's stage spaces offer audiences footholds for the imagination[2] that are always present, yet continually changing and never concretised. Consequently, the audience's reading of the space is perpetually shifting over the course of a play, and likely to exist on an individual, not a collective basis.

This principle very clearly extends to the costumes, too. These offer a wealth of potential associations in their consciously undefined historicism and diverse, rich materiality. As light, set and sound offer shifting boundaries of space and place, costume extends this to the performers' bodies, and by extension, selves. Additionally, costume's crucial contribution to the generation of unstable, actively performed, and perpetually transformed subject identities of the characters on stage extends the destabilisation of boundaries from the tangible, spatio-temporal (in terms of the active reshaping of the body through clothes, and the active process of restructuring its edges) to the intangible, conceptual (construction and interrogation of the notion of subject identity). In this, the processes of costume in performance are analogous to the ways in which this principle is already present on and in Barker's stage spaces, and the imagined places these attest to. The notion of an unstable subject identity as performed through costume marks another strong connection of Barker's scenography to postmodern theories of the sublime. The anxiety that arises from the transgression of supposedly stable boundaries such as those imagined to contain subject identity harks back to Kristeva's writing (1982) which details the close relationship of the sublime to the abject (in the context of psychoanalytic theory). She offers a negative complement to the both/and principle I have identified with regard to Barker, neither/nor, which could arguably act as an expansion of the both/and principle on a conceptual level (as Kristeva discusses it at length in terms of subjectivity). The fundamental lack of neither/nor is crucially implicit in both/and, which suggest an infinite proliferation that cannot be completed nor comprehended. Consequently, the cumulative and therefore overwhelming effect of the both/and principle in Barker's scenography generates precisely that sensory overload and conceptual excess that brings to mind the terror and ecstasy of the sublime experience. It revels in the rejection of Kantian superiority of reason over the senses and instead offers a suspension of space, time, and self that denies conventional meaning-making processes.

Crucially, Barker seduces the audience into repeated attempts at meaning-making by way of the next principle discussed here, that of 'grades of likeness'. In the multiplicities of content that arise from the both/and principle, there are spectres of the recognisable. Drawing notably on Western European art and cultural history, Barker's scenography avoids eclecticism insofar as the multiplicity of its reference points do not remain separate, or individually identifiable, but instead generates something new and whole, with an internal coherence that attests to many different possible points of origin (cf. Berrigan, 2015: 58). The recognition of potential references within Barker's work (be they literary, historical, or aesthetic) is dependent on an individual awareness and understanding of European art and art history as much as literature and politics. The process of synthesising core aesthetic developments of European art and a radical innovation in their presentation as new, independent pieces of art allows a transcendence of patchwork. The notion of grades of likeness features centrally in this process: Barker's stage spaces conjure up places that are reminiscent of a vestry (*The Twelfth Battle of Isonzo*), a rich woman's manor house (*Und*), a bombed out home (*A House of Correction*), or Beachy Head cliff (*The Forty*, playlet 25); the time period is somewhat like 13th century (*I Saw Myself*) or post-Second World War Europe (*Found in the Ground*); the lighting raises associations from throughout Western cultural history from the Renaissance to the modern day, with possible connections to Bosch, Velázquez, Rembrandt, Goya, and Tarkovsky. The costume brings to mind 1930s to 1950s European *haute couture* (particularly the work of Cristóbal Balenciaga and Dior's New Look), but also other times, different and elusive geographical locations and seasons. The sound offers incomplete recognition, in terms of its sources: clangs, clatters, and drones offer uncanny sonic content that brings to mind invisible processes beyond the onstage space that are both firmly post-Industrialisation and yet strangely timeless in their existence without knowable origin. At the same time, Barker's scenography presents audio-content that is situated in avant-garde music, such as Stockhausen (which Barker uses extensively) and Bartók. The aurality therefore offers the same multiplicity of potentially familiar fragments that serve as short bursts of supposed recognition, only to descend into the unfamiliar again at the next moment, keeping the audience on the edge of the known, and firmly between frustrated alienation and the relief of comprehension.

Crucially, however, these processes of recognition are incomplete: places, time periods, and sounds conjured by the plays are 'like' but also fundamentally 'not like'; the cultural memories evoked are drawn from the cultural subconscious of the audience, stirring associations without completing the process. Only in sustained reflection and contemplation after the event might one concretise the comparison to somewhere else, sometime else, and then only with the caveat of 'like': association by gradation, not by equation, resulting in a sense of intangibility (both of the play itself, which remains inexplicable, and the ineffability of content attested to without conclusive specification). The meaning-making processes that Barker's scenography invites are perpetually frustrated by a combination of multiplicity – of what would be considered relevant content, following the both/and principle – and elusiveness, in which associations are hard to grasp, elusive, and ultimately become unstuck as grades of likeness are layered atop each other.

This decidedly liminal situation, and the oscillation between partial recognition and its subsequent loss, is reflected in Lyotard's writing (1989) on the sublime which haunts the state of being thrown into a confrontation with the thing (in this case scenography) on its terms, by the simple virtue of its occurrence that disarms thought. Instead, one has to experience it, and in the process admit the unfixedness of subject identity. This movement of being thrown can also be related to Kristeva's image of bursting (recurrent in *Powers of Horror*, 1982) that she relates to the cancellation of personal existence in subjective perception (Ibid.: 210): a sublime experience, both terrible and ecstatic. Between Lyotard and Kristeva we find suitable description of the effects of Barker's scenography that draws on both individual and collective memory[3] in order to seduce the audience into the encounter with that which triggers a proliferation of imagination. The irresolution at the heart of this experience (cf. Johnson, 2012: 131), its resistance to complete comprehension and analysis – both of which it nonetheless invites – attests to the central tension of Barker's work. Furthermore, the suspension between (individual/ collective, known/unknown) that grades of likeness throughout Barker's scenography conjure acts as a complimentary principle to the multiplication of content achieved through both/and. This might be considered as an expression of what Barker considers the condition of being European (cf. in Brown, 2011: 129–130).

The proliferation of potential associations that are generated by the grades of likeness that Barker's scenography evokes at every turn furthermore resonates strongly with Lyotard's notion of the landscape (1991a) which refutes opinion and offers desolation in its stead;[4] it requires the loss of (concrete) place and the interruption of conventional narratives, both structurally and in content. These are effects that in Barker's work are centrally generated by the complexity of the scenography which offers an overwhelming sensory and conceptual environment that vies for the audience's attention with the seemingly familiar (offering grades of likeness in all aspects of the scenography) only to leave them wrestling with the deeply unsettling (un)familiar[5] instead. In addition to the layering of content in terms of conceptual and associative complexity – which challenges audiences to make repeated choices in assigning significance to aspects of production, all of which are presented as equally relevant – conventional meaning-making strategies are further complicated by the third principle arising from this study of Barker's scenography: it lies beyond the realm of the rationally comprehensible, and beyond audience's capabilities to situate it in a concrete socio-political and historical context. This 'beyond' is achieved by the complimentary processes of denaturalisation and theatricalisation.

Denaturalisation and theatricalisation lie at the heart of Barker's aesthetic, and are instrumental in thwarting the recognition processes instigated by the grades of likeness presented in all aspects of scenography. Denaturalisation[6] in this context refers to a conscious and deliberate distancing from the everyday reality that audiences experience outside the theatre, which is achieved by making strange – 'not like', and therefore in immediate close relationship with the previously discussed principle of 'grades of likeness' – those elements of scenography that are apparently recognisable. Denaturalisation should be considered in relation to and in conjunction with theatricalisation: where the former focuses on processes of distancing (from everyday life, from naturalistic imitation), the latter engages more explicitly with processes of heightening aesthetic expression. Evidently, the two usually work in tandem, and as with much of this book's analysis, the somewhat separate consideration of their appearance in Barker's scenography is to some extent arbitrary, and founded in subjective weighting of their effects.

In their extreme visual simplicity, Barker's sets offer openly theatrical approaches to the generation of places on stage through denaturalised space. Offering no indications of quotidian life, the near-empty spaces Barker's characters inhabit are thoroughly theatrical (in that they expressly foreground aesthetic, not practical qualities) and evidently designed for intricate choreographies of energetic speaking bodies that engage in conscious performances of self. Even seemingly domestic activities (e.g. the weaving of tapestry in *I Saw Myself*) are pulled away from the dreary reality of the process to present instead an intricate ballet of heightened gestures that attest to, rather than imitate, the action. The decidedly industrial materials that prevail throughout the set designs further enhance the sense of distance between the audience's lives outside the theatre, and the action on stage. The near-emptiness of the spaces serves to focus attention on the living, breathing, and speaking bodies of the actors. These are literally highlighted by select beams of lighting that serve an illuminating and sculpting function, not the more-or-less accurate imitation of particular times of day, or seasons, nor the manipulation of audience's emotional relation to the stage by way of colour temperature, etc. (cf. Morley in Kipp, 2016: 261). Lighting in Barker's scenography emphasises shape (especially that of the performing body) and disguises dimension (often of the physical stage space): it renders the stage space unlike anything the audience might encounter in their everyday life, denaturalising the suggested places of the plays' worlds. It emphasises the affective potential of the stage visuals, rendering them openly theatrical.

Similarly, the conscious historicisation of costumes at work in Barker's scenography engages in active processes of denaturalisation by distancing the visuality of the plays even further from everyday reality. Additionally, the combination of different elements of design from a range of time periods – though most often drawing on *haute couture* from the 1930s to the 1950s in key elements, particularly accessories such as gloves and hats[7] – allows a distancing from perceived historical reality as well: the stage world is not in the 1940s (as *The Fence* might be perceived), nor concretely 1st century (for the historical context of *Ursula*) or post-Second World War Germany (*Found in the Ground*). It is like those times and places (invoking the principle of grades of likeness) and also not (both/and): it is sometime else. The deliberate amplification of details differentiating the onstage attire from audiences' everyday wear is heightened further by the restriction of the colour palette to one that is mostly monochrome (subsequently imbuing any colours with heightened significance; this technique is also in use with the lighting) and the quasi-emblematic functions many of the figures attain through the combined semiotic impact of their roles and attire. The proliferation of high-status figures, especially women (queens, duchesses, etc.), that are designated as such through their attire is presented alongside service personnel (maids and valets), a juxtaposition which immediately opens up manifold socio-political contexts and diverse historical connotations.

In the same vein, the iconic qualities implicitly at work in an audience's reading of Barker's many brides and widows fragment the particularity of the characters across multiple times and places, whereby their artifice is magnified: both distinctly unique and potentially generalisable, the costumed bodies of Barker's figures are consciously and notably theatrical. Overall, the visuality of Barker's scenography emphasises beauty (in terms of aesthetic composition of the stage image, and its choreographic development over time) and affect over conventional storytelling in order to approximate the extremes of human experience, and seduce audiences to explore these limits imaginatively (cf. Johnson, 2012: 122). This process of presentation, rather than representation, closely aligns Barker's scenographic aesthetic with Lyotard's writings on the sublime in postmodern art (cf. 1989) as well as with contemporary scholarship on the sublime more generally (e.g. Johnson, Etlin, Zuckert, et al., 2012).

The aurality of Barker's plays equally engages the principles of denaturalisation and theatricalisation. It offers audiences a complex sonic scenography that clearly also engages the principle of 'grades of likeness', which are perhaps even more ambiguously perceived by virtue of the intangibility of the medium. This precariousness of potential (mis)identification of sounds and their sources already becomes part of the denaturalisation process due to the physical and conceptual separation of sounds from their source of origin,[8] which denies audiences the rationalising mechanism inherent in a clear assignation, and thereby rationalisation, of a sound and its genesis. Both sound and silence in Barker's scenography are rhythmical and choreographic in structuring time and space on and offstage, yet fail (deliberately) to concretise either. Consequently, audiences are left to make sense of the soundscape only ever in approximation. In conjunction with the visual components of scenography, the decidedly non-naturalistic sounds serve to further enhance the artificiality of the stage world. The combination of live performed sounds, including the often musical, poetic and expressive vocal performances by actors on stage, with abstract, non-diegetic and often acousmatic sound, atonal music as well as (pre-recorded) locational sounds, and denaturalised sounds (see Chapter 5, but also cf. the notion of *acousmêtric* sound, Home-Cook, 2015) offers a complimentary sonic scenography to the denaturalised visuals established by other scenographic means.

Barker himself uses this terminology of denaturalisation (cf. in Brown, 2011: 124) to describe aspects of scenography, which he sees as a means of ensuring the dominance of voice and performed text. However, I argue that the denaturalisation processes at work in all elements of his scenography contribute centrally to the overall effect of the plays, which greatly exceeds the already significant impact of the complex poetry of the spoken words. The seductiveness of Barker's scenography – beautiful, coherent, stylish, stark – undermines its own potential reduction to mere sensation by a twofold engagement of audience's imaginations: in denaturalising, the scenography is made uncomfortable, as conceptual resolution remains absent; the theatricalisation further foregrounds the dissimilarity of onstage and offstage worlds and heightens a sense of the scenography as an aesthetic event in its own right.

The principles of denaturalisation and theatricalisation work in tandem to generate conceptual distance (after the scenography initially fosters engagement by way of multiple possible, though never completed, associations), which is then in turn heightened by the intentional amplification of those aspects that are recognisably artificial. It is important to note here that this process is one of calculated oscillation that moves from fascination (with the stark beauty of the stage image) and curiosity (in identifying, consciously or unconsciously, associative content) to frustration and confusion (with the irresolvable and/or contradictory aspects of the scenography). The explicit thematic explorations of cultural taboos surrounding sexuality and death – recurrent centrally throughout Barker's playwriting – intensify this process. The unease inspired by these possibly contentious subject matters, but more importantly by the way in which they are explored, is scenographically furthered by a fundamental destabilisation of conventional meaning-making processes. These push not only towards a crisis of self (cf. Kristeva, 1982) and the dismantling of supposedly stable markers of the *status quo*, but also seek to trigger an ecstatic proliferation of imagination (cf. Guyer, 2012). The conscious and deliberate processes of undermining conventional meaning-making that are at work in Barker's scenography therefore can be compared to the processes of negative presentation (cf. Johnson, 2012; Lyotard, 1989, and Kristeva, 1982) that approach the failure of reason, and the suspension of self, both of which lie at the heart of the postmodern conception of the sublime. The close proximity of Barker's scenographic working principles to theories of the sublime is even more apparent in the next principle discussed here: playing with the limits of perception.

This play with perception involves both conceptual and physical limits, in which the latter often inform the understanding of the former. In terms of the stage spaces, the deliberate absence of concretising spatial markers that result in associative multiplication also serves to establish a sense of unreliable visual perception: with so few clues to locality, the spatio-temporal properties of space become conceptually unfixed. This process works in tandem with the lighting techniques – in particular side-lighting – which obscure the physical dimensions of the stage and skew depth perception. Not only is the audience left to repeatedly reassess the 'where' of the stage, its capability of discerning the 'what' is fundamentally destabilised by pushing their visual perception to its limits by use of select highlighting and deep shadows. The notion of the *Ganzfeld* effect ('complete/total field'; cf. Abulafia, 2016; Karasek, 2010) might be considered in particular relation to the ways in which lighting functions in Barker's scenography: the presentation of (seemingly) unstructured colour fields causes a disorientation that spectators may seek to ameliorate by looking for the apparently missing visual clues (cf. Abulafia, 2016: 58–61).

The select highlighting employed in the Wrestling School's productions might provide such a relief, carefully placed, which simultaneously results in a theatrical equivalent to filmic zoom: in the absence of other clear stimuli, the brain instinctively attaches importance to what few signals are clearly perceptible. However, the decidedly historical, yet essentially placeless costumes that would draw visual focus actually provide little, and mostly confusing, information to the spectators. The conscious absence of strong colour in the costume and lighting palette (cf. Morley in Kipp, 2016: 258) not only further skews depth perception, but might also contribute to an effect comparable to the *Ganzfeld* effect by further reducing sensory stimuli, leaving audiences to search for triggers in order to derive conceptual clues. The abundance of darkness flowing around and across the stage between thin corridors of very low light brings the visual scenography conceptually close to the process of privation which Lyotard locates at the heart of the sublime experience (cf. 1989): in the absence of sensory stimuli, imagination proliferates, and in the incongruity of reason in the face of multiplicities of meaning (cf. Kristeva, 1982), experience takes precedence. This process of imaginative excess that is triggered by a lack of concrete stimuli is in tension – and works in tandem – with the excess of stimuli that is present at other points in Barker's scenographic work, in particular the sonic content that includes the dense performed text with its multiple layers of possible meanings, and its affective impact as part of the overall soundscape. Consequently, Barker's scenography is both 'too much' and 'too little'.

The tension between the visible and the invisible in Barker's scenography complements that between the known and the unknown in a conscious cultural echo of Enlightenment thinking, in which the latter two (invisible/unknown) always appear as proportionately larger (physically and conceptually) than the former. This negative presentation of excessive content is a fundamental technique at work in Barker's scenography, which always foregrounds suggestion over declaration. The austere and minimal sets, so deliberately sparsely lit, deal in imaginative potentiality to the point of plethora, which paradoxically here is an effect of minimalism. What the space is, and is not, pales in view of what it could be, and mean, both of which are presented as (irresolvable) challenges to the audience.

This play with perceptual and conceptual limits also extends to the aurality of Barker's plays in multiple ways. On the one hand, the layering of live and recorded sounds of various volumes, pitches, and directions generates such a rich tapestry of sonic content that it may result in a sensory overload for the audience's hearing. In this excess, the resultant process of delocalisation (cf. Augoyard and Torgue, 2005: 38 and 130 ff.) – the (possibly consciously) erroneous identification of a sound's source – may be pushed to the point of ubiquity, in which the failure to identify the source of the sound is complete: it comes from nowhere and everywhere. George Home-Cook's definition of the *acousmêtric* (2015, following on from Chion, 1994) offers a useful extension to the notion of the ubiquity effect that also contains the both/

and principle: *acousmêtric* sound is located both inside and outside the stage image. The multiplicities of sounds that are perceptible to different degrees (in terms of their origin, direction, or volume) engage Barker's audiences in a sustained struggle to make sense of a play's aurality. The impossibility of identifying not only the source ('what') of a sound, but also its direction ('where') results in auditory straining, similar to the increased, frustrated search for concrete visual stimuli in the face of overwhelming stage images (even though what overwhelms might actually more frequently be the absence of conventional locational markers and visual narrative content). The overwhelming nature of this encounter leads me to consider the ubiquity effect as an acoustic equivalent to the *Ganzfeld* effect, both of which are at work in Barker's scenography, playing with the audience's limits of perception. This is furthered by the deliberate and careful use of punctuating silences that structure space and time on stage. These silences arise both from the performed text in tense pauses at the points where Barker's figures' eloquence fails them (cf. Placida in *Ursula*), and the sudden noticeable reduction or cutting out of ambient noise (cf. the opening of *Found in the Ground*, or *Blok/Eko*). In the wake of this abrupt change to the aurality of a production, the audience is left to strain their hearing for stimuli to replace those it suddenly lost. In particular the silences generated through the paring away of ambient sound content draw attention, on the one hand, to the sound that was quite possibly only registered subconsciously, and on the other to its sudden lack. In this auditory lacuna, any other sounds attain much greater significance (in an acoustic 'zoom') as the process of attending comes to the fore (cf. Home-Cook, 2015).

Simultaneously, Barker plays with the incongruences that arise between diegetic and non-diegetic sound, the distinction of which is not always entirely clear (cf. *Und* and *Blok/Eko*). The intentional deprivation of clearly identifiable sound content (in terms of both origin and perceptibility) acts as a complimentary sonic strategy to the visuals of resonant emptiness that dominate the onstage space and its conceptual expansion beyond. The concept of totality, or the absolute, that lies at the heart of both *Ganzfeld* and ubiquity effect once more draws Barker's scenographic principles and postmodern conceptions of the sublime into a close relationship: the attempt to negatively present the absolute and engage an unbounded imagination (cf. Johnson, 2012) is an endeavour that not only runs up against the limits of art (cf. Lyotard, 1989), but also refuses comprehension and analysis in equal measure. The audience is left with a potentially devastating experience that transcends reason and crucially throws their understanding of selfhood into question. Using the physical limits of human perceptual ability, Barker's scenography engages the reflexive relationship between lived experience (phenomenology) and abstracted, often retrospective analysis (semantics and semiotics) thereof, frustrating the latter in order to throw attention back again to the former, which in turn generates further attempts at comprehension: the aporia at the heart of this process is where I propose to situate the final working principle of Barker's scenography as identified over the course of this book, the scenographic sublime.

The scenographic sublime is not so much an individual principle or clearly definable process, nor a specific moment, but rather the culmination of effects that result from the interaction of the other working principles here identified: the principle of both/and results in a proliferation of potentially meaningful content, which in turn conjures the grades of likeness that become starting points for cascades of incomplete associations, and subsequent attempts at meaning-making. The oscillation between the various incomplete associations leads to a process of denaturalisation and theatricalisation in which the distance to everyday reality is repeatedly affirmed and the artificiality of the onstage world is heightened.

As outlined above, the scenographic sublime is situated in a processual and relational gap between experiential and cognitive engagement with the scenography. By foregrounding affective encounters with the work, without completely rejecting attempts to comprehend it in a conventional, rational, and narrative manner, yet frustrating such approaches repeatedly, audiences are challenged to contemplate the limits of their rational understanding as much as they are invited to engage in a process of unbinding their imaginations from habitual (personal and collective cultural) constrictions. In Barker's scenography, beauty, affect, and expressiveness supersede rationally comprehensible meaning and conventional narrative. However, it does not simply take those principles (beauty, affect, expressiveness) as their own ends in a cultural vacuum. Instead it offers them as potentially contradictory carriers of significance[9] that seduce the audience into wrestling not only with the 'object' presented (the scenography) but also with their fundamental conceptions of existence (in a socio-political context) and subjective identity. In engaging the full range of emotions onstage in separation of their conventional value (where beauty is good, disgust is bad, and desire is problematic), not singly, but as a conceptual and experiential multi-track, in which contradictions are open to exploration and new relations between them generated, Barker's scenography offers audiences a rupture of thinking and being that sits alongside the trajectory of the postmodern sublime. The scenographic sublime might therefore be identified as an experience arising from a series of interacting processes between different aspects of scenography that aim to heighten and proliferate sensation (often by privation/lack; cf. Lyotard, 1989), undermine reason (by a conscious absence of unambiguous resolution; cf. Johnson, 2012), and deny value judgement and conclusion (at least in the moment in which it is experienced). It does so by presenting the diverse aspects of scenography as of equal importance, and force a radical re-evaluation of the supposed stability of individual subject identity (in its particular cultural and historical context; cf. Lingis, 2000; Kristeva, 1989; Lyotard, 1989, 1991).

The existence of scenography in a liminal circumstance between real, physical time and space, and the multiplicities of possible times and spaces it may conjure or attest to in production, highlights its fundamental potential for radical difference in the experiences it triggers in audiences. This radical difference does not only extend to alterities of being that are presented onstage and their subjective reception by individual audience members, but also contains the possibilities of spilling offstage, inciting a crucial re-evaluation of selfhood and being both individually and collectively. Barker's scenography actively harnesses these potentials by way of selectively employed principles (discussed above) that complement the conceptual content of the plays which are so frequently focussed on difference, performance of self, and the limits of imagination and being. The irresolution at the heart of Barker's explorations of death, desire and the 'ecstasy of vanishing meaning' (Rabey, 2009: 18) leads me to the long-standing philosophical concept of the sublime, which over time has come to signify the attempt to articulate the limits of being and experience in their irreconcilable contradiction.

The development of discourse for the exploration of intangible, mutable concepts such as the sublime – in particular regarding philosophical developments following the Second World War that sought to address the absolute failure of Enlightenment thinking in light of the unspeakable, incomprehensible horrors of that time – is efficacious insofar as it generates the possibility of constellational (cf. Weber-Nicholsen, 1997) and negative (cf. Lyotard, 1989; Kristeva, 1982) presentation of concepts and ideas. However, this approximation is necessarily partial, subjective and unfixed. The sublime therefore resists the efficacy of discourse at the same time as it invites its own development and analysis through discourse. Similarly, the practice of scenography, and the academic field of study accompanying it, require structure and invite analysis but are ultimately resistant to a fixed imposition of both. Barker's emphasis on tragedy, the beauty of pain, and the ecstasy of suffering actively seeks out the limits of reason, a thematic movement that is echoed by the complex interactions between different aspects of scenography, which further open up the aporia between expression and the unpresentable (cf. Lyotard, 1989). The imaginative movement of conclusive description and analysis of both scenography and the sublime is therefore asymptotic: towards, but never touching.

Notes

1 Barker's scenography very much utilises absence in this regard, too, as it results in a straining, searching for rationally comprehensible content.
2 Thank you to Prof. David Ian Rabey for coining this phrase in conversation with me.
3 This is necessarily a Western European cultural context. The exploration of a European identity and sensibility notably recurs throughout Barker's work, explicitly or implicitly; he also addresses it frequently in interviews and in his theoretical writings.
4 In fact, Barker argues that the landscapes of his plays are 'manifestations of consciousness' (1997: 21) that attest to 'spiritual despair' (Ibid.) and 'frustrated longing' (Ibid.) that become a ground for 'potential reconstruction' (Ibid.: 22) of self, and society.

5 This is a term which presents an excellent example of the interplay between the principles of 'both/and' and 'grades of likeness'.

6 Though this process may bring to mind the distancing effect sought by Brecht through *Verfremdung*, I would argue the crucial difference is that Barker seeks to distance theatre from everyday life, not the audience from the experience of the play; in fact, the denaturalisation process in Barker could be seen to undermine attempts at critical distance, which would rely on establishing points of contact with everyday life and contemporary issues.

7 Shoes present a somewhat different matter, as Barker's choice of high heels is more crucially connected to the notion of status, and the generation of a seductive body through movement, than to the historicising and denaturalising process.

8 Whilst this might once again bring to mind Brecht's working methods, I think it is important to distinguish: both Barker and Brecht seek to express that the stage world is not real; however, Brecht's intention is to establish a critical distance from what is on stage, whereas Barker seeks distance from the outside world. Brecht seeks to appeal to the audience's reason, Barker to their imaginative capabilities.

9 Significance here foregrounds a sense of importance without necessarily being able to concretely identify how it arises, or what it might attest to, rather than the term 'meaning' that one might otherwise employ.

Appendix

Transcript Interview Cardiff 20th October 2014
Ace McCarron (lighting designer)

LK: Are you familiar with the term scenography? If so, how would you define it?

AMcC: Scenography is a term that people don't use so much in this country (the UK). It's an academic discipline in America and people tend to use that term in Europe as well, in the Netherlands and Germany, where I worked. As I understand the academic discipline of scenography in America, it takes to cover all the design of a show. You will find that a lighting designer in a show in America frequently has a degree in scenography, whereby they have also had to study costume and costings, and so on. Scenography as a discipline in America is a much broader thing compared to over here where courses tend to be more narrowly structured, even though one specialises later on (in the United States). Scenography is maybe a more useful term that should be employed over here because it refers to the design as a component of the experience of the performance. If you look at very old British opera programmes, they will have 'settings by' or 'cloths by'; the cloths were painted and flown in. There is now a movement in Germany to do opera with cloths and people in costumes as the composer intended; it is a retrograde step because we demand a little more of scenography nowadays as the experience of the show. If you look at an artist like Robert Wilson, sometimes the scenography is the main feature of what he does, which may move it closer to the notion of an installation; which is arguably part of the Wrestling School's way of creating a show as well.

LK: I read your article for the forthcoming publication by Andy Smith and Jim Reynolds. It is entitled 'Amplifying Catastrophe' and in it you write of the 'amplification of the moment'. Is this how you might define your role when working with the Wrestling School?

AMcC: With the Wrestling School I would say this amplification is always part of the task. When I worked with Théâtre de Complicité many years ago, in certain circumstances my role was not to amplify the action. This was because a lot of their work was gestural; there was a physical invention of the scenography at play, which invites the audience to imagine. As such, if I applied my skill, knowledge, and experience to that, I am subtracting from such moments. In such cases, my job is to let them do the scenography. This is a rule for me: who is doing this moment? Where is this moment arriving from? Can I help? Should I help? Should I step back from this moment and say, no, we must not notice a change of lighting here, we must not be distracted. We have built some kind of original continuum for the show to take place in, and that continuum can frequently be very fragile. Therefore, if the lighting becomes a distraction, it breaks it. As such, I am a kind of dramaturgical lighting designer, as opposed to an artistic, graphic, or impressionistic lighting designer. It is not about spectacle. I have always been very interested in the plays I have been working on. For me, becoming a lighting designer from working as a technician was a way to get into the rehearsal room. For a stage manager, becoming a deputy stage manager is the same process. Some deputy stage managers get a lot of experience, but they do not get promoted, as that would take them out of the rehearsal room again. This has been a long fascination for me, ever since working at the Citizens' Theatre in Glasgow. In becoming a lighting designer, I placed myself in a position where I had access to the decision making process, understanding that, and contributing to them.

LK: In your article, you also mention your experiences in opera. Does that shape your approach as a lighting designer?

AMcC: Working in opera makes you aware of rhythms, which can exist in silence, as much as anywhere else. It makes you think about what will govern your decision making with regards to how you place your work in time, changes of lighting in time. Sound will heavily dictate what I do, as it is usually there before I come into it. The rhythms with the performers are already there and I must fit in with that. I think that Giacomo Puccini is one of the world's most underrated dramatists. Most people studying drama in the world of academia rule out opera. Puccini is very skilled as a dramatist, he placed it very strictly in the tempo of the music, as opera composers should do. I remember working on a production of *Tosca*, which was revived by a director who said to me, referring to the eight bars of music between Angelotti hiding in the church and the jolly sacristan's arrival at the beginning, 'listen, Ace, Mr Puccini has written us a lighting cue'. That has always made me listen harder to operas to find out if there are structures within it that I necessarily have to obey. Surprisingly, that also happens with Arthur Miller. If you ignore those structures, you do it at the cost of transmitting the play to an audience. The audience is charmed and enthralled and also engaged by such rhythms. Therefore, in every play I have done, I have written down these sound-light cues.

LK: Would you extend that to include Barker's writing, which I would argue is quite musical itself?

AMcC: Yes, it is. Normally, I know precisely what to do, what is being asked of me. Occasionally I can even pre-empt it. However, Howard is not a particularly slavish follower of his own stage directions, so until I join

rehearsals, I only have the text to work with. Therefore, I can begin to conjecture plans in my head of how the cue structure will work. Sometimes
I then find out that Barker as director has moved in a slightly different
direction. I come in with a 'chapter and verse' structure for a piece only
to find out there is something else happening. But then there are plays
like *Judith*, which is one scene. A lot goes on in it, but the sense of location never changes. This is very unusual for Howard; but perhaps it is
more common nowadays. The first plays I worked on, *Seven Lears, The
Europeans* and *Victory*, were epics in comparison to what he does now.
When we returned to the Sheffield Crucible a year after doing *Seven
Lears*, with another show in the same time scale, we wondered how we
had achieved so much content, so much staging activity into that show
because we must have worked very, very quickly to do so. *Seven Lears*
was the first Howard Barker play that I lit, in which I had to find out for
myself what exactly that role entailed for me.

LK: Do you find that there are any challenges that are particular to working
with the Wrestling School and Howard Barker?

AMcC: I think it is the extreme level of ambition that makes it special. When
the Wrestling School was formed, Kenny Ireland (the director at the
time) invited a lot of his friends who had been with him at the National
Theatre to work on those productions. They seemed to fall into a pattern
of working. It is remarkable how much you soak up from the mood and
the energy in a room, regarding pace and transitions, etc. Those were big
shows for me. I worked very, very hard on them. After that, you kind of
walk out into the rest of the profession with a sense of what can be achieved
of a play and also how good a play has to be to invite that. To me, a good
play invites strong theatricality in its performance. Shakespeare invites
immense theatricality in every instant of his plays. I really believe that the
experience of watching drama in a theatre space should be different to
other media. There is something about being in the room, which makes
that drama more powerful. You look to a text to acknowledge that that is
an effect of voice from a good actor. Howard Barker is consistently able
to deliver that. You may find that other playwrights achieve that occasionally. The whole notion of poetry has been extremely unfashionable,
I do not know why, since it is still core to our actor training. Maybe the
realism of 1960s drama made that unfashionable and remains so until
today. I am mystified by this. Notably, Howard, despite his ability to
deliver this, is not significantly more popular. It is another mystery.

LK: Could you talk me through the stages you work through when working
with the Wrestling School?

AMcC: It has varied. Especially with Kenny Ireland as director it was markedly different, planning *Seven Lears* because it was such a complicated
show; *Victory,* too, as he was originally in that piece. He had asked me
about that play, as I saw it when it played at the Royal Court. There is a
scene in which they bury a rifle. The whole of the design began from that

necessity to have lift-out sections in the floor, so that the rifle could in fact be buried. This idea carried over into all the scene changes in which where sections of the floor were lifted up and shuffled around. I told him that the effect of that, to me, was that it turned into seven little plays, with great discontinuity. On the final incarnation of that production in Greenwich Theatre I sat in to watch and realised that he had really taken on that problem to the extent that people would invade a scene towards its end, there would be a short musical piece and the character that would remain for the next scene would be picked out by lighting. The next scene would begin as people were still leaving the stage from the scene change. The gaps between scenes had been minimised and there was an emphasis on the character that remained to enter the next scene. This was a year before the production, so a very long timeframe. On the other hand, I now have done so much work with Howard Barker and the production budgets are now so small that I walk into rehearsals quite late. I try to be there as much as I can, but they mostly rehearse in London. I do not live there anymore. There is almost an unspoken dialogue happening between Howard and me by now about what needs to happen. For *The Ecstatic Bible* in Adelaide I attended quite a lot of rehearsals prior to going to Australia. When we got to Adelaide, we had two weeks to merge Brink Company with the Wrestling School. I was sitting with Howard and the director of Brink and would turn to them and say 'lights will come on over there and here and will develop like this', and look at them to ensure they understood what I was saying and give them a chance to raise objections. I did not ask them directly, there was so little time, in a 7 hour 45 minutes play with a four day technical rehearsal you have to keep the pace up. We were forced to work at that speed. The play includes my favourite scene of any Howard Barker play; it is called *A Museum*, which was done with four lanterns, in which the dead reawaken to listen to a poem. In the middle of all that pace and excitement, you sometimes get to your good stuff. I've had a similar experience with Philip Glass' *The Trial* in London just now, which we lit at great speed.

Sometimes when working with the Wrestling School I have to ask actors to, say, come downstage by 30 cm. It is not that you are trying to alter the blocking that the actors and directors have worked out. Doing fast deals about things, you are trying to police it. Especially when using razor-thin slices of light. We do not quite have the resources to do the fabulous sets we used to have with the Wrestling School; we are not able to do that anymore. But we have simpler ways of doing such things now. Of course, I usually try to achieve something that is simple and tourable most of the time. Again, we do not tour so much nowadays. Once, when working at the Riverside Studios, we took down the masking and revealed their lantern rack, which was in one corner; eight bars of lighting, one on top of the other. There were maybe 30 fresnels we had not used. There was a sort of gallery opening after the show, so I asked the crew there whether we could plug all these unused lanterns in and to my surprise they agreed. It was a fabulous effect and it happened quite accidentally. You always have to work from a basis of knowing the play and what excites the people you are working with.

LK: Could you elaborate on the exchange and input you get from Howard Barker and also from other designers, such as Paul Bull (sound design)?

AMcC: When Paul creates a soundscape – and I remember particularly *Ursula: Fear of the Estuary* where we had a factory hooter; Howard found this a useful sonic parenthesis in the show; he kept moving the sound cues around from day to day. This was something I did not have to follow as it was just a sound effect. But sometimes, Howard will turn to Paul and ask about other sound cues that feed to me, when the sound becomes a character in the play with which the actors have to interact. Very rarely will I ask for the sound to be changed. I used to work with John Leonard, a sound designer at the Royal Shakespeare Company, who used to say lighting designers are lucky, as usually the directors will request some changes of them whereas it will be immediately apparent when a sound cue has failed. Lighting is usually more reflective of the mood on stage. Sound therefore takes precedence, also with regard to interacting with the sound of the actors' voices. So I follow the trail from Howard to Paul to me in many circumstances, though not all. Occasionally, quite violent music will interject into a scene, indicating a character's torment and I have to ask myself does that need to be reflected in the space in terms of what I do with lighting? If I do it there, do I then have to do it repeatedly throughout the play, by which time it loses its effect? This is the kind of question I ask of Howard, I point out things that might become tedious, things that might be distracting or draw too much attention to themselves. If you are engaging with an actor as a spectator in a moment in which their character is going through something terribly profound, you will pay less attention to the forces of the production that alter their environment, such as lighting and sound. You engage instantly with that person, if you are capable of empathising with them. In such moment you can get away with quite violent changes in sound and lighting and sta-ging; this leads you into very interesting areas. Whilst we might not con-sciously notice those changes, you feel them subconsciously. You make that moment stronger, amplify it in effect, without drawing any attention to the scenographic means by which you do that. The point is to make them feel the emotions of that moment without distraction, as much as possible. When discussing such choices with a director, one has to become quite articulate about one's understanding of the scene and the emotional affect it has that governs the decision making process in the design. The director can then disagree with your response or not. That is perhaps the most creative aspect of my job, figuring out my emotional responses to the performances I am watching and then articulating those. The tech-nical aspects are much less interesting to me. As a lighting designer you have to fulfil both those roles, the technician and the informed audience member, which involve highly different intellectual standpoints, respectively; which may not have any crossover in the end. I am no longer excited by equipment. I no longer know how to operate the current lighting control consoles. I normally get someone else to do that for me nowadays.

LK: You have mentioned the exordia, both in our correspondence prior to this meeting and in your article. I wonder if you could elaborate on that: do you see a special scenographic significance in them? To me, they work as a kind of thematic preview.

AMcC: Yes, they do. It is rather strange, because this year we went to France to do *The Gaoler's Ache for the Nearly Dead*, which was the first play in which an exordium appeared in the text for a Howard Barker play. But then it disappeared again. Maybe this is something you could conjecture as a trend in Howard's writing, that he would try to create a world for the play to begin in, but then again not. The written exordium of that play is the gaoler of the play appearing at a hatch, looking at the stage. The exordium we actually used was entirely different. Maybe *Judith* was the first exordium we had, in Howard's production. He perhaps saw that his roles as writer and director could be separate. His own detachment from his text when he is directing a show is alarmingly good. Maybe he saw that the creation of the exordium was something that did not come from the play script, but rather arise out of rehearsal. Of course, he always had the chance to do that. So rather than pluck a moment out of the play and place it in the exordium, it is more about finding a harmonisation of an event in the exordium that then relates to an event in the play. I think it is fair to say that when the play actually begins, there is a surprise that the actual text will arise out of this exordium. Because you experience the exordium and then the play begins, which does not immediately grow out of that exordium. It is another device to do some work in the imagination of the audience before the play actually begins. They are hard to tech; they are very hard to do. Perhaps *(Uncle) Vanya* was before *Judith*? It had an extremely elaborate exordium which took hours and hours to tech, in almost every venue we took it to. Howard then went on to write *The Forty*, which to me reads almost like an extended series of exordia. This may have been based on me turning to Howard and telling him that the process of creating the technical rehearsal for the show was extremely boring after creating the exordium. Sometimes they contain these incredibly loud sound effects, just to suppress any kind of conversation that audience members might have with one another. To place them into this experience from the moment they walk into the theatre. Part of the exordium for *The Ecstatic Bible*, which only had four elements in it, were about 12 refugees that would appear on one side of the stage with suitcases and overcoats and cross the stage; when they were in the middle, a fast jet would cross overhead and they would all duck until the noise of the jet was gone, go offstage, and come back round to do it again maybe three minutes later. The man who did the sound for that show had recorded an F/A-18 Hornet at the Australian Grand Prix; your first experience of the show would be those jets, which you could hear a block away from the theatre, so you would not even know where the sound was coming from. Once in the foyer, you would then realise that it was coming from behind the theatre's doors and you had to consider that you would have to walk in there. It was not dangerously loud, but loud enough to be uncomfortable. It was great.

LK: What would you say are the guiding principles at work in the Wrestling School's work? You mention in your article 'a judicious use of darkness', for example.

AMcC: Many of my friends come out of a Wrestling School performance and have been quite affected by something someone has said in it. Howard's plays talk about things that are not popularised on the media. He looks for those silences about certain kinds of ideas. In one particular production, five or six of my friends came up to me afterwards to say that what he had written contained an idea that they might not have been prepared to hear; something that reaches deep down into your psyche and shakes it up. The poem *Hated Nightfall* is incredibly strong, I remember when I first read it. It had all sorts of resonances for me that I would not usually realise are affecting my psyche, that I might not usually be paying attention to, but they are at work. That, for me, is the primary effect of these plays. Maybe they are shaped up to elucidate certain moments, moods, and terms of sensibility. Just in the course of discussion of those things, there will be an idea that you have not considered before which may have a profound effect on your thinking. Or the play may contain something you have been thinking about which then is uttered, is said, and given credence as a legitimate human response in the course of it. You have to be aware of that when you are delivering those scenes, this crucial articulation of an idea any moment might contain. For example, the idea of virginity in *Ursula* is something that I had never participated in a conversation about, its potential value, and how that has changed over time. Howard wrote an entire play. Some people were quite hostile in their reaction to it. There is a debate in Howard's plays about the viewer and what they bring into the theatre and how they might be transformed. The events that forge a curiosity about one's self, other people, and how society and the system work have to be served up very carefully. It is something the Wrestling School does very well, to enter into conversation about that. Howard has a great instinct for that. In the coffee breaks, I have come across actors discussing life itself and the events of the play; it is very reassuring that actors of that level of experience can and do still draw so much from the work. Perhaps the single strongest effect of Howard Barker's plays is that they excite actors. Not many playwrights have that kind of force in their performance. These plays use an actor's full training: their full voice, their intellect, their access to their animal being. All these are needed in the performance of those parts. For me, Barker has strong resonances with Shakespeare. There is a very strong resonance between their respective ambitions; they use the same kind of actor. That is why it surprises me that not more people see the merit of Howard's work and that it is not more influential. It is a mystery.

LK: Would you consider there to be a hierarchy of production elements? Does that depend on the piece?

AMcC: Part of the reason of my long-standing relationship with the Wrestling School is based on the fact that the technical aspects of lighting are a mystery to Howard, as is the case for most directors. Kenny Ireland did know and that shapes the way we worked together on light. It was reasonably easy to harmonise with what he thought a show can and should do in terms of lighting. Howard is perhaps less capable of isolating the individual components because he is so influential in the overall appearance of the show, from a physical point of view. He is more trusting towards me in the work that I create; he notices everything. But because I know his work so well, I can somewhat anticipate what is needed, what can, and what should happen in terms of lighting at any one point in time in his plays. In terms of precedence, it is difficult to say. Throughout the Tomas Leipzig era, there were less and less resources to create staging effects. As such, the spaces became plainer, which afforded me greater freedom, allowing me to place lights more freely throughout the space. As a result, I could do a lot of work with a small number of lanterns, which is desirable for a touring piece. The set is designed first; if I have a chance to raise any pressing concerns or objections, I get a chance to do that. I very rarely do that, though. I also like a challenge. So the set design will govern what I do, but I have a great freedom within that to do what I want to, to achieve certain things. When we did *The Gaoler's Ache* in Lyon, there was a moment when Howard wanted to emphasise someone climbing a ladder and I informed him I did not have a light to do that at that moment. I had to stop the technical rehearsal, which I really dislike doing and try to minimise as much as possible, and thankfully was able to solve the problem very quickly. There are few instances of this happening, where Howard will request an emphasis or change; I might have a lantern standing by, ready to show him some options. The effect of what I call 'enhanced presence' is done in a certain way; there is not a single Barker play I know of that does not call for this effect, where you contrast an actor against a dark background or are in control of how you contrast an actor against a background. You can cue this so the audience suddenly feels close to an actor. Other than that, a hierarchy or precedence is hard to quantify because the productions are built on long-term relationships. If I was working on a Barker play with a different, new director, and new designer, there would likely be a clearer definition of precedence in the different elements of the production than it would be with the Wrestling School. I suppose that would hold true for any organisation in which people tend to work together a lot over time. The nature of that relationship is rather hard to articulate, though. Also, there are not many organisations in Britain that have been working together for such a long time. I have worked almost as long with the Wrestling School as I have for Music Theatre Wales. But perhaps because the latter involves music, it warrants less discussion. However, something like *The Trial*, which I am working on at the moment, has a lot of details in the staging, which then again results in more discussion. The last few Wrestling School productions have been studio-based and therefore much simpler. Howard is very clever in the way he uses space and has never stretched the budget. The stage for the production of *The Gaoler's Ache* in France was made from cardboard boxes, which appeared unlikely to work, but it did, and incredibly well. A lot can be achieved with a few elements, such as the boxes, a white ladder, and then lots of lighting. There is a lot of trust built into working like this.

LK: Could you elaborate on your term and concept of 'enhanced presence' and how this works through light?

AMcC: I was interviewed for the position of lighting designer for a production of *Idomeneo*, together with two others. I was asked what I could do for the production and replied that I could have *Idomeneo* standing downstage centre, yet make an audience feel he was right next to them. I got the job. I then certainly made that effect happen. What I did was to put a follow spot in the most inconvenient point, next to the deputy stage manager, and in the opposite corner. It was doubly inconvenient as the beams ended up blinding the operators and deputy stage managers. But the rest of the theatre was in complete blackness and there was a glowing man standing in front of an orchestra pit. This production won the Olivier Award for operatic achievement that year. Critics that usually never write about lighting mentioned it in the reviews. One even wrote 'spot-lit by Ace McCarron'. He clearly did not know how to express himself in this regard, but he felt compelled to mention it. The lighting was in complete control of the creation of such a moment in that instance.

Enhanced presence is about the level of light on an actor in relation to what is behind them and changes in that relationship over time. It is achieved via affect, it is not something the audience necessarily consciously notice, but they feel it. In an opera, the starting point of such changes are quite easily identified as they are written into the music. The best way to achieve this effect is with side-lighting because you avoid hitting the floor as much as you might otherwise; instead you lose the beam of light in the wings on the other side. This is something we have always done with the Wrestling School. That way, you can get a high level of lighting on the actor, without disturbing the picture on stage. I have to say that Andy Phillips, the lighting designer that worked on the first Wrestling School show, was a particular master of this technique. His concentration was immense and he worked very quickly. He was a great plotter of lights, rather than someone who arrives with a fully drawn plan. Consequently, I already knew those techniques when I started working with the Wrestling School. I found that I was trying to get this way of lighting into every show I did; sometimes there are no front of house lights, all lanterns are on stage. This might then make it difficult to rig on tour. But I am more relaxed about such things nowadays. *Seven Lears* was perhaps the peak of my side-lighting mania, you might say. It was hard work, but it did produce astonishingly good result.

I met Sean O'Callaghan last week who was performing in Cardiff; he reminded me of something he said to me when we were in Copenhagen with *(Uncle) Vanya*: 'Where is the fucking light in this scene, Ace?' I told him that it was there, if he moved as had had done in rehearsals, he would find some light on him. He expressed doubts, so I suggested – and this is what he reminded me of last week – that he sit in the auditorium. He did and saw the lighting was working very, very well. He said that this then made him work much harder, especially when finding his lights. That production would be an extreme example of enhanced presence, because often the light would come from behind the actor and the beams of light existed inside a dark space. It is a tricky thing to do when you are forming a corridor of light, to ensure that it is straight. When the beam of light then hits the floor and an actor stands on it, then they are actually lit. If you slant the beam, then their heads are not lit. *The Trial* is a good example, as we chopped up the light in quite an unusual way and somehow we still ended up with the actors in the light. To some extent this is due to me examining rehearsals and deciding where to place lights to that they do a lot of work for me. I think it worked so well that the performers were drawn to the light; they felt comfortable in their positions then. I have worked with most of the singers before and they are very disciplined about their movements, and very aware. The deal you have to make, the balance you have to strike between where you place a beam of light and where you want the actors to be is quite crucial to the concept of enhanced presence. In *(Uncle) Vanya* there was only one actor who had no sense of where their lights were. I do not disparage actors like that at all; they have a lot of other things to worry about at any one point. In that production it did mean that I had to take them around the stage to make sure they knew where to be when in order to make sure they would be lit. Andy Phillips used to say that actors are either moths, who will find the light, or moles that will gravitate away from it. It is true. Nowadays, the moths vastly outnumber the moles. But I like the challenge to make sure everyone is where they need to be.

In *The Europeans*, there is a scene when Staremberg is hiding in a room, witnessing a conversation between two people and the curtains are drawn. The Empress comes in and demands the curtains be flung open. At this point, there were two beams of light, maybe six inches wide, diagonally down the back wall. I had stood in the beams myself, identifying a brick of the wall on either side for guidance. I had then gone up to the actor playing Staremberg, whose radar for such things was perhaps not the best and shown him how to orient himself by using those two bricks to find his position. When we were about to begin the technical rehearsal, Kenny Ireland asked me about the lights in the back and I replied that those were the specials for the actor playing Staremberg in that scene. He immediately asserted that he would never find the lights. As they came up, the two lights came down the actor's face and across his chest, just as intended.

On the same stage, we had an actress in a chair in a fixed position, which is great for me as it allows me to make the beams very, very small. But if she turned her head, because of what she was wearing, she effectively disappeared. The show also had a wonderful set that was on casters with structures called 'periactoids'. Whenever we were at a new venue, I would focus the lights and then we would arrange the set accordingly. One of the periactoids had an actor inside, to move it; they had to find their places extremely well in order for my lighting to work. There was only one moment when it did not work.

This show was important to me for another reason. The final stage direction reads 'a firework trickles down the sky'. We had a fireworks display with lights flashing from the wings but we did not quite have the time to really solve this direction until Kenny Ireland and I were at Greenwich theatre and were told the set would be four hours late. Kenny and I marched out into Greenwich market and came back with four very large golfing umbrellas. We hammered the spike of one into a flat shape, drilled a hole into it, and hung it upstage with the fabric stripped off. Then we attached little lamps to all the spokes and created this device whereby these little points of light would splay out as we faded them up. It was technically very difficult and we had to train the stage management to get it just right. My relationship with Howard Barker was not particularly well developed at that time, because he was merely the playwright who sat in on rehearsals and Kenny dealt with him, but not me. During the dress rehearsal for the show, Howard leapt out of his seat at the fireworks, saying this was brilliant and we had to get it more into the show. I disagreed at this point, as I felt the repetition would become tedious. He agreed.

LK: In your article you write about 'identifiable style': would you consider there to be a distinct Wrestling School aesthetic, or a style? What would it be and would you see a difference between style and aesthetic?

AMcC: I think there is definitely an aesthetic and/or a style associated with the scripts. I also think that productions by other companies that have failed to take this into account have failed massively. I would say the aesthetic of a Howard Barker play is strong in that it is set in a world that is plausibly human, but fictional. The style of it has more to do with the language and the structure of the play that has been created. I would probably attribute that to style, rather than aesthetic. There is probably a particular cocktail of these two things that varies from play to play, but remains strong and identifiable throughout. As such, if we have succeeded as a company with the Wrestling School it is because we have identified that particular aesthetic and used the different production elements to support it. The available resources always place some restrictions, of course. Time is a great restriction in particular; and the limited opportunities to stage these plays. I think if we are successful it is because we have used our resources well and identified the best way in which to use them to create this balance of style and aesthetic. The most frequent question asked by actors who come to see these productions is 'how do you do it?' One could be pragmatic and say, we open the text at page one and take it from there. Actually, if you have worked with the same company for more than one production, you can stay up all night talking about this company's processes, personalities, and aesthetic decisions. But if I compare it to, for example, the Citizens' Theatre in Glasgow, because their style was equally theatrical, you would not be able to identify how they arrived at their decisions. There is just something in the air with such companies that arises out of people working together again and again over time. This atmosphere informs the entire work process. The same holds true for the Wrestling School, where you will have a varying mixture of old and new company members, and either the new ones get it, or they do not. If they do not, they might even be quite hostile to it all. It is fascinating to watch how the aesthetic is taking hold of people and the harmonisation of the new people with the existing core. It requires dedication, technique, and imagination. Having Howard Barker in the room with you helps the development of those, of course.

LK: I keep returning to your article, because it is lovely to encounter a scenographic practitioner that is so articulate about what they do but moreover what their work does. You note a 'change of rationale in set design' over time, would you say there is an identifiable evolution of scenography in the Wrestling School productions? How would you consider that to be evidenced?

AMcC: In a similar way to Kenny involving friends in the casting of the shows, the design was also approached. It was certainly considered an equally important task to find good designers for the shows. The Wrestling School has had some wonderful designers involved with them. Some of them were more successful than others. Obviously, Howard must have had ideas prior even to the formation of the company; an aesthetic bubbling away beneath the surface that is premised on sparsity and primacy of language which could only really emerge once he became the director. With simpler designs I of course had more to do, too. I think Howard's influence over the design processes and his increasing specifications of what the designs should be became stronger and probably a little more refined; though I have to say that they were refined very carefully and when he got more involved from *Ursula* onwards, things became very exciting. They were very strong designs. *Ursula* looked terrific. It looked brilliant and actually was quite a flexible space. The technical realisation of the set had a cable system in the floor that could be used to pull set pieces and furniture on and off. It was also a metal floor, which afforded me immense lighting opportunities. Howard's imagination has always been very theatrical and he has been very skilled in deciding how that imagination could manifest itself in very strong moments. At the same time, he has always afforded me great flexibility in what I do so that I can assist him in achieving that. Furthermore, the work operated on a similar principle to the exordia, whereby something tangential to the potential expectations regarding the setting is taken and made surreal. It is something unformed, so you have to take what you are watching and the text and tie them together for yourself, which makes you engage deeper and think harder, also afterwards, regarding public or private context, or social and historical context. You have to do some work. I do not know when this particular imagination began, but Howard is a visual artist as well, of course. For all I know, his dissatisfaction with the process goes way back. I am now a dramaturge with the National Theatre of Wales and part of my remit is to ensure that the thinking of a playwright that is truly original is not suppressed by the production that it gets. Perhaps that is why Howard took on those roles because he was dissatisfied with the ways in which his work was being realised in terms of the scenography. My contribution was perhaps facilitated by that, too.

LK: The remit of my study is from 1998 until 2012, so from *Ursula* to *Blok/ Eko*. Do you have any production within that time that stands out in your memory?

AMcC: There are actually quite a lot. It is hard to detect a movement in all that, since it is the great quality of artists to address themselves to many different things. Yes, there may be an overriding aesthetic and a style of the Wrestling School and Howard Barker, but alongside that there are the different views on what Howard is portraying in the context of the play; therefore, considering my contribution in a play like *Und*, for example, in comparison to *Ursula* is very difficult because I do not just address an aesthetic and a style, but also a topic and a spatial contextualisation of that topic. *Ursula* is much more of an epic for example, but I think *Und* is one of Howard's strongest pieces. The extremely variable degree of resources available for different pieces also shapes the way in which they are produced and perceived. It likely predates your time-scheme here, but Howard's production of *Judith* was the one where suddenly there was an exordium, suddenly the stage is a blank space with three heads hanging in it, suddenly there is lots of space for actors to move in, but also a mystery to the space and the ominous feeling that there may be a decapitation coming along any minute. That worked very well. *Ursula* was one of the most complex shows, with one of the most blinding moments, I believe. A copulation is taking place on stage between the Mother Superior and Lucas, where we had 40 scaffolding poles swinging above them, lit by a powerful flash head, blinding. The movement and the flash were coordinated with the music. This produced amazing reflections, amazing shadows, and really created an indelible moment. It could not have been stronger. The metal floor amplified the effect massively. Maybe the overriding thing that influenced scenography over time is the diminishing resources. The plainer spaces of course afford me a greater freedom to do more extreme things with lighting. From my point of view, that is what has happened. The last one I worked on, *The Gaoler's Ache*, was a black space with artefacts lying around in it. *The Dying of Today* was a chair and some newspapers hanging on the wall. With stages like that, you have to sit down and consider how the lighting can provide variation in how you read those things. It is a very creative task. A lot of other shows are not that creative and you are working within quite severe limitations of what you can do. The Wrestling School productions are always rather exciting to do. I did not get to light *Found in the Ground*, which was a pity because I had been reading it for a long time beforehand but there was a clash with another production I had agreed to work on. I have to stress that it was a result of my working in opera, where a production is booked at least a year in advance. The Wrestling School Company work on a much shorter notice. I did not work on that production, but I did see it. To me, it is a play that works almost in a symbolist kind of way and the way it was staged was necessarily part of how the audience was invited to read it. I think that production was done very well. *Found in the Ground* to me was a play that was perhaps even more designed than others. The lighting was done very well and made me think of how that something that is in the ether surrounding the Wrestling School will inform a designer and influence what they do. I quite like *Slowly*, as well, as an example of a play that seems fairly simple in terms of lighting design; it contains very few cues. But the world that is created for that performance to take place is quite specific. So I do not really know; I do not have a favourite.

There are things we have always avoided, like colour. We do not use colour and if we do it is not the kind you notice. White light is very prevalent. We use sidelight, which models the performers very well; and those principles give you a starting point. For me there has not been a distinct aesthetic journey of the company. The topic and the setting have been much more dominant factors for my work with them. You always have to consider what is needed and what you can and cannot achieve. What are the demands of the play, the limitations of the set? I always like a challenge, set with ceilings, sets that are completely white: many lighting designers would throw their hands up in despair, but I think 'bring it on'. I think the Wrestling School is my favourite company to work for, because it is always a challenge. My dilemma always is: am I working towards a lighting design as an artist or a technician? It is a mixture of achieving a technical solution to an obstacle and responding to an aesthetic challenge. I have a freedom with that company that I relish. In my schedule over the course of the year I try to make as much space for the Wrestling School as I can.

LK: Thank you very much for your time.

Transcript Interview Exeter 15 December 2015: Paul Bull (sound designer)

LK: Are you familiar with the term scenography? Could you define it for me?

PB: Yes. It's hard to put it into words. It is the whole ethos of a production to finding all the design elements and concepts, I suppose. How would you define it? It's trying to place all those little elements into the way a theatre show is presented for performance.

LK: Could you talk a bit about your role when you are working with the Wrestling School Company?

PB: Let's actually go back to the very beginning: the Wrestling School started as a company to perform the works of Howard [Barker]. Howard wrote the plays, but didn't direct them. They were directed by director Kenny Ireland. Back in those days they were co-productions with Leicester Haymarket, in our studio. I say 'our studio', because I was working as resident Head of Sound. So I [my work with the Wrestling School] go back to the very early days [of the company] of *Golgo*, *Seven Lears*, and so on. So in those days, it was almost a traditional theatre company: the director would take the words of Howard, and come up with a design, possibly relating to some of Howard's physical, visual, and auditory ideas. But then at that point we actually had a composer, Matthew Scott. The audio content was actually composed by him. He has done a lot of work for television now, and earned a great fortune on that, but still works a lot in the theatre, in Chichester. So ever so often I meet up with him, as I have friends in common. After I left [Leicester] in 1990, I parted company [with the Wrestling School] for ten years until 2000. I was working in Germany at the time and got a phone call from the production manager. Because I have never lived in London, his exact question was 'Paul, who would you recommend as a sound designer in our shows?'; this happened because the previous sound designer John Leonard was becoming so busy he wasn't able to spend the necessary time [with the Wrestling School]. My response was 'I'll do it'. He said 'We don't have a lot of money to pay you for it'. and I said 'I don't care; I can make some of my money elsewhere to help subsidise this'. Since then, I have been their resident sound designer; there have been a few projects that Howard [Barker] didn't direct and other people have used other sound designers. So that's the background to me getting involved. Probably 10 or 12 different productions, which I can't all bring to mind at the moment.

LK: I've written a list of productions you worked on within the parameters of my enquiry, since I am actually looking at works from when Barker himself began engaging scenographically. That was in 1998, with *Ursula*.

PB: I wasn't involved with *Ursula*. *He Stumbled* (2000) would be the first I was involved in. Along with blocks of words and images, I feel we [the company] have come up with blocks of audio content that reflect a whole vision. It's a really interesting way of working, which I think most people would think to be quite frustrating as you tend to be given a long list of things [of desired sounds]. To me, as a creative sound designer, I take this list of things and see them as planks of wood to be turned into something else, building blocks; and we've come to quite an interesting and useful short-hand [Howard and I]: he might say 'I want [the sound of] starlings' and I will present him with something slightly different, or seagulls, but bird sounds. We use bird sounds quite a lot. Howard will have a name for them, though they may not be precisely that sound (e.g. starlings). I suppose that is the first thing to talk about, the building blocks. We've used Stockhausen and other avant-garde music a lot. Howard gives me a list, and I know I will have to find a way of looping the samples. He will provide me with a sample timing, and from experience I know that might not work, samples may have to be longer, or shorter, or looped, so the creative process of making these samples usable is entirely left to me. It's a wonderfully versatile way of working. Howard continually brings in samples, apparently handed to him by a next-door neighbour (who that might be, I do not know) that he embraces. It includes electronic compositions as well as classical avant-garde pieces. So it is my job to magically make this collage of excerpts and samples into a soundtrack. Yes, it appears very dictatorial, but I actually find it very collaborative. I have experienced it many times that a director says they have no con- crete vision and charges me to come up with something, only to dismiss it when I present them with what I came up with, because it suddenly doesn't fit. By having a very clear visual, audio, and verbal direction from one person actually makes the life of a creative person much easier; I find working with Howard very creative. The concrete structural frame- work helps; I find it gives quite a lot of freedom. It is an unusual way of working, even within my profession.

Naturally, the immense changes in technology also helped our way of working. In the early days, we had to pre-plan a lot more. We were working from mini-discs which allowed us to run up to six tracks at any one time. It also created a lot of pressure on the DSM who would have to operate the sound equipment. In the early days, a lot of my time was taken up finding a way by which a person not trained as a sound designer could easily operate the sound. It really was very heavily focussed on pre-planning, and also re-recording to adjust the length of loops, as they might have been too short, etc. Often I used cassettes and CDs as well, for example a long running wind sound effect would be realised by those means. Similar to the birds I mentioned earlier, we have come up with several wind formats [like a catalogue both Howard and Paul are familiar with], artic wind is one we use a lot. Very often we go back to previous years and poach a lot from those productions where I know the necessary audio materials exist already. There is one that combines a breeze and the distant sound of hydraulic hammering of a pole driver. All of these specific effects are named and become part of our repertoire. So really my work is a combination of technicalities and creative realisation of Howard's ideas. We also use quite a lot of actual cast recordings to give us some screams and shouts, though we often use the Stockhausen screams and shouts in the recordings, too. Metallic drops of cutlery and trays are also a common sound effect, though it may be used for ambient sound, rather than as a concrete cue that coincides with a physical action on stage. All of it has to work with the stage and costume designs, of course. It took me two years to realise that the stage and costume designers were not actual people, but Howard under different guises. I suppose that unity of vision was incredibly helpful once we had established a rapport, when I could almost second-guess where Howard would like to cut a sound cue, which parts he would want to loop, where I might have to rework it. I then also got to embellish these sounds, for example in *The Fence* – we were still on mini-disc at that time – we had a faulty disc, or one that disappeared during rehearsal, but we came up with alternative sounds created by banging on the wire fence which again was just left to me. But since we already had worked together we had, like an artist in a studio, a palette; we have a palette of sounds that I know work for Howard's pieces. It is not surprising, since Howard is also an artist [painter and photographer]. So bringing together sound, colours – also through lighting – became second nature. We did another piece in Birmingham which was not actually directed by Howard, and that was quite difficult, because suddenly I didn't work with the same restrictions I had become used to and thought to myself 'I've had an easy life [being directed by Howard]'.

My predecessor, John Leonard, is somebody of my age, my generation, and we were of the few that were actually calling ourselves sound designers in dramatic theatre at the time. We came up with ways of working, in John's [Leonard] case with Howard, which despite its seemingly prescriptive manner demanded a deep engagement; so when John [Leonard] could not be there during the production period, it became a problem. Which is how I got involved with the Wrestling School. So the challenge then was, and is, making it work with limited time, very limited budget, very limited equipment, and not with sound operators operating it, but having really complex sound. Moving on to computers, especially QLab, has opened up the world. Especially things like the opening exordium, using images and feelings as an overture to a piece have been made so much easier by technology; they are often repetitive, but we wouldn't know how many repeats would have to play, so when we got to more complex exordia when playing at the Riverside Studios, for example *Found in the Ground*, would have been extremely challenging had it been done on mini-disc. *Found in the Ground* is actually, I believe, one of the first productions that we used computer playback on. We did use it before then, on small-scale productions, but we simply did not have the resources to have a computer at that point.

LK: I find your use of the analogy of the painter very interesting. I am currently working my way through the Exeter digital archive's Barker resources and I felt very strongly that there is a through-line, certain snippets of sound reappear and are – in immediate juxtaposition – extremely recognisable, for example a man's shout that appears in *Ursula, Gertrude – The Cry, The Fence*, and then again in *Found in the Ground*: there really is a sense of a shared vocabulary that extends across productions and developed over time.

PB: Some of those sounds will be from before I joined the company, like that shout, and as time went on we have expanded and given our sound library more nuances. I don't know if Howard has this palette, these noises, in his mind when he is writing or if he writes, and then takes up the work as a director and keeps his writing self apart – which is certainly something he does when he directs, almost as if he is having a conversation with two different people in the room, which is not something everybody can do, and does. There are many who write in order to direct and then direct as it is written, which I find a very frustrating way of working since they tend not to be open to any options [of theatrical solutions and realisations]. On the other hand, Howard's usual focus on few core characters makes it much easier, particularly with very short rehearsal periods, to achieve something coherent, even on a bigger scale. To work with people who really know each other makes the process much easier, and quicker. Understanding the text is crucial, which is made much easier by having people who have worked together on work of this kind before, and for a long time. We all share a common language; the stage directions are not always simply 'dog bark up left'; not having to be literal about everything is a real joy. The developments in technology, though they make many things a lot cheaper, do not necessarily make things faster, but they enable an even greater complexity and afford repeatability. For *Blok/Eko* they even came here, to Exeter, we opened up the back wall of the theatre, and had nearly 100 people on stage. Which was an absolute liberation, something we had never done before.

LK: In *Found in the Ground* there is the wonderful stage direction 'the sound of infinite distance'; it's one of my favourite directions by Howard Barker, simply because it shows his disinterest in feasibility whilst writing.

PB: My favourite stage direction, maybe it was in *He Stumbled,* or the next one, *A House of Correction*, the stage directions read something along the lines of 'the stage floods with a hundred nuns', which left me speechless when reading the play. That is the joy of working with Barker. I also suppose when writing he might not know whether it will be a stage show, or a radio play. He just churns them out, I never keep track, all I know is that there will be yet another collection from Oberon full of new plays – it's like a collection of novels. Which may or may not be produced, in different times and different eras.

I have to say, having seen a couple of productions that were not directed by Howard, and not with the Wrestling School, some of that type of scenography is still present. I saw *Und* up at the Edinburgh Festival by a company called Mechanical Animal Corporation that felt very reminiscent of the Wrestling School work, there was a lot of steel, a lot of wire, and there were a lot of very strange thumps and bumps; similarly, the show that was recently at the Print Room under the direction of Robyn Winfield-Smith [*Lot and his God*] – but Howard was involved with it – felt very reminiscent of our style, the crockery crashes offstage, the voice of god, the presence of god, and yet not. Whether other people watch Howard's productions and decide that is a good way of approaching the pieces and therefore shape other productions so much stylistically … I can't say, but it would be interesting to see something not done in that style.

LK: Do you think there is something in the plays themselves that invites those sorts of solutions?

PB: I think there is. Because how else would you do mechanical dogs swathed in bandages [in *Found in the Ground*]? Surrounding Howard is a group of really great people that work on realising his ideas, the costumes, the mechanics, the clever ideas we have to work with. That has been the joy of the Wrestling School, just people working together towards common solutions, for quite fraught and difficult scenographic problems. Certainly in the case of Ace McCarron, who does the lighting, we have worked together on several of the shows and we complement each other because he has a knowledge of sound and music and I have a knowledge of lighting. Therefore, if we feel something isn't working, we can talk to each other in a way that is useful and helpful, articulate beyond 'Oh, I don't like that', which is a reaction you do get in other circumstances. Howard and all the others [of the Wrestling School and associates] tend to work with a common vision, which we have not necessarily worked hard to come up with, it's just that Howard and his work attract people who work in that kind of way. Of course, that brings its own challenges when funding dwindles and venues get smaller and smaller, as do the company and its finances, and we are unable to sustain it in a meaningful way. Especially in the way the Arts Council always wanted Howard to give post-show talks and discussions and I'm sure you're aware of Howard's attitude to those.

LK: I am indeed. There is currently a double bill of Barker plays at the Arcola, under Winfield-Smith's direction, which apparently featured a pre-show talk, which perhaps he will find preferable. Could you outline the stages of your working process with the Wrestling School for me?

PB: It always starts with a phone call 'I hope you're available' and in general I will do anything I can to make myself available. Usually I am at least available by the time we get into production week; there was one time – mind you, the play was not directed by Howard, but by Gerrard

[McArthur] – where there was a conflict of dates, but I had a close collaborator that I have worked with. It's not the same though, and that is always the problem, when you are unavailable, and are asked 'Who would you recommend?' – well, I don't want to recommend anyone, I want to do the work myself, my particular way, which you are looking for, since you asked me. So really the working process depends on my movements, timetables, and schedules. But at some stage leading up to production week I will clear a bit of time and meet with Howard. I have sometimes managed to meet with him in Brighton, but sometimes it will be a phone call, which is absolutely necessary because the script tells me next to nothing in my terms of sound design, because it is all in Howard's head until we sit down. I try to get as much as possible done as soon as possible and get it into rehearsals. That's the desire, often not realised. Though again, this has been more possible in recent times with the increased access to technology, also file sharing samples via DropBox and so on. We are lucky in that we have often had the same DSM on the book, and operating sound, so they know the method of working. Really it's about developing and cultivating a team over a long period of time. I will then come up for some rehearsals and talk with Howard some more, check the edits, get a new selection of samples of music, and do some recordings. I tour with a little zoom hard disk recorder. So I sit in the corner of rehearsal rooms through pots, pans, shouts, and screams. I could likely blackmail a lot of people with my collection of sexual moans and orgasm noises that I've accrued over the years, recorded as parts of different soundtracks. I'll then take those recordings away and work in my studio with my big box of tricks including a big hard drive of other noises: explosions, pile drivers, thunder, gun shots. Talking of gun shots, it takes quite some time to find the right one sometimes, and we work hard at it. We try several, which becomes much easier with modern technological developments. Thn follows the tech rehearsal period in which we make it work in real time. It's no magic, it's no secret. It's working very closely with all involved, like set collaborators, and have some fun through that as well.

LK: The vocal aspect of Barker's work is so crucial, especially in pieces such as *Blok/Eko* that present such an overabundance of spoken text. Do you feel the relationship between spoken text and other sound on stage has developed over time, especially with more easily available technologies?

PB: Probably, because it is more repeatable. Once we got away from the minidiscs, it became more creative. A lot of the early days were more heavily focussed on organising, which tracks had to be on which discs, and so on. New technologies freed that up and allowed us to do a lot more subtle underscoring, as we are no longer relying on DSMs hitting very precise marks. The cueing is all recorded into the technology now. I think we have been able to get a better balance between recorded and live sound and that has been a very fluid opening up of our sonic horizons. I suppose the biggest challenge we ever has was *Gertrude* [– *The Cry*, 2002] because

I was only able to do the opening in that wonderfully bizarre Knight's Hall at Hamlet's Castle during a Hamlet/Shakespeare festival where we had the full length of the hall, about 60 meters long, with a runway of about 55 meters. So we had a set of stereo speakers that far apart, with Stockhausen playing very loudly. Stockhausen is very aware of spatial distribution anyway [in his compositions], so it was a real joy to play with that. But because so much of it was done on the fly, it was almost created live in that space; I was operating the opening, but had to leave thereafter and had to recreate the sound design in an easier format for when the piece went on tour afterwards. I suppose that was the biggest challenge.

LK: I watched *Gertrude* this morning and was wondering about the echo: the recording has a significant echo on the actors' voices, though I don't think the recording was made at the festival, in that large hall – so was this echo deliberate?

PB: No, that would likely have been the microphones: their placement in relation to the actors. We rarely use treatments on the voices. If we do, it is for very particular reasons. We tried it in *Blok/Eko*, for the old man's voice and it did not quite work. Again, it also comes down to the fact that it has to be repeatable by someone who is not necessarily trained as sound specialist. There were a couple of treatments on the voice … we also tried to pick up the squeak of a boot at one point and I think ended up with a recording after all. Quite often, in situations like the squeaking boot, we end up with recordings, but we are not trying to Mickey Mouse it, we are not trying to make it happen in time with the footstep, it is an ambience. It is very unnatural in style overall anyway, so we make sure that the sound is removed from the action on stage. That is another frequently employed technique of disassociation on stage, strange noises that are apart from what is happening on stage.

LK: The only example of a treated voice would be Macedonia, the headless woman in *Found in the Ground*, whose voice was amplified and morphed, making her even more strange.

PB: Yes.

LK: Occasionally, there is a slight echo in *I Saw Myself*. I wonder if that was an effect of microphone placement again: whenever someone was up the steps next to the wardrobe, their voice gained an echo.

PB: Yes, true. We had a microphone hidden behind that. It really also depends on budget, if a sound operator cannot cope with an effect, and it is not repeatable, then we will usually cut it.

LK: Thankfully, I have had the opportunity to talk to Ace McCarron and Helen Morley (lighting designers working with Barker), who you have also worked with. Could you outline for me the exchange and inputs that take place between the different parts of the scenography?

PB: It's not a conscious sitting down in which we discuss our approach as a team because I think that ultimately the cohesiveness comes from the solid rock that is Howard who has the vision and the overall concept and as much as anything, the process is really us [the scenographers] helping to realise what is in his head. By the time I came on board, Ace had already worked with Howard for quite a while and established their style, with very strong, stark lighting and a limited palette of colours; very stylised and unnatural at times. This is a style that has now become fashionable with all sorts of other work, the extreme highlight and lowlight use, the side-lighting, not illuminating faces completely. This is something I do myself whenever I have to do some lighting design, it is very conceptual, very much like dance lighting. As much as anything, Howard is placing the actors very deliberately, like mannequins. Placement, rhythm, timing, pauses, and style of speaking are all part of the overall effect. I think if one little thing was out, or missing, the whole concept falls to pieces. It is not something we all consciously sit down to discuss in a production meeting, because I think we will have all had our individual conversations with Howard prior to that, which bring us to that common ground from the start which then becomes such a wonderful vision. Our production meetings are therefore fundamentally about practicalities: have we got the puppets, the starlings, how will they move on the stage? Will they be on a stick, moved by a person on stage, or tracked across? How do they turn around? This gives me the time to figure out the accompanying sounds, birds panning left to right; in the days of mini-discs, I would get that recorded. Now with current computer technology we can sort these things out much later. In the old days, it was very much about timings, which was always difficult to do. Now it is more fluid. It was never a sit down in which we all came up with the concept, because the concept was already formed, probably as soon as Howard put the last full stop down with the typewriter on his foolscap paper. He always writes on that paper, so we would have to ask him to write within the dimensions of an A4 page, so we could photocopy the script, rather than redrafting it before sending it out to the cast.

LK: You have already touched on this, but could you talk a little more about the input you receive from Howard? What exchanges take place between you and him during the scenographic process?

PB: I suppose if you sit down and analyse it, it feels very mechanical: here is the list. Or two lists, perhaps three. Here is the list of music, here is the list of sound effects, and here is the list of things we have to record, all expertly notated in Howard's handwriting. So we have long conversations, usually over the course of a lunchtime and evening, since I am usually only over from Exeter for a day. I might visit him three or four times during the rehearsal period, depending on the complexity of what we are doing. In the early days, there would have to be a lot of preparation, as I mentioned previously, and a lot of technical queries. The actualisation of the sound-scape, the realisation of the score, if you will, was left to me. For *Found in the Ground* we had a disagreement, because Howard described himself as 'sound designer' and me as 'sound realisation', which seemed a demotion to me, so we had long conversations about that and came to a compromise. I suppose, that is what sound design is to me, the realisation of somebody else's vision, if vision can be used to describe an aural landscape. What would be the sound equivalent to vision?

LK: Soundscape? Imagined soundscape?

PB: Yes, but you can have a visual landscape, which is different from vision. So what is the sonic equivalent? There's a question I have never asked myself before. What is the aural equivalent of vision? I'll work on that and let you know.

LK: You have already identified the guiding principles of the Wrestling School's productions in terms of sound and your contributions to them; would you say they are different from other dramatic work you have done? In what way?

PB: Yes. They are not 'dog bark up left', basically. How to describe the work of Howard Barker? They [the plays] are these epic vocalised poems that would probably have as much rhythm if you closed your eyes and listened to the production because they have a rich lyrical quality that can – on the surface – feel very confusing, almost like Brechtian alienation, but actually when you look at it in detail there is just an epic flow of humanity which nobody else writes. Which brings us back to the initial phone call I received, and I was in Cologne doing a very physical production, and Chris phoned me and I said let's find a way of making it work for the money you are going to give me. I think that was it. There was no debate. Howard's work touches me, it is my sort of work and there is no one else doing it like that. It just provides you with such a journey to go on, both as an observer and as participant, collaborator with Howard. It is exciting in a way that very few other writers do.

LK: You have made the comparison to dance in terms of lighting. Would you also make that comparison in terms of sound? Or would you compare it to something else?

PB: Hm. I would not make that comparison. It is almost like a live radio play because in radio they tend to take more risks with underscoring, with strange noises, which very few other people do in live performance. I wouldn't compare to dance – and if it was, the comparison would be with Merce Cunningham and John Cage – because the visual aspect is at times totally unrelated to the aural aspect. Particularly at the time of a scream of shout, you may only realise what that is at the end of the play when it has been developed with the narrative of the performance. Quite often it could feel as though it is a Cunningham/Cage sort of thing. But at other times there can be lyrical things in the soundscape that underscore and drive the momentum of the piece; I would say it [the sound design] is more alienation than lyricism because I think quite often the lyricism arises from the poetry that is the spoken word Howard has written.

LK: Would you say the soundscapes you create present a counterpoint to that lyricism?

PB: Yes. It helps bring out emotions that possibly are not present in the words at times and that can be all sorts of emotions; even if it is just utter abject horror. Sometimes there is some lyricism [in the sound design]. What to me is really exciting is that in a "dog bark up left"-type show, when I have toured it, I get to the end of a tour and most of the sound cues have been cut, but nothing of the emotional content of the play has changed whereas if you took out even just one element, one little bit of piercing Stockhausen or the like, out of the Wrestling School productions, something would be missing. You would not be able to put your finger on it, but I think it just would not feel whole. It has been very good reflecting on all of this.

LK: I'm glad to hear that. I have found that scenographers often do not necessarily talk about their work; they do. They are makers, doers, realisers. Which is in part why I am doing this project: to find a vocabulary for expressing and analysing these processes; this is currently still woefully lacking. You have been wonderful in your responses in this interview; I have hardly had to ask you anything. Would you say there is such a thing as a Wrestling School aesthetic and what is it?

PB: I would say there are two: there is Kenny Ireland's aesthetic and Howard's. I'm trying to remember who the designer was in those early days. The whole Barker approach – I think he only took up directing because no one else was available at the time – I don't think he had any particular ambitions to engage with those aspects of production. I cannot be sure, since he took up directing before I came on board. I suppose they probably had it all set up, but Kenny got the offer to become artistic director of the Lyceum up in Edinburgh. All of a sudden, I suppose, it was forced on Howard. I think he has taken it to great heights. As I said earlier, most people who write and then direct their own work, direct it as they have written it and have a great attachment to their text, whereas Howard does not. The work is very much centred on the word, the spoken word, then the vision, and the aural vision (whatever that term might become; I'll have to invent something to go along with Howard's 'exordium'). I think the style of the Wrestling School comes from that: Howard's unifying vision. But I have other directors whom I have worked with where we have a shorthand and a developed style, which may become a little bizarre, but often it is circumstance that gives birth to a certain style, but sometimes it comes from a person. I think in terms of the Wrestling School, it is Howard with whom that style originates and it works, whether it is in a studio theatre or in the Knight's Hall in Denmark.

LK: Looking at the productions from when you joined the Wrestling School (*He Stumbled* in 2000) up until *Blok/Eko* in 2011, are there any productions that really stand out to you? If yes, which ones and why?

PB: *Gertrude*. Who could fail to be astonished, amazed, blown away by that absolutely oddball look at a dysfunctional family, vaguely related to *Hamlet*. At the time we were doing in Hamlet's castle in Elsinore. It really was a great one to experience because we were all able to live in a commune-type place. At the same time there was a conference happening that focussed on one very particular enzyme. So we had this absolute dichotomy of art and science. My wife came out with me, it was in 2002. We flew out from the Edinburgh bubble into another bubble where we were all working together, supporting each other, eating together – which rarely happens with the Wrestling School to that extent – so we really became enmeshed there. So out of that came this real understanding of how we all worked, and a great show that I was actually sound operating as well, like a live radio show, as it was changing each time. My wife was working with a training organisation, so they came up with the first Wrestling School weekend school. Wonderful people came together from around the world to take part in that.

The other one would be *Found in the Ground*, where for the first time, it became easy to realise what Howard wanted, what I wanted, with new computer technologies. That play actually had quite a dense soundscape, where for the first time I was able to paint on stage with sound, to overlay and create, rather than work it out in a small back bedroom, something that was very much part of the reality of the audio-visual reality of the stage. Those two would be the most memorable productions. Lastly, I have to mention the joy of *Blok/Eko*, which I was able to do in my – then – home town. To be able to do it in a theatre that I know a bit, in my home town, being able to go home to my own bed, creating a Barker production – was a great experience. I don't think there has ever been a bad production with Howard and the Wrestling School. Whereas with other directors there have been. The relationship with Howard really is a special one.

LK: Thank you, it has been so great to have a complimentary viewpoint, since I spoke with both Ace McCarron and Helen Morley (long-standing lighting designers of the Wrestling School) about their work on light with Howard. I think sound is so often overlooked, literally, because we afford so much importance to the visual aspects and only notice certain sounds when they interfere with our vision.

PB: Quite. When I started working in 1978, I knew I wanted to go into sound. Most people at the time would do a bit of sound because they wanted to get into lighting but the only way you would get into a department at the time was doing a bit of both. In those days you would take things off the BBC Sound Effect series, which was only about ten records, so any thunder was always the same thunder. So by the time I went to Leicester I was searching out record shops, on the hunt for bizarre American vinyl so much so that everything for a production like *Woman in Black* came from my collection. Had I requested royalties for that, I would be a millionaire now.

LK: You say you had this immediate interest in sound. What is it that sound does in the theatre that makes you so interested in it? It can do lots of things, but to you, what can it do, and does it do, when it is done well?

PB: It just enhances. I suppose I would like to think that if the sounds I produce were not there, something would be missing from the production, just as if you had turned the lights off. So many of the sounds I use are so subliminal, but still essential to the whole. They might appear to be actual ambient noises, like traffic, that interfere with the real traffic noises to give it a different quality. These may come about purely by accident, when the director hears a noise in rehearsal, like an ice cream van, and then it gets put in. So then I work my way through various ice cream van jingles until we find the perfect one. Each show creates its own palette.

LK: Have you found that with the advances of technology that you have identified here, the role of sound has changed in theatre?

PB: Yes and no. It depends on who you are working with. I'm lucky now that I do not have to take everything and anything that is offered to me. I would like to do a bit more sound design. The new, younger generation have grown up with computers and so on. But you get shows where, for example, someone on stage puts on an LP and the sound designer does not put down the noise of the needle hitting the record, or the whispering and clicking when it runs out; and I wonder why not. For me, this is somewhat frustrating, because when I still had to hand-cut tapes, I would always do that: clip the needle sound at the right volume in relation to the record, and so on. It is an attention to detail that I occasionally find lacking, perhaps because it is all so much easier and sound designers do not have to put so much preparation into their work. To me, a tape loop is called that, because we had to make actual, physical loops that go round my living room, and I'd have to try and keep my cat from interfering with it. So to be able to just cut and paste takes some of the fun out of it for me. But you can't get in the way of progress. I quite often use the analogy of building blocks; my sound designs are based on that. You can get a bit of wood from the wood store and put it on stage, but it is not a set then, is it? You have got to do something with it. It is the same with sound. That is how I treat sound: layer it, change the frequency, change the tonal balance, change the ambience it is in, turn it upside down, reverse it ... that way, you can create the sound of a dying elephant. Which probably has been my biggest challenge to date. It involved cricket balls and baseball mitts and the slowed-down sound of a king penguin, among other things at a time where the technology to mangle and manipulate sound just was not in existence yet. We eventually got more technical, using delay units, etc. To be able to get quick, easy access provides a lot more options nowadays. Back in Leicester, they had a joke, if you can't find Paul: he'll be at the record library. Back then you had to go out and really dig deep to get access to weird and wacky noises. I make wacky noises. That's what I do: weird and wacky noises.

LK: Thank you very much for your time.

Transcript Interview 4 Brighton, 15 January 2016: Howard Barker (dramatist, director, scenographer)

LK: I am interested in your scenographic processes. You began directing your own work in the early 1990s; then in the late 1990s, with *Ursula* you started doing set designs, costume designs followed shortly thereafter, and then sound. I wonder: how has the process of designing developed for you?

HB: It's funny, I don't quite know. You could almost ask why I started directing; the reason I started directing was that Kenny Ireland, who was the original director [of the Wrestling School], left to pursue a career in Scotland and we did not know who else to turn to. Over the years, all the directors who had done my work had nearly always failed, in my opinion, and in his, actually. So I could not see much point in then going back to directors from the RSC like Bill Alexander, to invite them back to the Wrestling School because they would just do what they did before, so there would be no point in having the company. So I stepped in with that first one, which must have been *(Uncle) Vanya*,[1] I believe. I'm not sure. That set was designed by somebody I knew, as was the sound and it was okay but I suppose what I said with that first *(Uncle) Vanya* show, 1996 I think that was, I told the designer what I wanted. Robin Donne was his name. I asked him 'do you mind if I show you? It can't be a Chekhovian set, because it is an anti-Chekhovian play. Can we set it in an old, sunken freighter, a rusty freighter, with decks and iron staircases?' So he designed that. At some point in the play, the wall collapses and the sea comes in. So in fact, I initiated the design, and he was very cooperative. He was not egocentric at all, he accepted that. Having done that, I then thought, since I instructed him, I might as well do it, and work with someone as an assistant who knows the technical stuff, can go to the workshops and do what I can't do: make the stage models, do the arithmetic. So all I would do would be to produce the drawing. And she – it was always a she, a very good girl, especially the last one I worked with was very good – would maybe make some suggestions, not many, and then she would carry it through. When it came to putting the set up, I was just watching. So I did half the designer's job, I did the design and handed the practical stuff to somebody else. That's how that happened; I just kept doing it. Because I am a painter, I have got a visual sense, of course. I wouldn't let anyone else design now. Every time I would have to do it myself. As I've said before I don't collaborate.

LK: I suppose that extends to costume as well?

HB: Absolutely. The two go together. Even with the costumes for *(Uncle) Vanya*; I told Robin I want this to look roughly 1900, but I want all the costumes to be exactly the same colour because a very small chromatic range is important to me. I don't like colour. In my paintings I don't use colour. So that would be the style; and it slowly became what might be called the second Wrestling School style because Kenny Ireland's style was spectacular, very lavish; he always worked with professional designers who brought in their designs and whilst he influenced it, it was theirs. They were very colourful and luxurious. Whereas I thought, theoretically, you must concentrate the audience tightly on the language and the body. We can't have people looking at the furniture. The items, the props, and the set must be exquisitely beautiful, but pared down to the minimum; then we will listen to the voice more. That is my theory anyway; so all my sets have been very austere. Functional and austere. The costumes are more lavish. I do enjoy costumes, especially for women. I don't design so interestingly for men. They tend to follow a very narrow period of *haute couture*, basically. Probably 1930 to 1950, that sort of period; with hats, as you know. I want the actors to look beautiful, so when they move properly, the costume moves with them, and that is very important to me. Actors are not ordinary people, on stage. Offstage they are very ordinary, but onstage they are not to be ordinary. That is why I insist they look exciting, whether they are dressed or undressed, they should always look good. It is exactly the same thing [with the set]: I do the designs – we can look at them later, if you want – and then a very good wardrobe super-visor – who I have worked with on nearly all the shows – comes in and she turns them into something the wardrobe cutters can work with. That is the process.

LK: You mentioned the movement of the costume there. We had one of the Billie Kaiser designs – the wedding gown from *The Twelfth Battle of Isonzo* – in the second production of *The Forty*; I noticed that you use very interesting materials. This one consists of a white faux leather corseted bodice (unlined) and layers of white tulle skirts. I also recall a production photograph from *The Fence in its Thousandth Year* in which Algeria wears a wonderful, stiff dress, or coat-dress in what appears as burnished copper colour. So I wondered about how you choose your materials.

HB: Are you sure that it was not *Ursula*? She [Placida, played by Victoria Wicks] had a very extraordinary thing on which looked like it shone; it was not leather, but it might have implied that. I can't remember that being in *The Fence*.

LK: I suppose I am generally very interested in your material choices, whether that is something wardrobe brings back to you.

HB: I like wool on both men and women. If you can't get wool, make it look like wool, because wool hangs properly. It's not light, it doesn't flap around. So if you want good movement, especially on a woman who walks well, Victoria does, of course – I always try to cast women who move well – then you get that movement of the body and it is tremendous. That is what clothing should do, I think, it should enhance the body. So I have some very clear ideas about the materials I like. If I wanted to change material, I would ask the wardrobe supervisor Bushy Westfallen: 'Bushy, what have we got, if we don't use wool?' and she might say 'well, it's tweed' or something like that, which might do it; but of course we are constrained by cost. As you mentioned earlier, the costumes are not lined, and they do not last. I am not an expert in materials; I have never been a costume designer in that sense.

LK: But you have an idea of how they should move which will then influence your design.

HB: Yes. As far as men go – *The Fence* isn't a bad example, *Gertrude* is another – I try to enhance the traditional shape of men's clothes. To remove them from a specific time period. Nearly all the suits [in *Gertrude*] had rolled top seams on the shoulder, which marked them out from the ordinary. The trousers are nearly always very full. I don't like men's trousers to be tight; then again, the trouser material should move with their bodies. In that way my designs are not dissimilar for the two genders.

LK: I just saw the recording of *Gertrude* in the Exeter archive. In it, Hamlet has this wonderful, distressed one-sleeved jacket that is shorter on one side. It's a play with traditional shapes.

HB: Yes. He has a messed-up school uniform. He always has two ties on. It was very important to me to evoke a mischievous school boy.

LK: You mention the minimalism of your designs; is it also related to your desire to distance your work from everyday reality, to set it in its own world and give it an ambiguity of time period?

HB: It is not so much ambiguity as absence of. The answer to that is yes, you put that perfectly.

LK: You make reference to your paintings and sketches, which I will look at in a little while, if I may. Has the process of creating the paintings that you do alongside the writing changed since you started engaging with the design processes?

HB: No. It hasn't changed. I may write in the morning and come here in the afternoon and I reproduce as a picture the scene I have written in the morning, or a moment from the scene; and I do that with a pen and ink wash. That is the end of it for me. I don't refer back to that ever again. Certainly not in the directing. It is to excite myself, perhaps; to visualise what I have just written. It is quite personal. When Kenny Ireland directed, he sometimes asked to see these books; maybe he used some of those ideas, but I don't. When I come to direct the thing, it's from scratch. Just from the text and the actors, I don't use those drawings. The other drawings are the set designs; obviously I know the budget is very small but that is irrelevant because I don't want much there. If I wanted much there I would be frustrated by the budget. The budget doesn't allow that. I wouldn't say I was forced into an aesthetic because I would choose it anyway. I'd rather spend money on the costume than on the set. You can see the set there for *Gertrude*: it's simply actually a lot of overalls that are made into surfaces which in turn move on wheels and that is about it; and there is a white floor. It is more or less the same with the *13 Objects* set: moveable walls of corrugated iron, or rather plastic made to look like iron that slide sideways to expose actors in different places on stage. It is designed to draw your eye to the actor all the time.

LK: Yet you never neglect material. It is something I noticed in production stills, but also looking at these stage models here. The idea of texture is still prominent in the set designs.

HB: Yes. I suppose that is true. The first one [*Gertrude*] is made of masses of suspended linen [the overalls], that one [*13 Objects*] is made of ribbed iron, and the set for *I Saw Myself* is made of raw timber, completely untreated. In fact, people kept getting splinters off it. So yes, I like surfaces. I am also aware that a surface can be lit better if it has some rhythm within it. Of course it is also a question of what size theatre you are playing in. The Wrestling School is mostly condemned to play in studios. So you could play it with no set at all in a studio. In a bigger theatre it is somewhat different. This model is from when we did *The Fence* in Birmingham, which was essentially a huge flying number, because Birmingham Rep has a lot of fly bars, more than anywhere else I think. So you can keep bringing things in, one after the other; they tended to be bits of significant fencing. I'd say that was simple, too.

LK: You already mentioned that you approach the text again when you come to it as a director. Does the same apply to your design processes?

HB: I try to approach it freshly when directing. Yes, I would say it holds true for the design, too. Regarding the play I finished a couple of days ago, I haven't thought about the set at all. I just try to play the emotions and the relationships. I don't think of the set. If it was to be staged – and the way things are going it never will be – I would then come to the idea of 'what is the design for this thing?'. Probably, I would produce something austere again, I might use railway tracks, because I like movement across that parallel line with the audience; in the particular play I have just written, parts happen after death and one of the ways I want to demonstrate the post-life element of it is to bring the actors in as dead on a track, looking directly ahead; and that is completely informative about where you are. Also, it is economic. Railway tracks are cheap.

LK: I wasn't aware that tracks were cheap; in any case, they provide wonderful lines on stage, as they do for the dogs in *Found in the Ground*.

HB: They also have a wonderful sound. In my designs, you see the pulleys and the wires, they are not disguised. That is also why I like things to fly, which you can't do in studios, but in a big house I like things to come in, and when they do I want to see the cables illuminated. So I always use high-polished chrome or silver wires, so they catch the light and we are not deceived. Of course that is part of the beauty of it.

LK: So that then informs your suggestions to Ace McCarron regarding the lighting, I would imagine?

HB: Well, I tell him I'd like the cables lit.

LK: You have such a diverse range of interests: you read Rilke, Cioran, Celine, and many others, the aesthetic of the costumes is clearly informed by haute couture of the 1930s to late 1940s; what other inspirations or influences would you see in your designs?

HB: Listen, I am a European, I am steeped in European culture. Whenever I go to Europe, I will go straight to the museums, the art galleries; we all do that. There isn't much I haven't seen in terms of visual materials over the years. But it isn't the case where I would say 'I want it to look like a Rembrandt'. I particularly despise theatre or film – and it is usually film – where the reviewers will say 'it's like a van Gough, it's like this or that, isn't it amazing, like Piranesi'. That is a defeat. All these things should be contained in the mind of a serious artist; you shouldn't have to reproduce somebody else. That is why I am profoundly grateful to Béla Tarr, as a director, for his mere existence. I will say that about hardly anybody in life, but he has totally absorbed what it is to be a European, visually. When you see something like *The Turin Horse* or *Satantango* you sometimes see a moment and think that shot owes its origin to something, what is it? Oh, it's Hammershoi, that Danish artist, oh no, it's in fact Canaletto. It's there. But he doesn't go around trying to imitate, it is in him, he has absorbed it entirely and his brilliance is to continue the tradition of what it is to be a European by renewing it again and again; and that is what I try to do. Why do I go back to Chekhov, why do I go back to Shakespeare, why do I go back to Lessing? Why do you bother, they say, just write new work. Well, I say, the work is new. It's completely new. It's revisited. I did it with the Velázquez painting, *Las Meninas*. Why revisit it? Well, Picasso did it. *Las Meninas* is an incredibly important painting. Velázquez died almost as soon as he finished it, which is a sign of something; and Picasso goes back to it, other people go back to it, because they are so infatuated with it, they want to rework it. Well, that's the sign of a great culture. You can't be forever innovating, being novel all the time. Of course a lot of my work is innovative. But at the same time I want to know that I am an element of this huge river of culture which is what being a European is, and why it is so difficult: because there is so much of it. How marvellous to be an African, because you haven't got that incredible weight of accumulated visual and intellectual material through which we are constantly wading. I hate eclecticism, you see. When David Bowie died some days ago, somebody said 'what's remarkable about David Bowie, he was marvellously eclectic'. I thought, what's good about that? Eclectic is copying. What's clever about scooping up other people's ideas? No, you must let it come through you and emerge in a form you would not recognise. If I am eclectic, you would find it very difficult to prove because all the material is recirculated through me.

LK: So there is a sense of ghosting, a sense that you are steeped in European culture?

HB: Yes, I am steeped in it. But you cannot produce the new without being deep in the old. As it says in that scene in *The Europeans*, 'we need the new, but we need the new to come from the old'. You can't just cut off.

LK: Maybe it's a redundant question, and you'll tell me if it is: do you feel that engaging increasingly with your plays scenographically, when realising you could work so well with your own designs, it influenced your playwriting at all?

HB: No. I don't think so. If I am writing for a certain actor, say Gerrard [McArthur], say Victoria [Wicks], I want *them* to play the role – maybe they never will, but as I write it, I see that actor doing that. That's natural and inevitable, because they are both very distinctive. Gerrard's amazing, beautiful face, his extraordinary voice, his slightly damaged body: all that makes him, to me, a very powerful stage image. Victoria's presence is immense. She is like a ballet dancer, she can do anything, and she is not young. So those things excite me, visually, and they presumably produce something in the text, too, though I couldn't say how that occurred. Suzy Cooper, as well: there are at least three actresses I've written for a lot, because physically they move me. They all carry a huge sexuality with them but not in a louche way; it's very contained, it's very elegant. It comes from elegance. That fits the rhythm of my writing, which – as I needn't tell you – is never naturalistic. The body to carry that voice can't be naturalistic. We always get amused when we get those nauseating post-show talks; sometimes you get a very young audience with a dismissive attitude and they say 'we thought they were acting', to which we just don't know what to say. Of course they were acting: it's not the real world, it's performance. So I try to tell that all the time, in the production; you come into a theatre, it is not the street. That is the street, this is the theatre, so when you come in, let's tell you straight away: ditch all your presumptions about entertainment, if you can, ditch your morals, don't bring those in; and I do that by the exordium, as you know. I continue trying to create a theatre.

LK: I suppose there is a culture of self-effacement at work in mainstream theatre. I recently had a conversation with someone studying in Denmark, where they have the principle of Jante Law, a social law which states that no one is to be better than anybody else.

HB: All societies have that problem.

LK: I wonder if that attitude then shapes the perception of those things that are deliberately and decidedly different, like your theatre.

HB: My theatre is very high status. The characters are high status. They are not round-shouldered. They are trained in the body. These are all ostensible signs of aristocracy. That you stand properly and you speak a language that is very specific, and it is not the language of the populace as a whole. Isn't that the case with Shakespeare? You have to establish that difference. If people find that offensive, I don't know why, but that is how democracies decay, isn't it? When beauty is ridiculed, you know you are in trouble.

LK: You mentioned the budget, or lack thereof, earlier, and I wonder how you develop your designs. In other places, you have written about the fact that you never consider feasibility when writing because it would cripple your imagination.

HB: The problems are for the director.

LK: But also for the designer: you. So how does that process take place?

HB: Well, I don't set myself problems that are insoluble. But then, as a matter of fact, no problem is not soluble in theatre. If I wanted to write about the Battle of Waterloo, I wouldn't hesitate because I know you can do it. You can do it with three actors and a bare stage. There is no problem that is not resolvable in terms of design, so I don't think the process ever struck me as difficult. I've never had a problem with it. But you have to think metaphorically, you really do. If you can't think metaphorically, you can't do this. Which is why I keep saying: the poetic instinct is very important in theatre. You don't ask for the literal, you cannot keep asking for the literal. How did we create the opening of *Gertrude*? The opening stage direction is 'A king is lying asleep in an orchard', isn't it? Right: you can't have an orchard on stage, unless you are the Schaubühne in Berlin. He would have an orchard, sadly. You don't need the orchard. So what do you do? Well, he is asleep, and orchards are about apples. The public knows *Hamlet* a bit. So I gave him an apple, a huge apple in each hand. He's asleep on the ground, a sunhat over his eyes: that's an orchard to me. There was a fan suspended overhead, spinning very slowly, creating a certain summery idleness. That's the picture. Then we have the wired birds flying across, rather worryingly, slightly neurotic birds, shrieking. That is the picture when the audience comes in. Then one of the sliding walls goes back and you see Gertrude. The other one goes back and you see Claudius; and the sounds immediately become more anxious because there is a murder about to occur and we all somewhat know that. That is a simple and effective way of rendering the scene, I believe.

LK: You just mentioned sound there, and of course language is so incredibly important in your work, too. With *Found in the Ground* (2009) you took more control regarding the sound design, so could you talk about your processes for sound design? Your soundscapes consist of various ambient sounds, with great expressive potential; it is not 'a dog barks upstage', it is stage directions like 'the sound of infinity'.

HB: I find that hard to talk about. I don't even quite know when I start thinking about the sounds. I don't think I think about them when I am writing it, unless it says specifically something like 'a rifle goes off', of course. The general sound picture I don't think I come to until I know I have got the show on and I know I am directing it. Then I will go down to my CD collection and then I'll pick notes, or half-phrases from five, maybe, European composers, whom I admire, but beyond that, are suitable for theatre. My favourite composer is Bartók. But you can't really use Bartók in theatre without it sounding like music, because it is intensely musical. Whereas if you use Stockhausen … there is an awful lot of *noise* in Stockhausen. Noises, not music. There is, for example, a wonderful piece which I have used a number of times, which is like the sound of a gate creaking. I don't know how he creates it, but that is what it sounds like to me. So I'll pick that out and I might put that in, or some clicks, or some tinny noises, or crockery clattering, and I will go right through the text, on my own, with those sounds, and place them: I want this here, I want that there. I can normally hear them, so if it's Paul [Bull], and it usually is, we'll then go through it together, and he'll take the CDs away if he hasn't got them, and he will cut them as I want them. He'll then bring it back and we'll talk it over. It's a kind of punctuation. It is to heighten the effect, but it is not in the way that is the curse of contemporary documentary or drama. It is not mood music. I can't bear manipulating an audience like that. It's horrible. It's degrading. You degrade the audience, if you give it mood music.

LK: It is really interesting you should say that, because it is almost word for word what Helen Morley said about the lighting [in Wrestling School productions]: you don't prescribe a mood, or tell the audience how to feel. It just is. You might have a sense of place, of size, of temperature, but there is no value judgement or emotional content that is prescribed within that.

HB: In terms of lighting, there is a certain part of the palette I don't want in there. I know nothing about lighting, but I don't want certain parts of the palette in there, for example golden, warm hues. It has to go. When Gerrard and I directed together in France about two years ago, we did *The Gaoler's Ache*, the Marie Antoinette play. Ace [McCarron] came out and lit it, and I said to Gerrard 'this is all too colourful, too picturesque', so I asked Ace to go through the lighting stages and he would bring them up one by one, working towards the whole effect and I'd say 'no, stop there!' and I know Gerrard felt exactly the same, 'don't add that red, don't add that orange, don't add that amber'. It is severe, and that is what we want. I always want the severity of that restricted colour palette. I use white make up with actors, I don't mean it in the way of Asian theatres, but I want them to look pale, I want them to look as if they don't go out, they are a bit anaemic. That, again, is part of that process of taking away shades of colour. Working down to the basic all the time. Near to black and white, always. I mean if you look at my pictures, just for a moment, I have a few on the walls here, they are all in a tremendously restricted palette. You can see, there are only four or five colours on there. There is white, black, Naples yellow, and yellow ochre. I don't know if we use those colours on the stage that much, but the idea of presenting everything within a narrow palette, a limited range is still present. The lighting, too, as I do it on the stage, always from the side, at sharp angles, giving the *chiaroscuro* effects. When I do photography, the same principles apply. The light is always from the side.

LK: You are a painter, and as we have discussed, steeped in European culture, so the *chiaroscuro* is fundamental to canonical Western art.

HB: Yes, it is. I suppose, it has been a form since the 17th century.

LK: A form that has been recognisable, in the sense of providing precisely that moment of familiarity that one cannot quite place, and then on to the next moment of anxiety of the almost-familiar.

HB: Yes, that's right. For me, in a way, I suppose, the best moments of intimacy between actors – and there is a lot of intimacy in my work – are those in which you just need them isolated. The woman and the man – love is usually heterosexual in my work – if they are there and there, whether they are dressed or naked, the gap is important. I really believe in distance. The more intimate you want to be, to speak intimately, the more interesting it is if the distance is great. Then you just pick them out with light in that space. You don't want to see everything else; you just want to see them. That should be the focus.

LK: The restriction of your colour palette in set and costume, and lighting all work together. How do you deliberately shape the space with that?

HB: I try to lose the horizons. I don't want the edges to show. Once we have the side-lighting set up, then I don't want to see the floor. Which is very difficult, because light bounces. That would be my ideal at certain points, to have the actors coming out of a low mist, so you wouldn't see the floor. The floor is normally boring. There is not much you can do with a stage floor. The interest is in the body. I'm all for limiting it all, keep on limiting it.

LK: It is interesting you mention the floor; when I spoke with Helen Morley, she mentioned the light floor you had in *13 Objects*, which you emphatically did not want lit. Which makes it all the more difficult.

HB: Yes, I often have a white floor. I know it makes it more difficult. That is a conflict. The reason I want a white floor is to say 'you are not in the world' because we don't usually have white floors. Well, Victoria Station does, but on the whole we don't have them. So it is all part of the same effect of making you feel you are somewhere else, or nowhere, actually.

LK: I recently watched the recording of *Ursula*. When Leonora, the blind girl, approaches and Placida describes her rattling at the gate, and climbing over it, you had a wonderful isolation on Leonora's hand and stick, weaving in and out of a narrow beam of light.

HB: That's right. Of course, all you could see on the stage was Placida and the girls in their horseshoe-shaped arrangement of chairs.

LK: You mentioned the use of plastic walls made to look like corrugated iron in *13 Objects*, and I suppose it is practicality as much as budget that informs that decision, not to use the actual material?

HB: You can get the plastic to look like corrugated iron, it is cheaper, it is easier to transport. You have to remember, the Wrestling School had to tour, always. So the logistics of truck size, how many people have you got to help, and so on, all featured in those decisions. Lightweight things were better. I didn't let that dominate me, but it is a thought.

LK: So as long as the same sense of materiality is achieved, you are not obsessed about the actuality of the set?

HB: No. I don't think so. But whatever it is, if it failed to be visually right, I wouldn't have it.

LK: This brings us to the end of my written questions, which are not exhaustive at all. So if we could have a look at some of your sketchbooks and designs that would be wonderful.

HB: Certainly. Let's start with the sketch books then. They may not be of much use, because as I said I do this when I am writing, and then I don't use them again. How many of these have I done? About 18 books, over the years. Not everything is illustrated because I didn't always do it. Take anyone at random. What's the play?

LK: *Wonder and Worship in the Dying Ward*.

HB: That's never been performed. But the pictures are there.

[...]

HB: Ah, yes, it's the girl on the trolley that runs electrically on rails. I have mentioned my fondness of rails. There's the protagonist's boyfriend, who happens to be undressed in front of her. A rare example of male nudity. It does happen.

LK: Quite. There is Modicum in *I Saw Myself*, and the man in the queen's wardrobe in one of the plays of *The Forty*.

HB: Yes, it does happen. So that's *Wonder and Worship*; there's the opening scene, with the mad boy on the ladder and he describes what he sees. There's the car, here are all the sick with their pets.

[...]

LK: There is a great sense of movement in the drawings.

HB: Yes, exactly. Putting tension into a still figure is very difficult. It is easier to achieve vigour through movement. [...]

[...]

LK: You have some recurring motives. I mention this, because I just saw a drawing in here of a woman with a coffee cup and it reminded me of *13 Objects*.

HB: Yes. I like tea tables. I like cafés. That's probably why I put *Lot and His God* in a café (*turning pages*). That is a film.

[...]

LK: You have your 1930s to 1950s aesthetic in costuming that is very prominent in your works, but if you think of something like the maids in *I Saw Myself*, with their big sleeves, they are quite differently historical.

HB: Yes, and their medieval headdresses. The funny little hats. But the protagonist I put in very much 20th century attire. It was only the servants who were, if you will, in period costume. That gives you that mix of times to confuse specificity.

LK: I recall, in *13 Objects*, but also in *I Saw Myself* – and it took me very close watching to notice this – that they are not in fact one-piece dresses, but very high-waisted, cropped short jackets, and extremely high-waisted skirts.

HB: That's an element of my style. Victoria [Wicks] wore something similar in *Gertrude*. A tiny little jacket.

LK: What is that appeals to you about that cut across?

HB: I just love it. It's why I'm wearing this (*gesturing to waistcoat*), I suppose. Why do I love it? God knows why. My mother? Who knows?

LK: What I find so lovely about it is that it cuts across the body in an unexpected place: it sits above the waist, but is not an empire line. It sits in between them.

HB: Yes, that's absolutely right. Also: these garments should open. I like things that open. […]

[…]

HB: Yes. I wouldn't use colour. Or I would desaturate it, so the colour disappears, or put a filter on it. So it might be ochre or sepia. (*referring to book*) So that's them. I use coloured inks and water. As I said, these are made during the writing and are irrelevant to the rest of the production process.

LK: So they only came back into play when Kenny Ireland asked to look at them.

HB: Yes, if he wanted some guidance.

LK: Do you feel he asked for them when he felt something was particularly difficult?

HB: Maybe. To be honourable to Kenny – whom I disagreed with on a lot of principles, towards the end especially; his idea that the audience needed seducing, which I agree with, but coming from a different place. He wanted to seduce them by a kind of familiarity and caring: 'do identify with this girl'. He never liked Victoria [Wicks], he never liked Melanie [Jessop]. He said, 'they are too hard, the women are too hard. People won't sympathise'. I said, 'No! I don't want them to sympathise. I want them to adore. Let these women mesmerise the audience, instead of the audience sympathising with them'. It's a choice, isn't it. Anyway, Kenny asked for the sketchbooks perhaps to be close to me, trying to serve my work. He was a very honourable man, uncommon in all ways. (*picking out stacks of costume designs*) I don't know what these are. There you are.

LK: That's Gertrude [from the play of the same name].

HB: Yes, that's her opening costume. I do all that, I put the notes in.

LK: You have an idea for a fabric that you want to use because you have an idea of how you want it to move.

HB: Yes. Here I think I said I wanted muslin, but the costume woman might have said that's no good, and changed it to something suitable.

LK: I think it was a chiffon in the end.

HB: Yes, that would be right. Chiffon, that's what it was. You see, I might give a note.

LK: (*reading costume notes*) Yes, the blue shoes. 'Always blue now'.

HB: So there's that. Here's a later costume. I don't know if we ever did that.

LK: I don't recall that design appearing in production.

HB: I wanted it to be fur, a lot of fur onto black. (*referring to notes*) But you see, again I'm emphasising how small the colour range is. (*turning page*) Now this one, we did make.

LK: Yes, the skirt that's 'too short'.

HB: It's quite short on one side, and much longer on the other.

LK: Of course, it's her mourning attire when we see her after the funeral.

HB: That's right, it's not the same one as the one that makes Hamlet cross.

LK: Which incidentally I find rather funny, as in production the whole dress was translucent, making Hamlet's objection to the length of the skirt ridiculous.

HB: Quite. There is a hilarious story about that. The show opened in Elsinore, and we were given this enormous room, like a ball room, but it lent itself very well to the piece. There was a long deck – it was all on a deck, which I thought was the answer, because we had to get in so quickly – and the actors played up and down it, the full length of the room. In that scene 'the skirt's too short' happened – all the costumes were off to one end of the room – and Victoria was not in the preceding scene, but she was about to come on in that little dress and had to do a change preceding it. Jane [Bertish] and Tom Burke were playing and got to Victoria's cue but she didn't appear. They were desperately trying to keep going, and she still didn't appear, because that dress, the flimsy dress – it was like a handkerchief – was hanging on the rail and when she took it off, she got it inside out, or somehow twisted, and she couldn't get it on. She was struggling, trying to get into the dress and she told me, she thought 'I have to go out. Fuck it, I can't wait any longer' and she barely had it on. She was wearing high heels, and the twisted dress that barely covered her. She walked on, and Tom Burke gave the line 'that skirt's too short'; but of course, it didn't exist. I don't know if the Danes got the joke, but we did. (*moving pages*) Oh, there it is, that's the one.

    [...]

LK: Ah, that's the yellow dress, the one flash of colour in the production.

HB: That's right, I will use one colour only. It was the same with *Ursula*, I used just the one colour.

LK: What was that colour? It looked like – and that ultimately comes down to the quality of the recording – a peach colour. I'm referring to Placida's dress when the virgins arrive at the estuary, and she has the little hat.

HB: It was a kind of peachy colour, you're right. It was also somewhat beige, maybe.

LK: Yes, very muted and definitely infused with grey.

HB: The virgins were in grey suits.

LK: With their very heavy overcoats.

    [...]

HB: [...] There's Isola.

LK: Her hat is a beautiful thing.

HB: Yes, we had a very good hat maker. She would take my ideas away and comeback with precisely the thing.

LK: I suppose that is another way of removing the work from reality and especially contemporary society: hats and gloves. In winter people might wear them, but not otherwise.

HB: Yes. I'm sure it'll come back eventually. So many women look wonderful in hats; not all women. (*turning pages*) I also like this kind of thing: pleating. If I can get lots and lots of pleats, I like that.

LK: Is it the volume of fabric that appeals to you in that instance?

HB: It evokes history, somehow, like linenfold panelling. (*turning pages*) That one we have somewhere still. That's Isola's second one.

LK: What is it about that shade of yellow you like? It's present in your paintings, but it also appears in *Found in the Ground*.

HB: It's a bit like old army uniforms. If you look at military costume, it tends to be grey, like the Austrian army, or the German army. They are grey and the regimental flash of colour is very carefully chosen, for example pink on grey. Or yellow on grey. It's really good. The designers of uniforms know the effect of those highlights. So I evoke that same principle. It's very subtle.

LK: It's like punctuation on the costume itself, as well.

HB: Exactly. Sometimes, if flowers are among the props, I will match them in colour. (*turning pages*) Yes, we did that one.

LK: It's Cascan's uniform. That must have been quite difficult to make, since it has to fit Hamlet, too.

HB: Well, yes. But first it has to fit Cascan, Hamlet is second. Of course it didn't fit Hamlet very well, but that wasn't the point, was it? (*turning pages*) That's what I meant about men's suits: high-waisted. Who wears high-waisted trousers? Nobody, but they are brilliant. These are long, and wide-legged, with turn-ups; and the jacket is lifted there, at the shoulder seam.

LK: So it is familiar, but then you take it away from the expected.

HB: Exactly.

LK: Perhaps some people might not even consciously notice these little touches, but the effect is still present.

HB: They may not actually read it, but the effect remains. (*turning pages*) Yes, we made that one, in some form. That's Albert. I don't like giving men shirts. I always like them to have the jacket over the naked body. Shirts seem fiddly. In a way it says a great deal, that: if you put men in shirts you are constructing a very detailed period image. If you take the shirt away and just put the jacket on to the man's naked chest, you are really saying 'it's a man in a jacket'; you are not saying 'it's 1880, it's this time or that', so that's why I always do that. It saves money, too. Shirts are expensive. (*turning pages*)

[…]

LK: You don't have a costume archive then? You mentioned that actors might retain some pieces.

HB: No, there is no archive. Victoria has a few bits. They don't last. They fall apart. I have no room to keep them. (*pulling out a new stack of designs*) Here's another set. This happens to be in book form. I think it was done in Denmark. I think it's *Wounds to the Face* in Denmark.

LK: With two grand pianos on stage? It must have been quite a big space then.

HB: Yes, it was a big theatre. (*turning pages*) I like using men in women's slips. It has nothing to do with trans-gendering, or anything like that, just to play with the slight shock of it. (*turning pages*) Yes, I'm sure that's what it was.

LK: Here we have some more descriptions (*reading*): 'turned collar, transparent netting, heels and boots'. What about dark glasses? They are something that appears repeatedly in your work.

HB: Do they?

LK: Yes. I suppose it might be connected to the various blind characters, for whom dark glasses are an archetypal prop.

HB: Yes. Of course they are deeply sinister, too. (*referring back to page*) Yes, this is *Wounds to the Face*. (*turning pages*)

LK: (*reading annotation*) 'Plastic trousers'. There is an interest in material that comes through in these designs. I suppose it also reflects the sense of choreography that your writing possesses. It is composed. There is a musicality to the movement as there is to the lines.

HB: Yes and you did that so well when you assistant directed *The Forty*. As if you knew that the rhythm of the writing obliged the placing. The one follows the other. It is spiritual. If you can't do that, you can't direct my work. It is a spiritual thing. That line means he is there, she is there. (*turning to page*) I don't know what this is, if we ever did it.

LK: Interior lights in voluminous plastic gowns.

HB: It's a wonderful scene. (*turning pages*)

LK: You have the rabbit in the Balenciaga dress in the other room. Are there any other fashion designers, contemporary or historical, whose work may find its way into yours?

HB: No, I don't think there are. I knew Balenciaga from having picked up a massive book about his work at some stage. (*reading annotations*) '100 tonnes of earth'. What was I dreaming of? What play is this? (*reading annotations*) 'can set sustain interest for six hours?'. That's a question for me. Six hours. What show was that? It must have been *The Ecstatic Bible*. (*turning pages*)

LK: (*reading*) 'stiffened black wool, taffeta/organza dress, one piece, knee length, buttons on the side'. I think that's in *The Fence*. When people gather at the funeral and Algeria's friend urges everyone to demand to be her next husband.

HB: Yes, that's right.

LK: It's that wonderful line of buttons that is off-centre, but not entirely to the side.

HB: That's right. Where she gets married to Mr. Doorway. It could be that. (*turning page*) This is *Ursula*, the very last scene.

LK: Were the trolleys brought on stage manually?

HB: Yes, one of the actresses who had, in a sense, joined the enemy, and she brought them on, one by one. It took a long time, but it really held one's attention.

LK: And you had the wonderful sound of the castors.

HB: Sound is so important on stage. Silence, or just a drone, and then the clang as the trolleys clash against each other like trucks, railway trucks.

LK: The tiny, rickety trolley that we had in *The Forty* was one of my favourite props, with the giant wedding cake precariously balanced on it.

HB: Your instincts are very close to mine. (*turning to page*) That's from *Und*; it's a tea tray. I'm sorry I can't identify what all of these are.

LK: Please, you have so much work, some of which has been done in other languages, under different titles, one couldn't possibly remember it all.

HB: (*retrieving more designs*) Let's look at something more recent. What's more recent? (*reading descriptions on designs*) That is *Animals in Paradise*.

LK: Which was produced in France, was it not?

HB: Yes, and it was terrific. (*turning pages*) These are the set drawings for *13 Objects*. As you can see, the notes are quite specific there. I present different perspectives.

LK: That's a top down view.

HB: Yes. I do different angles and plans, elevations, to help. There's a drawing for the exordium on that one. I did a lot of work on it.

LK: Did you already know the space you would be in? These plans are very specific in their measurements.

HB: Yes, they are. I didn't know what size the space was, but I knew what size platform I wanted the actor to stand on. Here we are, there is another perspective, from the back this time. See how thoughtful I am (*reading annotation*): 'cylindrical drum, false bottom to reduce weight'. How thoughtful of me. Yes, that is exactly how it came out.

LK: These moving planes are a wonderful way of structuring the space, of making different spaces, just giving a visual, metaphorical clue that this is now a different space.

HB: One is always mesmerised by a machine that repeats its actions. Maybe two, maybe four; and that is quite enough to keep an audience sitting there for ten minutes. Some people always say 'your exordium's better than the play'. Well. You can't compete with a machine. A machine is so exciting.

LK: And yet the excitement of a human body, and a human voice?

HB: Maybe it is the setting up of one against the other. So you create the machine and then you bring the vulnerable body into the machine space. Naked people in Auschwitz. The tremendous pressure of the mechanical and the flesh.

LK: I suppose it might also be a question of weight. The machine's weight may be concealed – or not – and the perceived contrast to the human body to that might generate tension.

HB: Yes, the density of steel. I like steel on stage, though we can't have it, though we tried in *(Uncle) Vanya* because it was meant to be a ship, so there were rivets everywhere and it looked like it was heavy. It's fantastic when you can do that. I remember when I saw – I don't like *Scenes from an Execution*, but I've always been to see it – when it was done by the National Theatre in Denmark, it was a very sensitive director and he had an enormous tumble dryer. I don't know what it was there for, but it was interesting, the whole thing turned. I could never quite work out why he had done it, except the effect was quite something. I don't know what it was. Anyway, I like machines.

LK: I suppose the notion of something beyond, something uncanny, features frequently in your work. Things move on stage, they fly in. *Und* is a prime example: these invisible servants that the protagonist engages with.

HB: Yes, who don't exist.

LK: And maybe never existed. Yet increasingly strange objects arrive on the flying trays.

HB: Yes.

LK: The trays then reappear also in *Found in the Ground*.

HB: The nurses bring them in.

LK: But at the end they sway …

HB: Oh, yes, the girls put them onto wires and they just drift in the wind.

LK: You have mentioned the elimination of the horizon, which is common in your paintings, but this is counterpointed by the vertical line of suspended wire that pulls in a different direction and creates tension.

HB: Yes, that's true. As far as I'm concerned, the more wires, the better. This show had an awful lot of wires.

LK: It must be rather difficult for the actors to navigate.

HB: Yes, but that's good. Give them problems. What happened in *(Uncle) Vanya* was that the servants of the Chekhovian household were going along very high up indeed on this big stage carrying trays with teacups and so on; and every so often they would drop them, and it fell right down, 40 feet or more, and smashed onto the deck, which was also metal. It was a loud crash, teacups strewn everywhere. It continued to happen, so by the time the show opened, the floor was covered in trays. Some of the actors weren't so sure about that, but dear Victoria, she said 'I can manage that'. The actors were worried about falling over, they hate hurting themselves. I understand. At one point, the ship has split, and she goes off to the beach; she gets raped on the beach by Astrov, which is not far from Chekhov, actually. I said to her 'when you come back in, so we know you are in an appalling state' (she only had a slip on) 'could you come in backwards?' and she went 'well, I'll see'. So she did, she came in backwards, and of course the stage is covered in slippery trays; only

someone with a ballet sort of training could do that, without problems. She never fell over. Just as well, as she would have cut herself very badly. But in a way, to give that problem – to actors who are willing to do it, of course – adds hugely. The audience can see the danger they are in. It lifts the temperature of the whole moment hugely, if you see they are physically at risk. Do you want to go on? Is there anything I can show you?
[…]

LK: (*referring to the image of Suzy Cooper in wedding dress for* Found in the Ground) I love this particular piece of costume; we were talking about the hint of the recognisable earlier, I think this is a perfect example: you have the sort of medieval line, but then you have the French line, much later, baroque or even rococo, and then the very modern half-bust corset. So you have all these references, but none of them are determining.

HB: Precisely. And of course she can do it. Like Victoria [Wicks], Suzy [Cooper] can walk properly. How many people can walk? When I audition women, I say to them, 'would you bring a pair of high heels, please' – they think I'm a fetishist – 'can you walk across the room?'; often they can't do it. They can't walk; they are not trained anymore to walk. In the 50s the girls at RADA were trained, put books on their heads. Men, men of course can't walk, full stop. But somehow you expect women to be able to walk. Why would you give someone a costume like that when they can't move in it?
[…]

HB: Yes, I develop and print. I don't always do as well as that. On stage I never know the light readings. Those are lucky. (*turning page*) That's professional, that's not by me. That's Gerrard [McArthur] in *Found in the Ground*.

LK: (*referring to photograph of the character Macedonia*) I didn't know she was wearing socks, I couldn't see that on the recording, it was too far away.

HB: Collapsed stockings, actually; and very ancient underwear, all sordid; and no head.

LK: Yes. That I thought was a spectacular problem, and wonderful solution. As I said earlier, I set my students the opening stage directions of *Found in the Ground* as a task, and then showed them the little video extract I had access to, which shows the exordium and the first few moments of the play. They asked me how it was done, because you can't quite see it on the recording. So I explained the solution with the hat to them. I thought it was just such a splendid solution to an intriguing problem.

HB: Yes. In this, you meet the problem. With any problem in the theatre, you give it to the audience. When I went to see *Gertrude* in Paris, it was an extraordinary show, with a great opera director – things I would never want, or think of myself, but it was interesting – it opens to the fuck, virtually, doesn't it? You couldn't see it! He brought the actors right upstage, behind a tree, and there some sort of sexual act took place. I hate sexual acts on stage. Whatever it was they were doing, it was up there. You can't do that. You give the problem to the audience. So she has to be naked, so we have to solve the idea of an intimacy; stylistically, not naturalistically, thank you. So we brought the actors right down to the front. That is what you must do. It is the same here. You have a problem, which you can't solve, basically. So you invent a substitute. That's art, isn't it. That's what art is. (*turning to photographs*) That's *Victory* in Australia. A great actress. Judy Davis. (*turning pages*) There is that incredible imitation of Hitler. He did that so well. (*turning pages*) There's Victoria on the table in *Animals in Paradise*. There she is again. (*turning pages*)

[...]

LK: There is hardly any material for *Und* available.

HB: There are no images, no.

LK: It's such a shame. What fabric was that dress?

HB: White plastic. It had to be, because she gets smothered with liquid. It was white plastic and it creaked rather nicely. (*turning pages*) These are all *Animals in Paradise* again. That's *Found in the Ground*. That's my version of *Scenes from an Execution*. Kathryn Hunter in the trapdoor. That's the scene [in *The Fence*] you mentioned, when she gets a husband.

LK: This is after everyone else has left, though. I remember seeing the buttons on Jane Bertish's costume and noticing they weren't where buttons usually are.

HB: You have a very good eye.

LK: I am hoping I might submit an article to an Australian Journal on brides and widows in your work, because they recur so many times, in so many different guises. The brides become widows and the widows become brides again.

HB: Yes, that's right. I like brides. As for the widows, they always end up saying 'there's a lot to be said for being widowed'. They enjoy the new life. (*turning pages*) That's *The Fence* again, with a bit of fence.

LK: What kind of floor did you have in that production?

HB: I think it must have been a black cloth. You have to have something on the floor. I always wanted to take a floor on tour – sometimes people got upset about that – because you can't just work off the black studio flor that is there. It's all chipped anyway and you're not allowed to paint the damn thing. So I admitted the fabric covering by putting an edge around it. (*turning pages*) This is something I did in Denmark, that was *Wounds to the Face*. There's a bit more *Und*.

LK: The draping on the skirt is lovely, and being plastic it really would have held those lines.

HB: Exactly. She [Melanie Jessop] is also very good with the whole idea of the body's language. She is marvellous with gesture.

LK: You have spoken about the idea of an iconic gesture before.

HB: Yes. I am very interested in gesture, though I sense it could be a bit of a blind alley. I just wish people did it more and understood what it was. How powerful it is. It's very unusual for someone to be lost for words in my plays, but it does sometimes happen. I wrote the stage direction just the other day 'she is lost for words'; and in that moment, gesture fills in. It can be exquisite. If you know how to do it, as Suzy [Cooper] and Melanie [Jessop] certainly do. It's basically Roman, isn't it? If you read people like Cicero, who produced books of rhetoric, they always said the rhetoric had to be accompanied by certain signs. Then you get the Roman Catholic Church and the papal gestures. They are very meaningful and part of the equipment of acting, I think; or should be. [...]

LK: [...] Thank you very much for your time.

Note

1   Records show that in fact Howard Barker began direction before then, in 1992 with *Ego in Arcadia*.

References

Abulafia, Yaron (2016) *The Art of Light on Stage: Lighting in Contemporary Theatre*, London and New York: Routledge.

Alston, Adam and Welton, Martin (2017) *Theatre in the Dark: Shadow, Gloom and Blackout in Contemporary Theatre*, London: Bloomsbury.

Anderson, Benedict (2013) 'Out of Space: The Rise of Vagrancy in Scenography', *Performance Research*, Vol. 18, No. 3, pp. 109–118.

Aretoulakis, Emmanouel (1996) extract from 'The Unpresentable in Critical Thought' available at www.costis.org/x/lyotard/aretoulakis.htm; accessed on 21.11.2014.

Aristotle transl. Janko, Richard (1987) *Poetics I*, Indianapolis: Hackett.

Aronson, Arnold (2005) *Looking into the Abyss: Essays on Scenography*, Ann Arbor: University of Michigan Press.

Aronson, Arnold (ed.) (2017) *The Routledge Companion to Scenography*, London and New York: Routledge.

Aronson, Arnold (2018) *The History and Theory of Environmental Scenography*, London: Methuen Drama.

Augoyard, Jean-François and Torgue, Henry transl. McCartney, Andra and Paquette, David (2005) *Sonic Experience: A Guide to Everyday Sounds*, Montreal and Kingston: McGill-Queen's University Press.

Balme, Christopher B. (2008) *The Cambridge Introduction to Theatre Studies*, Cambridge: Cambridge University Press.

Barcan, Ruth (2004) *Nudity: A Cultural Anatomy*, Oxford and New York: Berg.

Barker, Howard (1997) *Arguments for a Theatre,* 3rd ed., Manchester and New York: Manchester University Press.

Barker, Howard (2004) *Dead Hands*, London: Oberon.

Barker, Howard (2005a) *Death, The One and the Art of Theatre*, London and New York: Routledge.

Barker, Howard (2005b) *The Fence in Its Thousandth Year*, London: Oberon.

Barker, Howard (2006) *Plays Two*, London: Oberon.

Barker, Howard and Houth, Eduardo (2007) *A Style and Its Origins*, London: Oberon.

Barker, Howard (2008a) *Plays Three*, London: Oberon.

Barker, Howard (2008b) *Plays Four*, London: Oberon.

Barker, Howard (2010a) 'Afterword: The Corpse and Its Sexuality', in Gritzner, Karoline (ed.) *Eroticism and Death in Theatre and Performance*, Hatfield: University of Hertfordshire Press, pp. 242–245.

Barker, Howard (2010b) *Plays Six*, London: Oberon.

Barker, Howard (2011) *Blok/Eko*, London: Oberon.

Barker, Howard (2012a) *Plays Seven*, London: Oberon.

Barker, Howard (2012b) 'Charles V', *Studies in Theatre & Performance*, Vol. 32, No. 3, pp. 359–368.

Barker, Howard (2014a) *Plays Eight*, London: Oberon.

Barker, Howard (2014b) *These Sad Places, Why Must You Enter Them?*, London: Impress.

Barker, Howard (2016) *Arguments for a Theatre*, 4th ed., Manchester and New York: Manchester University Press.

Battersby, Christine (2007) *The Sublime, Terror and Human Difference*, London and New York: Routledge.

Baudrillard, Jean transl. Singer, Brian (1979) *Seduction*, Basingstoke: Macmillan.

Baugh, Christopher (2013) *Theatre, Performance and Technology: The Development and Transformation of Scenography*, Basingstoke: Palgrave Macmillan.

Beacham, Richard (1994) *Adolphe Appia: Artist and Visionary of the Modern Theatre*, Amsterdam: Harwood Academic.

Bech, Sidsel and Hann, Rachel (eds.) (2014) 'Editorial', *Scene (Special Issue: Critical Costume)*, Vol. 2, No. 1&2, Bristol: Intellect, pp. 3–8.

Bennett, Susan (2019) *Theory for Theatre Studies: Sound*, London: Bloomsbury.

Berrigan, Hannah (2015) 'Directing *Slowly*', Reynolds, James and Smith, Andy W. (eds.) *Howard Barker's Theatre: Wrestling with Catastrophe*, London: Bloomsbury, pp. 51–62.

Black, Richard Harrison (1874) *The Student's Manual Complete; An Etymological Vocabulary of Words Derived from the Greek and Latin*, Oxford: Oxford University; available at https://books.google.co.uk/books?id=AnACAAAAQAAJ; accessed on 03.06.2016.

Blau, Herbert (1999) *Nothing in Itself: Complexions of Fashion*, Bloomington and Indianapolis: Indiana University Press.

Böhme, Gernot (2017) *Atmosphäre – Essays zur neuen Ästhetik* (3rd ed.), Berlin: Suhrkamp.

Booth, Stephen (2001) *King Lear, Macbeth, Indefinition and Tragedy*, Christchurch: Cybereditions Corporation.

Brandstetter, Gabriele and Wiens, Birgit (eds.) (2010) *Theatre Without Vanishing Points – The Legacy of Adolphe Appia*, Berlin: Alexander.

Braun, Edward (1979) *Meyerhold: A Revolution in Theatre*, London: Methuen.

Brown, Mark and Barker, Howard (2011) 'Art Is about Going into the Dark', in Brown, Mark (ed.) *Howard Barker Interviews, 1980–2010: Conversations in Catastrophe*, Bristol: Intellect Books, pp. 187–202.

Brown, Ross (2005) 'The Theatre Soundscape and the End of Noise', *Performance Research*, Vol. 10, No. 4, pp. 105–119.

Brown, Ross (2010) *Sound: A Reader in Theatre Practice*, Basingstoke: Palgrave Macmillan.

Brown, Ross (2020) *Sound Effect: The Theatre We Hear*, London: Bloomsbury.

Brownie, Barbara (2017) *Acts of Undressing: Politics, Eroticism, and Discarded Clothing*, London and New York: Bloomsbury.

Bugg, Jessica (2014) 'Dancing Dress: Experiencing and Perceiving Dress in Movement', *Scene (Special Issue: Critical Costume)*, Vol. 2, No. 1&2, Bristol: Intellect, pp. 67–80.

Butcher, S.H. (ed. and transl.) (1902) *The Poetics of Aristotle*, 3rd ed., London: Macmillan.

Butler, Judith (1999) *Gender Trouble*, 2nd ed., Abingdon: Taylor & Francis.

Calefato, Patrizia (2004) *The Clothed Body*, Oxford and New York: Berg.

Carney, Sean (2013) *The Politics and Poetics of Contemporary English Tragedy*, Toronto: University of Toronto Press.

Chion, Michel ed. and transl. Murch, Walter and Gorbman, Claudia (1994) *Audio-Vision: Sound on Screen*, New York: Columbia University Press.

Clough, Patricia Ticineto and Halley, Jean (eds.) (2007) *The Affective Turn: Theorizing the Social*, Durham, NC: Duke University Press.

Collins, Jane and Nisbet, Andrew (eds.) (2010) *Theatre and Performance Design: A Reader in Scenography*, London and New York: Routledge.

Connor, Steven (2004) *The Book of Skin*, London: Reaktion Books.

Costelloe, Timothy M. (2012) 'The Sublime a Short Introduction to a Long History' in Costelloe, Timothy M. (ed.) *The Sublime: From Antiquity to the Present*, Cambridge: Cambridge University Press, pp. 1–7.

Craig, Edward Gordon (1956) *On the Art of Theatre*, London: Heinemann.

Crisafulli, Fabrizio (2013) *Active Light: Issues of Light in Contemporary Theatre*, Dublin: Artdigiland.com Ltd.

Curtin, Adrian (2012) 'The Art Music of Theatre: Howard Barker as Sound Designer', *Studies in Theatre & Performance*, Vol. 32, No. 3, pp. 269–284.

Curtin, Adrian (2014) *Avant-Garde Theatre Sound: Staging Sonic Modernity*, London: Palgrave Macmillan.

Dahl, Mary Karen (2013) '*I Saw Myself*: Artist and Critic Meet in the Mirror' in Rabey, David Ian and Goldingay, Sarah (eds.) *Howard Barker's Art of Theatre*, Manchester: Manchester University Press, pp. 129–138.

Davis, Tracy C. and Postelwait, Thomas (2003) *Theatricality*, Cambridge: Cambridge University Press.

Doran, Robert (2015) *The Theory of the Sublime from Longinus to Kant*, Cambridge: Cambridge University Press.

Downing, Richard (2013) 'Setting the Fractal Clock(s): The Coordinates of a Spatial Expression', *Performance Research*, Vol. 18, No. 3, pp. 169–178.

Dubost, Thierry and Barker, Howard (2011) 'Not What Is, but What Is Possible' in Brown, Mark (ed.) *Howard Barker Interviews, 1980–2010: Conversations in Catastrophe*, Bristol: Intellect Books, pp.131–136.

Dyble-Kitchin, Emily in Rabey, David Ian (2015) '"A Gallery of Images": From the Aberystwyth Students' in Reynolds, James and Smith, Andy W. (eds.) *Howard Barker's Theatre: Wrestling With Catastrophe*, London: Bloomsbury Methuen Drama, pp. 225–240.

Eke, Norbert Otto (2014) 'Bühne als Wahrnehmungsraum: Stimme, Klang und Präsenz' in Eke, Norbert Otto, Haß, Ulrike and Kaldrack, Irina (eds.) *Bühne: Raumbildende Prozesse im Theater*, Paderborn: Wilhelm Fink, pp. 29–46.

Elkins, James (2011) *Against the Sublime*, available at www.academia.edu/163451/Against_the_Sublime, accessed on 14.01.2015.

Etlin, Richard A. (2012) 'Architecture and the Sublime' in Costelloe, Timothy M. (ed.) *The Sublime: From Antiquity to the Present*, Cambridge: Cambridge University Press, pp. 230–273.

Fakhrkonandeh, Alireza (2014) 'The Acousmatic Voice as the Chiasmatic Flesh: An Analysis of Howard Barker's *Gertrude – The Cry*' in *Symploke*, Vol. 22, No. 1&2, pp. 235–273.

Fensham, Rachel (2014) 'Repetition as a Methodology: Costumes, Archives and Choreography', *Scene (Special Issue: Critical Costume)*, Vol. 2, No. 1&2, Bristol: Intellect, pp. 43–60.

Francis, Penny and Barker, Howard (2011) 'On Puppetry and All He Fears' in Brown, Mark (ed.) *Howard Barker Interviews, 1980–2010: Conversations in Catastrophe*, Bristol: Intellect Books, pp. 81–84.

Freeland, Thomas (2011) 'The End of Rhetoric and the Residuum of Pain: Bodying Language in the Theatre of Howard Barker', *Modern Drama*, Vol. 54, No.1, pp. 78–98.

Gage, John (2000) *Colour and Meaning: Art, Science and Symbolism*, Berkeley: University of California Press.

Goebbels, Heiner transl. Roesner, David and Lagao, Christina M. (2015) *Aesthetics of Absence: Texts on Theatre*, London and New York: Routledge.

Graham, Katherine (2016) 'Active Roles of Light in Performance Design', *Theatre and Performance Design*, Vol. 2, No. 1–2, pp. 73–81.

Graham, Katherine (2018) 'In the Shadow of a Dancer: Light as Dramaturgy in Contemporary Performance', *Contemporary Theatre Review*, Vol. 28, No. 2, pp. 196–209.

Gregg, Melissa and Seigworth Gregory J. (2010) *The Affect Theory Reader*, Durham, NC: Duke University Press.

Gritzner, Karoline and Rabey, David Ian (2006) 'Howard Barker in Conversation' in Gritzner, Karoline and Rabey, David Ian (eds.) *Theatre of Catastrophe: New Essays on Howard Barker*, London: Oberon, pp. 30–37.

Gritzner, Karoline (2007) 'Adorno on Tragedy: Reading Catastrophe in Late Capitalist Culture', *Critical Engagements 1.2* (Autumn/Winter 2007), pp. 25–52.

Gritzner, Karoline, Rabey, David Ian and Barker, Howard (2011) 'Crisis is the Essential Condition for Art Forms' in Brown, Mark (ed.) *Howard Barker Interviews 1980–2010: Conversations in Catastrophe*, Bristol: Intellect, pp. 123–130.

Gritzner, Karoline (2012) 'Poetry and Intensification in Howard Barker's Theatre of Plethora' in *Studies in Theatre & Performance*, Vol. 32, No. 3, pp. 337–345.

Gritzner, Karoline (2015) 'Tragedy, Immanence, and the Persistence of Semblance' in *Performance Philosophy*, Vol. 1, pp. 126–132, available at www.performance-philosophy.org/journal/article/view/9/26; accessed on 10.08.2015.

Guyer, Paul (2012) 'The German Sublime After Kant' in Costelloe, Timothy M. (ed.) *The Sublime from Antiquity to the Present*, New York: Cambridge University Press, pp. 102–117.

Hann, Rachel (2018) *Beyond Scenography*, London and New York: Routledge.

Hannah, Dorita (2014) 'Alarming the Heart: Costuming as Performative Body-Object-Event', *Scene (Special Issue: Critical Costume)*, Vol. 2, No. 1&2, Bristol: Intellect, pp. 15–34.

Henry, Susannah (2019) Private email to author.

Holmberg, Arthur (1996) *The Theatre of Robert Wilson*, Cambridge and New York: Cambridge University Press.

Home-Cook, George (2015) *Theatre and Aural Attention*, Basingstoke: Palgrave Macmillan.

Howard, Pamela (2001) *What Is Scenography?*, London and New York: Routledge.

Iball, Helen (2006) 'Dead Hands and Killer Heels' in Gritzner, Karoline and Rabey, David Ian (eds.) *Theatre of Catastrophe: New Essays on Howard Barker*, London: Oberon, pp.70–82.

Johnson, David B. (2012) 'The Postmodern Sublime' in Costelloe, Timothy M. (ed.) *The Sublime from Antiquity to the Present*, New York: Cambridge University Press, pp. 118–131.

Johnson, Dominic (2012) *Theatre & The Visual*, London: Palgrave Macmillan.

Kane, Brian (2014) *Sound Unseen: Acousmatic Sound in Theory and Practice*, New York: Oxford University Press.

Kant, Immanuel transl. Goldthwait, John T. (1960) *Observations on the Feeling of the Beautiful and the Sublime*, Berkeley and Los Angeles and London: University of California Press.

Kant, Immanuel transl. Meredith, James Creed (2007) *Critique of Judgement*, Oxford: Oxford University Press.

Karasek, Christina (2010) *Immaterielle Farbräume: Lichtkunst im musealen und urbanen Kontext*, Graz: Leykam Buchverlag.

Kendrick, Lynne and Roesner, David (2011a) 'Introduction' in Kendrick, Lynne and Roesner, David (eds.) *Theatre Noise: The Sound of Performance*, Newcastle upon Tyne: Cambridge Scholars Publishing, pp. xiv–xxxv.

Kendrick, Lynne and Roesner, David (eds.) (2011b) *Theatre Noise: The Sound of Performance*, Newcastle upon Tyne: Cambridge Scholars Publishing.

Kendrick, Lynne (2017) *Theatre Aurality*, London: Palgrave Macmillan.

Kiese-Himmel, Christiane (2016) *Körperinstrument Stimme: Grundlage, psychologische Bedeutung, Störung*, Berlin: Springer.

Kipp, Lara Maleen in Rabey, David Ian (2015) '"A Gallery of Images": From the Aberystwyth Students' in Reynolds, James and Smith, Andy W. (eds.) *Howard Barker's Theatre: Wrestling With Catastrophe*, London: Bloomsbury Methuen Drama, pp. 225–240.

Kipp, Lara Maleen (2016) *The Scenographic Sublime – An Aesthetic Analysis of Howard Barker's Work 1998–2011*, Doctoral Thesis, unpublished.

Kipp, Lara Maleen (2017) 'Brides and Widows: Iconic Dress and Identity in Howard Barker's Costumes', *Studies in Costume & Performance*, Vol. 2, No. 1, pp. 27–42. DOI: https://doi.org/10.1386/scp.2.1.27_1.

Klingelhoefer, Robert (2017) *The Craft and Art of Scenic Design: Strategies, Concepts, and Resources*, New York: Routledge.

Koda, Harold (2001) *Extreme Beauty: The Body Transformed*, New York: Metropolitan Museum of Art.

Kristeva, Julia transl. Roudiez, Leon S. (1982) *Powers of Horror*, New York: University of Columbia Press.

Kristeva, Julia transl. Gubermann, Ross (1996) *Time and Sense*, New York: University of Columbia Press.

Lagaay, Alice (2011) 'Towards a (Negative) Philosophy of Voice' in Kendrick, Lynne and Roesner, David (eds.) *Theatre Noise: The Sound of Performance*, Newcastle upon Tyne: Cambridge Scholars Publishing, pp. 57–69.

Lamb, Charles (2005) *The Theatre of Howard Barker*, London and New York: Routledge.

Lamb, Charles (2013) 'Reading Howard Barker's Pictorial Art' in Rabey, David Ian and Goldingay, Sarah (eds.) *Howard Barker's Art of Theatre*, Manchester: Manchester University Press, pp. 180–182.

Lehmann, Hans-Thies (2011) *Postdramatisches Theater*, 5th ed., Frankfurt a. M.: Verlag der Autoren.

Leising, Günther (2006) 'Light and Order: The Nature of Light' in Weibel, Peter and Jansen, Gregor (eds.) *Light Art from Artificial Light: Light as a Medium in the Art of the 20th and 21st Centuries*, Ostfildern-Ruit: Hatje Cantz Verlag, pp. 56–67.

Lingis, Alphonso (2000) *Dangerous Emotions*, Berkeley and Los Angeles and London: University of California Press.

Lochhead, Judy (2008) 'The Sublime, the Ineffable, and Other Dangerous Aesthetics', *Women and Music: A Journal of Gender and Culture*, Vol. 12, pp. 63–74.

Lyotard, Jean-François, edited by Benjamin, Andrew (1989) *The Lyotard Reader*, Oxford and Cambridge, MA: Basil Blackwell.

Lyotard, Jean-François transl. Bennington, Geoffrey and Bowlby, Rachel (1991) *The Inhuman*, Cambridge: Polity Press.

Malloy, Kaoime (2014) *The Art of Theatrical Design: Elements of Visual Composition, Methods, and Practice*, Burlington, MA and Abingdon: Focal Press.

Mangan, Mick (2012) 'From Plethora to Bare Sufficiency', *Studies in Theatre and Performance*, Vol. 32, No. 3, pp. 321–335.

Mangan, Michael (2013) 'Places of Punishment: Surveillance, Reason and Desire in the Plays of Howard Barker' in Rabey, David Ian and Goldingay, Sarah (eds.) *Howard Barker's Art of Theatre*, Manchester: Manchester University Press, pp. 82–93.

McCarron, Ace (2015) 'Amplifying Catastrophe' in Reynolds, James and Smith, Andy W. (eds.) *Howard Barker's Theatre: Wrestling With Catastrophe*, London: Bloomsbury Methuen Drama, pp. 63–78.

McKinney, Joslin and Butterworth, Philip (2009) *The Cambridge Introduction to Scenography*, Cambridge: Cambridge University Press.

McKinney, Joslin and Palmer, Scott (eds.) (2017) *Scenography Expanded: An Introduction to Contemporary Performance Design*, London: Bloomsbury.

Monks, Aoife (2010) *The Actor in Costume*, London: Palgrave Macmillan.

Monks, Aoife and Maclaurin, Ali (2015) *Costume*, London: Palgrave Macmillan.

Moore, Tirin and Zirnsak, Marc (2017) 'Neural Mechanisms of Selective Visual Attention', *Annual Review of Psychology*, Vol. 68, Palo Alto: Annual Reviews, pp. 47–72.

Moran, Nick (2016) *The Right Light: Interviews with Contemporary Lighting Designers*, London: Palgrave Macmillan.

Obis, Eléonore (2013) ' "Not Nude but Naked": Nakedness and Nudity in Barker's Drama' in Rabey, David Ian and Goldingay, Sarah (eds.) *Howard Barker's Art of Theatre*, Manchester: Manchester University Press, pp. 73–81.

Oddey, Alison and White, Christine A. (eds.) (2006) *The Potentials of Space: The Theory and Practice of Scenography & Performance*, Bristol: Intellect Books.

Otto-Bernstein, Katharina (2007) *Absolute Wilson* [DVD], Leipzig: Kinowelt Home Entertainment.

Ovadija, Mladen (2013) *Dramaturgy of Sound in the Avant-garde and Postdramatic Theatre*, Montreal: McGill-Queen's University Press.

Palmer, Scott (2013) *Light: Readings in Theatre Practice*, London: Palgrave Macmillan.

Palmer, Scott (2015) 'A "Choréographie" of Light and Space: Adolphe Appia and the First Scenographic Turn', *Theatre & Performance Design*, Vol. 1, No. 1–2, pp. 31–47, DOI: 10.1080/23322551.2015.1024975.

Palmer, Scott (2017) 'Active Shadows: Light, Darkness and Scenographic Atmosphere', *Staging Atmospheres – Theatre and the Atmospheric Turn Proceedings*, 08–09 December 2017, QMU: University of London.

Pavis, Patrice (2011) 'Preface' in Kendrick, Lynne and Roesner, David (eds.) *Theatre Noise: The Sound of Performance*, Newcastle upon Tyne: Cambridge Scholars Publishing, pp. x–xiii.

Prégardien, Christoph (2006) *Gesang: Technik, Interpretation, Repertoire*, London: Schott Music.

Rabey, David Ian (1997) *David Rudkin: Sacred Disobedience*, Amsterdam: Harwood Academic Publishers.

Rabey, David Ian (2004) *The Wye Plays: The Back of Beyond and The Battle of the Crows*, Chicago: University of Chicago Press.

Rabey, David Ian (2006) 'Raising Hell' in Gritzner, Karoline and Rabey, David Ian (eds.) *Theatre of Catastrophe: New Essays on Howard Barker*, London: Oberon, pp. 13–29.

Rabey, David Ian (2009) *Howard Barker: Ecstasy and Death*, New York: Palgrave Macmillan.

Rabey, David Ian (2012) 'Chasing the Ellipses: Staging Howard Barker's The Forty (Few Words)', *Studies in Theatre & Performance*, Vol. 32, No. 3, pp. 285–304.

Rabey, David Ian and Goldingay, Sarah (eds.) (2013) *Howard Barker's Art of Theatre*, Manchester: Manchester University Press.

Rabey, David Ian (2013) 'Introduction: The Ultimate Matter of Style' in Rabey, David Ian and Goldingay, Sarah (eds.) *Howard Barker's Art of Theatre*, Manchester: Manchester University Press, pp. 1–20.

Rabey, David Ian (2016) *Theatre, Time and Temporality: Melting Clocks and Snapped Elastics*, Bristol: Intellect Books.

Reynolds, James (2006) 'Barker Directing Barker' in Gritzner, Karoline and Rabey, David Ian (eds.) *Theatre of Catastrophe: New Essays on Howard Barker*, London: Oberon, pp. 56–69.

Reynolds, James (2015) 'Going Underground' in Reynolds, James and Smith, Andy W. (eds.) *Howard Barker's Theatre: Wrestling with Catastrophe*, London: Bloomsbury, pp. 149–168.

Reynolds, James and Smith, Andy W. (eds.) (2015) *Wrestling with Catastrophe*, London: Bloomsbury.

Roberts, David (2011) *The Total Work of Art in European Modernism*, New York: Cornell University Press.

Roberts, Matthew (2014) 'From Pain, Poetry: Howard Barker's *Blok/Eko* and the Poetics of Plethoric Theater', *Comparative Drama*, Vol. 48, No. 3, pp. 261–276.

Schaeffer, Pierre (1977) *Traité des objets musicaux: Essai Interdisciplines*, Paris: Édition Seuil.

Schalk, Samantha Dawn (2018) *Bodyminds Reimagined: (Dis)ability, Race, and Gender in Black Women's Speculative Fiction*, Durham, NC: Duke University Press.

Schellow, Constanze (2013) 'In Actu Negotiations of the Stage as a Spectrum of Im/Possible Movements Grounding Alternative Spatio-Temporal Experience in Philipp Gehmacher's Series Walk Plus Talk', *Performance Research*, Vol. 18, No. 3, pp. 135–143.

Schneider, Rebecca (1997) *The Explicit Body in Performance*, London and New York: Routledge.

Shevtsova, Maria (2007) *Robert Wilson*, London: and New York: Routledge.

Sierz, Aleks and Barker, Howard (2011) 'Death as a Theatrical Experience' in Brown, Mark (ed.) *Howard Barker Interviews, 1980–2010: Conversations in Catastrophe*, Bristol: Intellect Books, pp. 111–121.

Sloterdijk, Peter (2010) 'The Open Clearing and Illumination: Remarks on Metaphysics, Mysticism and the Politics of Light' in Keller, Max (ed.) *Light Fantastic: The Art and Design of Stage Lighting*, 3rd ed., Munich and Berlin and London and New York: Prestel.

Stein, Gertrude (1926) *Composition as Explanation*, London: Hogarth Press.

Suthor, Nicola (2014) '(Theater-)Graben: Die Untere Bildkante als Grenzwertiger Spielraum des Betrachters' in Eke, Norbert Otto, Haß, Ulrike and Kaldrack, Irina (eds.) *Bühne: Raumbildende Prozesse im Theater*, Paderborn: Wilhelm Fink, pp. 267–284.

Tatari, Marita (2014) 'Bühne des Dramas: Primäre Exposition und Raum Ästhetischer Erfahrung'in Eke, Norbert Otto, Haß, Ulrike and Kaldrack, Irina (eds.) *Bühne: Raumbildende Prozesse im Theater*, Paderborn: Wilhelm Fink, pp. 85–96.

Tkatch, Daniel (2010) *Das Erhabene bei James Turrell: Materielles Licht und das Medium der Wahrnehmung*, Berlin: Freie Universität Berlin (university paper generously provided by author).

Trigg, Madaleine (2014) '(Ad)dressing the Female Body', *Scene (Special Issue: Critical Costume)*, Vol. 2, No. 1&2, Bristol: Intellect, pp. 127–132.

Verstraete, Pieter (2011) 'Radical Vocality, Auditory Distress and Disembodied Voice' in Kendrick, Lynne and Roesner, David (eds.) *Theatre Noise: The Sound of Performance*, Newcastle upon Tyne: Cambridge Scholars Publishing, pp. 82–96.

Voegelin, Salomé (2010) *Listening to Noise and Silence: Towards a Philosophy of Sound Art*, New York and London: Continuum.

Waldenfels, Bernhard (2014) 'Die Bühne als Brennpunkt des Geschehens' in Eke, Norbert Otto, Haß, Ulrike and Kaldrack, Irina (eds.) *Bühne: Raumbildende Prozesse im Theater*, Paderborn: Wilhelm Fink, pp. 13–26.

Warwick, Alexandra and Cavallaro, Dani (1998) *Fashioning the Frame: Boundaries, Dress and The Body*, Oxford and New York: Berg.

Weaver, Gareth in Rabey, David Ian (2012) 'Chasing the Ellipses: Staging Howard Barker's The Forty (Few Words)', *Studies in Theatre & Performance*, Vol. 32, No. 3, pp. 285–304.

Weber Nicholsen, Shierry (1997) *Exact Imagination, Late Work: On Adorno's Aesthetics*, Cambridge, MA: MIT Press.

Weibel, Peter (2006) 'The Development of Light Art' in Weibel, Peter and Jansen, Gregor (eds.) *Light Art from Artificial Light: Light as a Medium in the Art of the 20th and 21st Centuries*, Ostfildern-Ruit: Hatje Cantz Verlag, pp. 86–223.

Welton, Martin (2017) 'Dark Visions: Looking at and in Theatrical Darkness', *Theatre Journal*, Vol. 69, No. 4, pp. 497–513.

Wiens, Birgit (2014) *Intermediale Szenografie: Raum-Ästhetiken des Theaters am Beginn des 21. Jahrhunderts*, Paderborn: Wilhelm Fink.

Wiles, David (2014) *Theatre & Time*, Basingstoke: Palgrave Macmillan.

Zuckert, Rachel (2012) 'The Associative Sublime: Gerard, Kames, Alison, and Stewart' in Costelloe, Timothy M. (ed.) *The Sublime from Antiquity to the Present*, New York: Cambridge University Press, pp. 64–76.

Zyman, Daniela (2006) 'On "Making Room" or How Seeing Takes Place in a Light Space' in Weibel, Peter and Jansen, Gregor (eds.) *Light Art from Artificial Light: Light as a Medium in the Art of the 20th and 21st Centuries*, Ostfildern-Ruit: Hatje Cantz Verlag, pp. 466–489.

Index

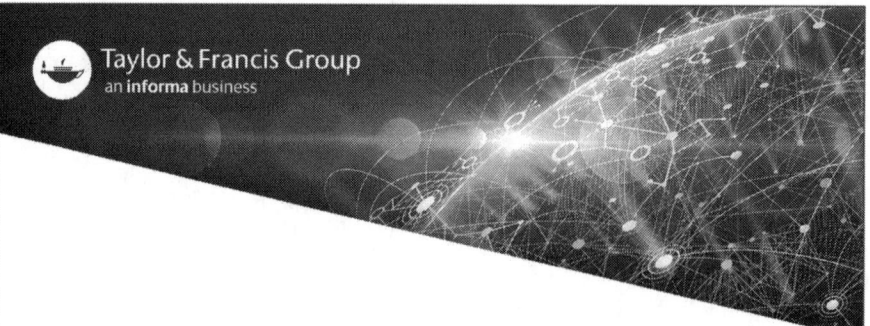
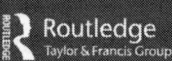
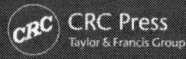